TRIBAL LIFE OF NORTH-EASTERN INDIA

TRIBAL LIFE OF NORTH-EASTERN INDIA

HABITAT ● ECONOMY ● CUSTOMS ● TRADITIONS

DR. S. T. DAS

GYAN PUBLISHING HOUSE
NEW DELHI-110002

Tribal Life of North-Eastern India

Rs. 630

ISBN: 81-212-0209-4

Published in 2006 in India by
Gyan Publishing House
5, Ansari Road, Darya Ganj, New Delhi-110002
Phones : 23282060, 23261060, Fax : 011-23285914
E-mail : books@gyanbooks.com
Website : http://www.gyanbooks.com

Laser Typesetting at : Shiva Infosystem, Delhi
Printed at : Salasar Imaging System, Delhi

PREFACE

The north eastern area originally comprised the composite Assam or old Kamarupa and the two native states of Manipur and Tripura. Assam alone, as it exists at present, no longer comprises the north-east region, is only one of the constituents forming the region. The other constituents are Nagaland, Meghalaya, Manipur, Tripura, Mizoram and Arunachal. Pradesh.

Although Assam of the past or the north-east region as it is called to day, had been known for its own civilization, its geographical position was not known to many people. According to the Chinese pilgrim Huen Tsang, Assam had attained a fairly high degree of civilization under the region of the Hindu King Bhaskara Varman in the 7th century. However, apart from a few copper plates and rock inscriptions, little is known about the Kingdom of Assam after Huen Tsang's visit until the arrival of the Ahoms in the 13th century.

The Ahoms were a tribe of Shans from a land called Pong, lying between Old Assam and Burma, who originally belong to north China. They entered the north-east region for the first time through the Patkai Hills as a small raiding party in 1215 A.D. Taking advantage of the political instability in the country, they gradually became the masters of the whole region and ruled over the land for nearly six centuries.

The Ahoms named the land Meung-dun-chun-khan or the 'Country of Gold' and later changed it to the Burmese name of Sham or Shan. The invaders pronounced it as 'Asham' or 'Aham' from which, it is believed, the Old State of Assam derives its name. The descendants of the Shan invaders were called Ahoms.

Since the Ahoms had a highly developed sense of history, they chronicled their stories on the dried barks of trees. They gradually subjugated the indigenous rulers—the Kochs,

Kacharis and Chutiyas—and organised a feudal system peculiar to themselves.

The north eastern region is very sensitive and important from the strategic point of view. No other part of India than the north-east region has boundaries which are clearly vulnerable to outside powers. The area is surrounded by four foreign countries, viz., Bhutan, China, Burma and Bangladesh. With her diverse population, speaking different languages and professing divergent faiths, may be regarded as an epitome of India. It is the land where waves of immigrants from Tibeto-Burman and Mongoloid stock have met and woven with the aboriginals a pattern of common condition and tradition. The people of hills and the plains have lived long side by side and followed common pursuits of life undisturbed.

The composition of population of the north-east and the immigration to this land throughout history offer a subject for worthwhile academic study. In the composition of its population, there are the Austric or the Austro-Asiatic elements, the Dravidian elements, the Indo-Aryan and the Indo-Mongoloid elements. The people of north-east India are composed of different races, speaking various languages, like Austric or Mon Khmer (one of which is Khasi), Sino-Tibetan representing the Bodo or the Kachari Tongue, and the Rai or the Ahom. These languages have influenced the phonological and morphological characteristic of the Assamese language which has developed out of the Sanskrit language from as early as the 7th century A.D.

India is the home of some 23 million naturvolker, who have lived through centuries their own life in the remote parts of the country and it is these people who still afford opportunities to social geographers and anthropologists to assess the influence of immediate environment on the culture, tradition and the mode of life.

There are many tribes in this north-eastern state. Each has its own culture, tradition, customs and beliefs. But the Mikirs, Dimasa Kacharis Zemi-Nagas and the Manipuris are the most interesting and important tribes. An attempt has been made to present a detailed and in-depth study of the tribes of this region. It is the outcome of my seven years' on the spot study of habitat, economy and society of the hill people. But greater emphasis has been given to the study of the Dimasa Kacharis, Zemi-Nagas and the Mikirs.

This in-depth study has been written to fill a gap in the literature of social geography and cultural anthropology. Particular emphasis is laid upon the way of life of the tribes which is one of direct response determined by the environment and the queer beliefs of the tribes, which spring from the fertile imagination. The various myths and legends are the result of the natural reaction of the tribes to their environment, a search for an explanation of the mystery of life. There is no set pattern of socio-economic development of the tribes. They are purely and strictly agricultural people, tied to their immediate environment which affords opportunity for cultivation. Though some of their customs are strange to us, others like the social system which functions at all levels are essentially democratic in nature.

In a book like this, I must acknowledge the assistance I have received from various authorities, writers and critics, who have afforded valuable suggestions and those whose books have helped me to draw inspiration. Omission if any was not deliberate.

Special mention may be made to Mr. B. Bhagavati, Mr. B.P. Chaliha, Ex-Chief Minister of Assam, Mr. Biman Kumar Dasgupta, Mr. Pradyot Mitra, Mr. P.D. Chaudhury, Mr. Jyoti Kumar Sarma, P. Pugh, Mr. K.P. Bahadur, Dr. K.B. Singh, Mr. T.S. Gangte, Principal, Churachandpur College, Manipur, Dr. H. Kamkhenthang, Sr. Research Officer, Tribal Welfare Deptt., Manipur, Dr. B. Pakem, Reader, N.E.H. University, Shillong, Dr. D. N. Barthakur, Director, I.C.A.R., North Eastern Region, Shillong, Mr. D.B. Ghosh, Deputy Director General, G.S.I., Shillong, Ms. Jaya Hazarika, Tinsukia College, Assam, Mr. Satish Chandra Kakati, Ex-Editor, Assam Tribune, Dr. D.N. Majumdar, Reader, Anthropology, Guwahati University and last but not least to Mr. N.K. Jain, Director, Directorate for Development of Tribes and Backward Classes, Manipur, for valuable material help and friendly suggestions. I am greateful to them.

I have also to mention my deep love and affection that I owe to my loving daughters Nivedita and Sunandita for their unending help and cooperation throughout the preparation of this book.

My wife Mina Das has shared the challenge of rethinking and reworking on the manuscript at every stage. My deepest love, intellectual and personal is to her.

I am also highly thankful to Shri B.P. Garg, Gian Publishers' Distributors for early publication.

Last but not least I record my sincere gratitude to those who have been quoted and to those from whom help and cooperation have been received.

S.T. DAS

CONTENTS

LIST OF ILLUSTRATIONS

CHAPTER I

GLIMPSES OF THE EASTERN STATES

The Assamese have always lived in isolation in a remote corner of India encircled by the mighty Brahmaputra. Nevertheless affinity of language and religion bind the Assamese to the rest of the country.

Since independence the State of Assam has lost territory—the district of Sylhet at partition, the Naga Hills in 1958, Meghalaya (Khasi, Jaintia and Garo Hills districts) in 1970, and Mizo Hills and Arunachal Pradesh (NEFA) in 1972.

Many States

The Greater Assam state has now been reduced to the Brahmaputra valley, where the State's official language, Assamese is spoken; the Barak valley (Cachar) where Bengali enjoys the status of the officially recognised district language; and the connecting Mikir and North Cachar Hill where tribal languages have official local provenance.

In the Brahmaputra and Barak valleys tribal groups like the Bados and Kachar's lived by fishing and hunting and spoke Tibeto-Burmese languages till about 2,000 years ago when people from Mithila speaking a dialect of outer group of Indo-European language came and settled. The immigrants brought iron tools to hack down thick semi-tropical evergreen forests and to work the heavy soils of the Brahmaputra valley. They produced more food and could sustain bigger population than the primitive people. The immigrants therefore multiplied faster. Their language and their culture ultimately became the language and culture of the valley.

In the Barak valley the Kacharis continued to hold their own till the 18th century when their king was given a fictitious Kashatriya lineage. Immigrants from East Bengal overwhelmed the Kachari indigenes, but the area retained its name, Cachar. The people are referred to as Kachari, but the district is referred to as Cachar.

Early Society

The Assamese represent the early Indian Society. Untouchability is negligible. Only 6% of the population are untouchables. All Assamese are equals, though some are more important than others and may be called *dangarias*, the respected. The elders enjoy a special status and the village headman is called the *gaonbura* or the village elder. The young are pampered and have rights and freedom of action. Bride capture was a usual form of marriage till recently, and gave youth options which the arranged marriages of other Indian societies denied.

The Assamese lived in a remote corner of India. The mountains which enclose the Brahmaputra valley make of it a blind alley. This geographical isolation of the Assamese has been further emphasised by the area having had a different historical experience than the rest of the country. The tribes, who held on to food gathering or shifting cultivation with the aid of hoes, were expelled into the backyard—the hills.

The natural landscape of Assam is of a naturally wooded tract rendered into a grass land by man's activities. If the grass is not burnt every year, the forest will take over and rob thousands of tourists of opportunities to see the one-horned rhino. Except for four months in the winter it rains through out the year and it rains heavily, thus providing the optimum condition for forest growth.

The forest is fought back by ploughing. The Brahmaputra valley is thus a man-made grassland. It is narrow (nearly 128 k.m.) wide and long (extending over 800 k.m.). Brahmaputra valley is the third biggest in the world.

Manipur, Nagaland and Tripura

Taking into account of the greater Assam, three of the most strategically situated states : Manipur, Nagaland and Tripura, on the north-eastern border, were the most neglected one.

Manipur and Nagaland, along with Tripura are three of the smallest states of the Indian Union. Tripura and Manipur were princely states with mythological accounts tracing back their history to the epic age.

Arjuna, the hero of the Mahabharata, during his wanderings in the forests, is said to have married Ulupi, the daughter of a Naga chief and had a son named Iravant. Later a Manipuri Princess also bore Arjuna a son, Babhruvahana. Years later Arjuna returned with a horse for Ashwamedh yaga. Conquering all the areas he reached Manipur. His son Babhruvahana came out to receive him. Arjuna asked him to fight as required of princess. In the battle Arjuna was beaten and badly injured. Ulupi the Naga Princess, is said to have arrived with medicinal herbs from the mountains and revived Arjuna.

Nagaland and Manipur have long borders in the east with North Burma, with its proximity to China, while Tripura on three sides is surrounded by friendly Bangladesh. The 8.2 lakhs tribal population in the hills have similarity to those in Nagaland and Tripura while 9 lakhs of people of the valley, owing to different topography, climate and religion have developed an entirely different type of culture.

The people of the Manipur valley are orthodox Vaishnavite Hindus by religion. The people and their houses are perhaps the cleanest in the world. Their greatest contribution to the country is the Manipuri dance, one of the four classical dance forms of India. The women work harder than the men. The Manipuris have developed from ancient days indigenous games and sports. Polo is said to have originated in Manipur. Manipuri is the common language among the people of the valley and the hills, even though the latter have a large number of dialects among the tribes. A Manipuri of the valley does not take meat in any form but relishes fish. Fishing in the ponds and rivers with especially made nets form part of the day's programme for any family.

Tripura with its five low ranges running from north to south has about sixty per cent of its area covered with forests. The tribal people with its shifting cultivation adhered to the hilly regions while the valley has been populated by the Bengalis. In the thirteenth century A.D. King Ratna Manikya, settled ten thousand Bengalis of various professions in Tripura. Surrounded by pre-partition Bengal, the culture and way of life of the people of the valley have been akin to those of any Bengali village and the tribal people in spite of their own dialects, dances and attire were closer to the people of Bengal.

About 30 per cent of the population of Tripura are scheduled tribes and ten per cent scheduled castes. Land for tribal people has never been surplus. The Jhuming cultivation has been reduced. Special schemes were undertaken to bring the tribal people on to permanent cultivation.

In Nagaland, the population has only a microscopic minority of non-tribals consisting mostly of traders and government servants. The villages are mostly situated on peaks of hills and far away from each other. Jhum cultivation which the hill people are used to from time immemorial continue as the jungles are still quite sufficient for the increased population to burn and to cultivate. They return to the same place after about 12 years.

There are 16 main tribes each distinguishable by its separate dialect, its dance and the colour and pattern of the shawls its people wear. The common language has been a kind of Assamese passed on by word of mouth, today known as Nagamese and used also in the Legislative Assembly. As a state, Nagaland has adopted English as the official language. The tribal people of these regions are perhaps the most musical of all the people of India.

Village Organisation

The hill people of these three states have certain similarities, the most important being an ideal village organisation. From the most democratically elected leadership, there are in some tribes on autocratic hereditary chiefship, which administer the village and dispense justice based on the unwritten traditional laws of the tribes. The village lands are owned collectively by the village. But the highly developed terrace cultivation, the result of hard work of individual, is owned by families who pass them on to their children. Small plots on which homesteads are built are also under individual ownership. Land disputes are almost unknown. But the vast forests used for Jhuming cultivation, the special jungles reserved for fuel and grazing, the trees preserved around the water points are all owned collectively. There are very few boundary disputes between villages and the traditional boundaries dividing miles of jungles are respected by both sides.

But in Manipur and Tripura there is a large population of tribes of Kuki origin. For hundreds of years these tribes have been migrating but today the villages have become permanent. A strong man with a sense of adventure and ambition went far away into pastures unknown, cleared the jungles and started a new village. He became the chief and those who desired settling in his village had to give him the annual rent in terms of paddy, parts of animals that had been killed and certain other services. These terms differ from tribes to tribes. The chief has his own mantris (ministers), who looked after various aspects of village administration. The natural forests are the most important resources of these three states. Geological mapping of these areas has not yet been taken up systematically though some indication of the presence of oil in Tripura, coal in Nagaland and lime stone in Manipur has been obtained and work on projects has started. Sources of hydro-power are in abundance, particularly prospects for micro-hydel projects.

The people of all the three states are rice eaters. Every family tries to grow rice whether in the valley or the hills. Jampui Hills in Tripura have been producing the finest oranges.

The Manipur oak 'Uyum' takes the Tasser worm. This tree grows wild in the Manipur and Nagaland jungles.

Meghalaya

Meghalaya came into existence in January 1972. It consists of the three districts of the Garo, Khasi and Jaintia Hill which previously formed part of Assam.

Although there is uncertainity regarding the origin of the Khasi and Jaintias, they are believed to be a remanant of one of the early population movement into India from Indo-China and their language belonged to the Mon-Khmer family of languages of that region. A customery law in the Khasi society is by which property is handed down from the mother to the daughter. The Garos, who inhabit the western segment of the state, are part of the Bodo race of the Tibeto-Burman family, with a matrilineal society as in the case of the Khasis and

Jaintias. They still practice shifting cultivation and their staple food is rice.

Arunachal Pradesh

Arunachal (previously known as NEFA or North-East Frontier Agency) also came into existence in January 1972. It consists of five districts, named after the principal rivers that form their drainage. It is bound on the west by Bhutan, on the north by the Tibetan region of China, on the east by Burma and on the south by Assam.

The inhabitants of the extreme northern and western regions have had age-long economic and social contacts with Tibet and Bhutan, so that their language, religion, dress and social habits have strong Tibetan affinities. The extreme eastern region, on the other hand, have been subjected to influence from Burma and there are number of small settlements of people of Burmese origin known as Khamptis and Phakials, who have maintained their identity as Buddhist communities in their adopted homeland. The inhabitants of the southern fringe of Arunachal, particularly the villages along the plains and lower hills, have had traditional economic and social contacts with the Assamese and have also some knowledge of the Assamese language.

The main bulk of the inhabitants in the interior hills, until recently, had little contact with the outside world. Of Mongoloid stock, they speak their own languages, which are mainly of the Tibeto-Burma family.

Until January 1972, both Arunachal and Meghalaya were constitutionally part of the state of greater Assam. Both the areas are tribal. The economy of the two areas is basically not much different. It is essentially an agricultural economy and the people practised mainly shifting cultivation, with rice as the staple crop. Both areas have rich possibilities for horticultural development.

The main charm and delight of the region is its flora and fauna. The significant feature of this area is the democratic process. Laws are framed by the people, sanctioned by the council and promulgated by the president or the chief. The chiefs have no right but to approve and enforce it. Hence, the people propose, the council sanctions and the chief promulgates.

Every evening all the men gather in spacious council room to discuss the topic of the day. The extension of democratic processes from the limits of a village over a wider sphere will provide one of the most exciting challenges to the people of Meghalaya and Arunachal Pradesh in the years to come.

Hot, humid, malarial but also green, mountainous and enchanting ; a land in which pagan worshippers of nature and Christians live in amity. It is Cupid's own hunting ground. In Mizoram love has no limits.

Mizoram

In Mizoram, every person from the plains is a 'Vai', an outsider. In Mizoram, there are two distinct groups—The Mizos themselves (mi=man, zo=hill, ram=country) literally the highlanders and their homeland, and the 'Vais', implying the Bengalis of neighbouring Cachar and all plains men in the rest of the country.

It lies in the north-eastern corner of India. Bounded by Burma in the east, Bangladesh on the west and Cachar and Manipur on the north and north-east. There is little flat surface land in the state.

Mizoram has three districts—Aizawl, Lunglei and Chhimtuipui. There are many rivers and streams, chief among them being Tlacong (Dhaleswari), Karnaphuli and the Kolodyne. Wet paddy cultivation and irrigation are very limited. Excluding the hot, humid and malarial tract inhabited mostly by the Chakmas, Mizoram has a pleasant climate and beautiful landscape. Rice is the staple food and all manner of meat goes into the Mizo diet. Pork (Vawksa) is the favourite meat.

The Mizo are of the Mongoloid family. One notices difference in stature, complexion, pigment of the eye, hair and other features among different sub-tribes. Among the major tribal groups Lushai, Hmar, Ralte, Paihte, Pawi, Chakma and Lakher deserve special mention. Traditionally, the Lushais were dominant and most of the chiefs belonged to the Lushais clans of Sailo, Rokhum and Zadeng. Barring the Chakmas and Lakhers, who prefer to call themselves Maras, all other tribes speak the Mizo language. The Chakmas speak a dialect similar to Bengali and Assamese while the Maras have their own language.

In the traditional religion of the Mizos, when a man dies his spirit enters the 'dead man's village' with the spirits of all animals and human beings killed by him in his life time. The more numerous the spirit of the slains, the better for a man's spirit after his death. This was a probable motive for head-hunting. A few teasing village belles could send a band of young men on a raid to collect heads as proof of their valour.

In olden days, the Mizos had an institution called 'Zawlbuk.' It was a dormitory for all the unmarried men and boys of the village. The inmates of the Zawlbuk were generally very noisy and the chief alone could admonish them. Games were played, wrestling was indulged in on a large scale, physical fitness was at a premium. The Zawlbuk enabled the chief to summon all young men for the defence of the village against a surprise attack. In some ways, the Zawlbuk was similar to the old 'Kalaris' of Kerala.

The Garos have a similar institution, 'Nokpante', which flourishes in some parts of Garo Hills even today. Now Zawlbuk has disappeared from Mizoram before the second world war.

The Mizo society has always been engalitarian. Even the chief were not particularly affluent. A sense of humour, along with the ability to sing, dance and make speeches, is the most widely shared quality of the Mizos.

Traditional dances like 'Cheraw Kan', 'Chheih lam' and 'Solokia' are popular, and one still hears about some one seeing spirits in the jungles (ramhuai).

The secular traditions are well-preserved, particularly in matters of love, marriage and inheritance of property. The youngman's right to court a young woman (nula) has not been curtailed, though curfew has placed severe limits on its nocturnal manifestation. The custom of a boy meeting and wooing a girl is known as 'Nularim'. In olden days boys would leave their homes after dinner and meet the girl in her house. If she rolled tobacco for him in paper and tied it with her hair, it was a declaration of love. These days, the boys are on the giving end and presents are said to include chocolates and cosmetics.

The Mizo society is tolerant of sexual peccadilloes. This does not mean permissiveness or laxity. The old custom of paying a price for the bride is still in vogue. The bridegroom pays this money to the bride's father and it is distributed among relatives.

Women bring water and firewood, work in the Jhums and weave clothes, with a rudimentary infrastructure, the economy of Mizoram is still based on the traditional method of shifting cultivation, 'Jhumming'.

From inter-tribal wars and spirit worship, the Mizo has come a long way in a short span of time. Today he is very westernised and restless.

A visual feast awaits the visitor to these Eastern states. Here history has taken a back seat and allowed Nature to enchant the tourist. Game sanctuaries, lakes and waterfalls, miles and miles of tea gardens, exotic orchids and the sheer greenery of hills provide a fitting back drop for the colourful fantastic costumes, customs, and handicrafts of the divergent people.

CHAPTER II

GEO-STRATEGIC SIGNIFICANCE

The need for an in-depth study of the geopolitical significance of the north-east region of India is readily suggested by misconceptions and confusion about the country. The people and their problems spread over this far-flung part of the country. The term 'region' is of recent use. In common parlance as well as official discussions the term is used quite often now-a-days, specially after creation of tiny States and Union Territories in about two decades of the post-Independence period.

The north-eastern area originally comprised the composite Assam or old Kamarupa and the two Native States of Manipur and Tripura. In mediaeval times the area was ruled by various indigenous dynasties such as Chutiya, Kock, Kachari or Bodo and later by the Ahom who came from Burma and ruled the country in the east for about 600 years. After the British annexation in terms of the Yandabo Treaty (1826) it was known as Assam more explicitly than before and formed part of the British Empire of India. However, no definite or conclusive explanation is available as to why the Area was called Assam. According to some well-known writers, the name was derived from *asama* bearing a topographical meaning; some others felt that Assam was equivalent to Ahom; still others were of the view that Assam meant 'peerless'. E. A. Gait, author of A History of Assam, however, held the opinion that 'Assameis a Sanskrit derivative and is a fair equivalent to Ahom'.

Whatever that be, Assam alone, as it exists at present, no longer comprises the north-east reagion; it is only one of the constituents forming the region. Theo ther constituents are Nagaland, Meghalaya, Manipur, Tripura, Arunachal Pradesh and Mizoram. Their population and areas individually are as follows:

Assam—Population 14,625,159 and area 78,528 sq. km.; Nagaland—Population 516,449 and area 16,572 sq. km.; Meghalaya—Population, 1,011,699 and area 22,489 sq. km.; Manipur —Population 1,072,753 and area 22,359 sq. km.; Tripura—Population 15,56,342 and area 10,477 sq. km.; Arunachal Pradesh—Population 4,67,511 and area 83,578 sq. km.; and Mizoram—Population 3,21,986 and area 2,398 sq. km.; (The population figures are given on the basis of the 1971 census). The area of the entire north-eastern region is 2,36,401 sq. km. with a total population of 23 millions which may have now reached the figure of about 26 millions. The peoples inhabiting the region are in all stages of civilisation. While Assam, Nagaland, Manipur and Tripura are five fullfledged States of the Indian Republic, Arunachal Pradesh and Mizoram are two Union Territories. However, demands for raising the status of Arunachal Pradesh and Mizoram to full Statehood have been voiced by the peoples and Governments there and it is most likely that their demands would be met by the Centre in the near future.

Although Assam of the past, or the north-east region as it is called at present, had been known for its own civilisation, its geographical position was not known to many people including those with a sense of history and geography. In 1908 Mahatma Gandhi, for instance, revealed a wrong notion about the people of this part of the country whom he mentioned in his Hind Swaraj or 'Indian Home Rule' as people like Pindaris and Thugs. During his first visit to Assam in April 1922 Gandhiji expressed regret for the observations he had made in his booklet, at a huge public meeting held in Gauhati. He said, "I have committed a grave mistake in my booklet Hind Swaraj in which I bracketed the Assamese with Pindaris and other wild tribes. I have made ample amends to the people. It was certainly a grave injustice to the great Assamese people who are every whit as civilised as any part of India."

Even as late as in 1936 many people in India and outside had no correct knowledge as to the geographical location of Assam and, for that matter, of north-east India. This is revealed in Dr. S. K. Bhuyan's London Memories. According to him, "Londoners who have heard of Assam can be counted on the tips of fingers" Dr. Bhuyan said, "When I told a lady that I come from Assam she greeted me saying 'Oh, I know the place. My brother lives in Bangkok.' She did not known that from Assain it was a long way to Tipperary and Siam. This ignorance is not shocking, as here in India ; Assam is Honolu to many a University product." He adds, "I told a London grocer that Assam grows abundant tea and the grocer readily said, 'I know it well. I sell Darjeeling tea myself." Dr. Bhuyan had to explain to the innocent grocer that Assam and Darjeeling were two separate regions.

Such misconceptions about the geographical location of the north-east region or Assam and its people can be multiplied. But there is little doubt that this region was till recently considered as a land of mosquito, kala-azar, rains, floods, earthquakes, head-hunting, sorcery and, of course, tea and oil. One may believe it or not, Assam was so much identified with, say, kala-azar, that in the admission form prescribed by the Cotton College authorities in the twenties there was a column in the form which said : "Do you come from a Kala-azar area ?" The column spoke for itself and revealed the strange ideas about this part of the country. At present also, there are persons whose perceptions in respect of the geography, history, politics, language, social customs, etc. of the people living in the region have not changed much ; if at all, certain events of the past few years have deepened the wrong impressions of many ill-informed but highly educated persons.

In regard to the geographical significance of the region it is necessary to understand its situation in relation to the world map. No part of India other than the north-east region has boundaries which are clearly vulnerable to outside powers. The area is surrounded by four foreign countries, viz. Bhutan, China, Burma and Bangladesh, touching 4,825 km. in length. The breakdown boundaries figures are as follows : Boundary between Assam and Bhutan—500 km. ; between Arunachal Pradesh and China—1,175 km. ; between Arunachal and Burma—475 km. ; between Mizorm and Bangladesh—275 km. ; between Tripura and Bangladesh—625 km. and between Meghalaya and Bangladesh—400 km. In the context of the Super Powers' hobnobbing with small countries in troubled water the significance of the N.E. region can be overlooked at the peril of inviting troubles of one kind or another. Students of Political Science and International Affairs would perhaps agree that the area is sensitive and its sensitivity is easily comprehended from another historical fact, that is to say, the population of the area is polyglot and a large percentage of them come of tribes whose links with India during the British Rule were minimal, if not non-existent. And, excepting Bhutan, the three other foreign countries close to India in the eastern part cannot be counted as permanent friends or permanent enemies. China's behaviour in any case is unpredictable; Burma's north-west parts have been found to be convenient hideouts for the Naga rebels while Bangladesh's Chittagong Hills areas are known to be a sanctuary for the Mizo extremists. The problem of infiltration from erstwhile East Pakistan has become intractable and its implications may be better imagined than described.

Notwithstanding their unparalleled capacity for formulating their defence policy the Britishers did not, it seems, have adequate perception about the geopolitical significance or north-east India nor the Government of free India realised after attainment of Independence that the area was ill-defended against foreign attacks. Similarly, the new Government did not properly grasp the political the problems in order to fix priority in solving them. It seems the Government followed the footsteps of the alien rulers in dealing with the problems of the region. A study for the foreign and defence policy of the British Government during the period 1858-1905 reveals that the Britishers were chiefly concerned with the defence of the north-west frontier of India. Britain's main anxiety was to prevent the danger of a thrust upto the heart to Central Asia posed by the inexorable advance of imperialist Russia, commonly described as Britains' Russophobia. The occupation of the Pamirs—the roof of the World was of vital significance in the latter half of the last century. A British military expert had apprehensions that the Russian posts on the Pamirs with Chitral in anarchy would constitute a dangerous neighbour for the British Empire in India.

This brief reference to the north-west frontier at the end of the 19th century is relevant to a study of the present-day position of the north-east frontier areas. It needs hardly to be stressed that the significance of the geopolitical situation of the region was not adequately appreciated by the British rulers nor by the successor Government after ndependence. For this lacuna in defence matter compounded by similar leeway in other spheres pertaining to this part of the country the nation had to face an ignoble situation in 1962 following the unprovoked and unexpected aggression of China on the northern borders. After Independence the Government of India should have recast the defence needs of the country in the proper perspective. Unfortunately, India's obsession with the Hindi-Chini Bhai Bhai philosophy was so deep that the Nehru Government did not apprehend any attack from China. But the events of October-November in 1962 exposed the Government's serious lapse in a vital field like national security. Even the none-too-happy relationship between India and Pakistan failed to suggest to policy maker in New Delhi that the north-eastern region was vulnerable to outside attacks and called for foolproof pre-preparedness for its defence. China's attack in 1962, however, impeled the Government of India to reorient the entire defence policy relating to this part of the country as all others together with building up the necessary infra-structure, specially road communications along the northern border.

Equally, if not more, significant and important are the political problems and issues. It is on record that excepting the people of Assam in the plains districts those of the other constituents of the region did not have any opportunity to join the mainstream of the freedom movement. The British Government had deliberately barred all contacts between the plainsmen and the highlanders in Assam and the neighbouring areas through various devices like introduction of an Inner Line, for instance. Though this system was ostensibly an economic measure to protect the peoples in the hills from any interference in their way of life the measure developed into an impenetrable barrier between the hillmen and the rest of the region which was further tightened by the Bengal Frontier Regulations I of 1873, etc.

The division of the Hills districts into Excluded and Partially Excluded Areas under the Constitution of 1935 was another political device by which assimilation of the hillmen with the plainsmen was hampered and thus the tribes were kept isolated from the winds of national awakening. This, in reality, constituted a sort of museum policy pursued by the alien rules Foreign missionaries were also working as handmaids to the British administrators in the tribal areas. The trading community among the Britishers was not lagging behind and, having the monopoly in tea, oil and coal industries besides its hold in river and rail communications, the British commercial section was also giving a helping hand to the then rulers in various ways. This is borne out by the fact that Lord Curzon, the most influential and reactionary among the Viceroys of India, told the tea planters of Assam in 1901 that the identification of interests of all classes of Englishmen in India was his constant endeavour which he repeated in a speech at Barakar in 1903 in the following words : "I look upon all Englishmen in this country as engaged in different branches of the same great undertaking my work lies in administration, yours in exploitation but both are aspects of the same question."

Lord Curzon's exhortation to the Englishmen of all hues serving in this part of the country is self-explanatory. All this had a very baneful effect on the entire population of north-east India. Despite the policy of the British rulers to isolate the hillmen from the others the message of the freedom struggle did penetrate some of the hill areas. This is evident from the anti-British agitation launched by Rani Gaidiliu in the inaccessible jungles of erstwhile Naga Hills district. Still, it cannot be denied that the unrest of the Nagas soon after India's becoming an independent country was one of the results of the then Government's museum policy applied to the tribals. Gradually, separatist tendencies affected the other Hill districts which formed parts of composite Assam for ages. Even, Arunachal Pradesh, that is, the erstwhile North-Eastern Frontier Agency (NEFA) which was by and large free from the operations of the foreign missionaries and other anti-national forces was separated from Assam. In the process the Assam part of the region was split and two new States Nagaland and Meghalaya were created besides two Union Territories—Mizoram and Arunachal Pradesh. Judged by the historical fact that the alien rule had neglected the region in the matter of the welfare of the people the Government of India should have initiated viable and time-bound schemes to develop the region. The answer to the separatist movement did not lie in the fragmentation of the composite Assam. Unfortunately, the Government created, in a huff, if one may say so, a number of States and two Union Territories. But it seems that the remedy has proved worse than the disease.

The problems of ethnicity in north-east India, let it be acknowledged, is a real one. But the problem has been made more complicated by the legacy of the British policy and has been overplayed by detractors of the national movement over the years. In order to take advantage of the situation arising out of isolation of the hills tribes from the rest of the country during the British days, a scheme was hatched by an Oxford Professor, Mr. Reginald Coupland, as transfer of power from the Raj to the Indians was imminent, to create a buffer State comprising the Excluded and partially Excluded Areas in the eastern most part of India to which a slice of northern Burma was to be added through negotiation with the Burmese Government. The Scheme prepared early in the forties is generally known as the Coupland Plan. For unknown reasons the British Parliament did not approve of the scheme and thus a potentially dangerous political design ended. Had a buffer State of Professor Coupland's conception been created in north-east India, the situation would have become internationally dangerous. However, the geopolitical importance of the region was not lost to the Britishers. The Cabinet Mission's Plan of May 16, 1946 to place Assam under Group C was another design by which the British Government in collusion with the Muslim League sought to keep up its hold in the area. Mr. M.A. Jinnah's bid to grab Assam into his projected Pakistan in the forties though Assam was not a Muslim majority Province lends support to the suspicion that some powers were sedulously working to detach Assam and the neighbouring area from India. Even Sheikh Mujibur Rahman had an eye on Assam, for he wrote in his book, Eastern Pakistan : Its Population, Determination and Economics : "Because Eastern Pakistan must have sufficient land for its huge population and Assam will give it full scope for expansion, and because Assam has abundant forests and mineral resources, coal, petroleum, etc. Eastern Pakistan must include Assam to be financially and economically strong."[38]

However, attempts of the aforesaid forces did not succeed. Following the attainment of Independence it was hoped that notwithstanding the harm that the alien rulers and their benchmen had caused to the integration of the various ethnic groups inhabiting the region, an outlook for national cohesiveness and understanding among all sections of the polyglot population would be promoted. That hope does not appear to have been brought to fruition even after three decades of Independence. This is an important aspect of the geopolitical life of north-east India that merits close attention of the Government, intellectuals, sociologists and others interested in peace and harmony among the people.

The unsatisfactory and inadequate communication system between north-east India and the rest of the country is also a relevant feature in the geo-political life of the area. The partition of the country in 1947 left this part high and dry. The only territorial link with the mainland was a narrow strip of land, 56 kilometers wide, spread over between West Bengal and Bihar, but without any rail facility or any worthwhile road. The importance of this corridor on consideration of strategy and transport was soon realised and Assam was linked by a M.G. rail line at Fakiragram within a couple of years. Admittedly, this was a remarkable achievement on the part of the Indian Railways authority. The complete dislocation of the inland and waterways between Calcutta and Gauhati which was the lifeline of transportation of goods to and from Assam in 1965 following the Indian-Pakistan conflict added to the transport bottleneck. The construction of a B.G. railway line from Delhi to Gauhati removed some of the difficulties in transportation of goods brought from outside north-east India for the entire region and the construction of Farraka Barrage has solved many long standing problems of this region.

In order to have an appreciation of the affairs of north-east India a reference has also to be made to the vast natural resources the region possesses and how these have been harnessed with fringe benefits to the population. In terms of natural resources the north-east is one of the richest regions but in point of economic development it is one of the most backward. This is an obvious paradox. To illustrate this point one needs only to refer to two very precious commodities, namely, oil and tea. Oil was first discovered in Assam and a British Company established a refinery at Digboi, the first of this kind in the country, in 1905. After Independence the first oilfield was successfully exploited at Naharkotiya in 1952. In the subsequent years several oilfields have been discovered in Upper Assam and the known reserves of crude oil in this part of the country are of the order of 69,27 million tons according to the Government of India's statistics compiled a decade ago, and the search is still on. The same official source says that there are 42,460 million cubic meters of natural gas in Assam alone. And yet a refinery in the public sector did not come up in Assam till 1962 when the people had to launch a massive agitation for fulfilment of a legitimate demand of theirs. The Gauhati Refinery established in the wake of public agitation continues in its original capacity of .75 tons.

Assam's tea occupies a prestigious place in the world's map of the tea industry. Approximately, 51 percent of India's total production of tea (575.12 m kgs) is produced in Assam. Since the Government of India earns a sizeable foreign exchange out of tea export every year Assam's contribution in that respect is considerable. (India's total export of tea in 1980 was 224.49m kgs. valued at Rs. 412.25 Crores). But Assam does not derive much benefit for a variety of reasons. Jute is another important agricultural produce, Assam produces the bulk of raw jute out of the country's total production of 5.3 million tons (1977), but there is only a small jute mill at Silghat in the cooperative sector. No effort seems to have been made to establish more jute mills. The earlier proposal to set up jute mills at Barpeta and Mangaldoi, the two main jute producing centres in Assam, has not made any progress. Water resources in north-east India are aboundant and can meet, if properly harnessed, the entire power requirements of the north-east region. Presently, some schemes have been undertaken such as at Loktak in Manipur and Kapili in Assam.

However, there seems to be a sense of awareness on the part of the Government of India for speedy removal of backwardness of the region, but unless the projects undertaken to that end are quickly and cohesively implemented the agony of the region with a host of problems, political, economic and social, is unlikely to disappear in the near future. The problems of the north-east people are multi-faceted and complicated and have to be solved in the right perspective. Indeed, the region is a miniature of India where, as in respect of the whole country, unity will have to be evolved in the midst of diversity so that a mosaic of Indian society can emerge.

CHAPTER III

TRIBAL SITUATION

The Tribes

The scheduled tribes of North-East India can be broadly be categorized into two broad divisions : (i) those who inhabit the hilly areas, or, the majority of the inhabitants of Arunachal Pradesh, Mizoram, Meghalaya and Nagaland and the inhabitants of the hilly districts of Assam, Manipur and Tripura; (ii) the tribes living in the valley areas of Assam, mainly the tribes of the Brahmaputra valley. Though these two categories are based mainly on the geographical situation of the habitat, they also indicate differences in cultural characteristics. The tribes in the hills (excepting a few, of course) remained isolated till the time of the British occupation. On the other hand, the tribes in the valley areas have been living with the other non-tribal communities since time immemorial and there has been a great amount of cultural give and take between the tribes and other neighbouring communities. In fact, the present Assamese culture is a synthesis between the cultures of the tribal inhabitants and the Aryan migrants. On the other hand, the habitats of the hill tribes are completely separated from the habitats of other non-tribal communities, but the valley dwelling tribes live amidst non-tribal communities, that is to say, their villages are interspersed between villages of other communities. Demographically scheduled tribes in the hills form a majority in the states of Meghalaya, Mizoram, Nagaland and Arunachal Pradesh, but in the valley areas of Assam and in Manipur and Tripura states scheduled tribes are minority as will be seen from the following figures:

State	Total Population	Scheduled Tribe Population	% of Scheduled tribes to total Population
Arunachal	4,67,511	3,69,408	79.01
Assam (Plain Areas)	12,456,477	1,344,026	10.78
Assam (Hill Areas)	4,55,357	262,622	57.67
Meghalaya	1,011,699	814,230	80.49
Mizoram	332,390	313,299	94.25
Nagaland	516,449	457,602	88.70
Manipur	1,072,753	334,466	31.17
Tripura	1,556,822	450,544	28.93

There is great variation in the population figures of different tribes. There are very small tribes with only a few hundred individuals and there are very large tribes comprising several lakhs in individuals. The population figures of some of the major tribes in different States/Union territories in North-East India according to 1971 Census are given below :

Tribe	Total Population of the tribe (1971)	% Population of State/ Union Territory
Arunachal Pradesh		
Adi	99,372	21.25
Aka	2,347	0.50
Apatani	12,888	2.75
Bongro	1,085	0.22
Hill Miri	8,174	1.74
Khamti	4,078	0.87
Miji	3,549	0.75
Mishing	3,359	0.71
Monpa	28,209	6.03
Nishi	80,325	17.18
Nocte	23,165	4,95
Sherdukpen	1,639	0.35
Singpho	1,567	0.33
Sulung	4,250	0.90

Tribe	Total Population of the tribe (1971)	% Population of State/ Union Territory
Tagin	20,377	4.35
Wancho	28,650	6.12
Meghalya		
Garo	4,11,532	40.67
Hajong	23,978	2.37
Jaintia	82,493	8.15
Khasi	3,84,006	37.95
Assam		
Boro-Kachari	5,43,615	3.63
Chutiya	9,103	0.06
Dimasa	37,900	0.06
Karbi	17,360	0.11
Lalung	10,650	0.07
Mech	12,919	0.08
Mishing	1,80,684	1.20
Manipur		
Aimol	108	0.01
Anal	6,592	0.61
Chiru	3,590	0.33
Chothe	1,117	0.10
Hamar	38,207	3.56
Kabui	17,360	1.61
Khoira	406	0.03
Maram	19,968	1.86
Tangkhul	58,167	5.42
Mizoram		
Mizo	2,70,312	81.32
Pawi-Lakher	21,427	6.44
Ralte	170	0.05
Tripura		
Chakma	68,711	4.41
Jamatia	22,446	1.44
Magh	12,378	0.79

Tribe	*Total Population of the tribe (1971)*	*% Population of State/ Union Territory*
Riang	74,931	4.81
Tripuri	2,68,948	17.27
Mariang	9,710	0.62
Nagaland		
Angami	43,569	8.43
Ao	65,275	12.63
Chang	15,816	3.06
Konyak	72.338	14.00
Lhota	36,949	7.15
Phom	18,017	3 48
Rengma	8,578	1.66
Sema	65,227	12.62

Political situation

The British first established their rule in the Brahmaputra valley as under the Treaty of Yandabo between the British and the Burmese. The Burmese king surrendered his claim over Assam to the British. Gradually they extended their administration to the different hill areas in North-East India. The date of extension of British administration in the hill areas of North-East India are shown below (Barpujari 1977-7):

Garo Hills	1816
Manipur Hill Areas	1820
Arunachal	1825 to 1875
North Cachar Hills	1829
Jaintia Hills	1835
Karbia Anglong	1838
Khasi Hills	1866
Nagaland	1878
Mizoram	1889

The Brittsh Government adopted a policy of keeping the tribal areas isolated from the rest of the country. The Government of India Act of 1935 provided for delimitation of Excluded and Partially Excluded Areas, which were kept practically outside the powers of the legislature and were under the direct administrative control of the Governor (Roy Burman, 1970). Simultaneously, the British Government established the Inner Line to control the entry of outsiders in Arunachal, Mizoram and Nagaland.

The political situation of tribal areas of North-East India became different after India became independent. Though in North-East India the struggle for political freedom was limited to the valley areas only, on the eve of the attainment of Independence political consciousness started to develop rapidly among all the tribal populations of this part of our country. The Constitution of India in the Sixth Schedule provides for district autonomy for the hill districts of erstwhile Assam. But the Nagas, from the very beginning of the Constitution, were demanding separation from Assam, and they did not co-operate in forming a District Council in Accordance with the Sixth Schedule of the Constitution. Only five District Councils, one each for the Garo Hills, the United Khasi and Jaintia Hills, the Mikir Hills (the present Karbi Anglong district), the North Cachar Hills and the Mizo Hills (present Mizoram), were set up in 1952. But soon there were demands for creation of regional Councils for the minority communities in Mizo Hills and in the United Khasi and Jaintia Hills and as a result in 1953 a regional council was formed for the Pawi-Lakher region in the south-eastern part of the Mizo district and in 1963 a separate District Council was created for the Jowai Sub-division of the United Khasi and Jaintia Hills district.

Soon after the Sixth Schedule came into operation in the hill districts of erstwhile Assam, it was felt that the powers of the District Councils were not adequate for all-round development of the tribal populations and so there were two sets of demands: some wanted the Constitution to be amended to give more powers to the District Councils and the others demanded a separate state comprising the hill areas of Assam. The movement for a separate Hill State was intensified in 1960 after the passing of the bill to make the Assamese language the official language of Assam. This movement was led by an organization of the leaders of various political parties of the hill areas called the All-Party Hill Leaders' Conference (APHLC). On 11th September, 1968 the Government of India announced its decision on the reorganization of Assam by forming an autonomous State comprising the hill areas within the State of Assam. On 15th October, 1968 the APHLC decided to accept the proposal. But meanwhile all the hill districts of erstwhile Assam except Garo Hills and United Khasi and Jaintia Hills districts decided to keep away from the autonomous State; so ultimately the autonomous State was formed with these two districts only. Ultimately at the time of reorganization of North-East India this autonomous State within Assam was granted full statehood as the Meghalaya State and Mizoram and Arunachal Pradesh were granted the status of Union Territories, and all the North Eastern states, namely, Asssm, Meghalaya, Manipur, Nagaland and Tripura were placed under one common Governor.

It cannot be said that after the reorganization of the states in North-East India the problems of the tribal populations of North-East India have been solved once for all. It wll be proper here to discuss some political problems of the tribal areas. It is very often said that the tribal groups have their political aspirations. But, political aspiration is a very elusive term. When India was under foreign rule the political aspiration of the whole nation was to become free from British rule. The people of a part of British India had the aspiration to build a state on the basis of religion. After Independence the political aspiration of the tribes of North-East India varied between complete severance of all political ties with India and formation of small administrative units (that is, states) for a group of communities having some affinities. This is very clearly reflected in the following words of Sonaram Thaosen, a Dimasa leader of North Cachar Hills (1967) :

"...the hill tribal people of eastern India are today divided into two groups depending upon two different circumstances. So also is the case with their problems. In the first group, they think that they have been turned into second class citizens and therefore want a separate homeland. They do not feel safe in the secular state of India. Thus their slogan is 'Better be a king in hell, than lead a dependant's life in heaven,' though actually they may not sincerely believe in such a thing.

"The other group of the hill people want to grow up in the Indian soil itself. They may not give away all they have, but they want to grow by mutual give and take."

But a question naturally arises, will the creation of administrative units (like Meghalaya and Mizoram) with groups of communities with some affinity amongst themselves solve the political problems of the tribes of North-East India? The indications of inter-tribal conflict were perceived by a mature Khasi political leader, B.M. Pugh (1962), who expressed himself like this :

"The outlook among the different tribes on North-East India has given rise to the demand in the Mizo Hills District for a Khasi-Jaintia State. So, while two decades ago the hills people considered themselves as one group, today, as instinct of self-preservation and mistrust, are making it more and more difficult for the tribes to get together or to look forward to living together in peace and harmony."

The remark quoted above is very appropriate because of the fact that each of the newly created 'tribal state' or 'tribal union territory' comprises more than one ethno-cultural groups, speaking languages of diverse origins, having different types of cultures. If ethnicity is the reason for establishing administrative units, it will ultimately be necessary to subdivide the present states and Union territories of North-East India into still smaller fragmentary units.

The late Professor Nirmal Kumar Bose, who was a stalwart of Indian Nationalism in the academic sphere, emphasised that political and economic co-operation can be achieved between different states though there may be a multiplicity of cultures within these states. He said:

"Let every state preserve its right to worship, to promote its language and literature, arts and crafts in its own way Let all these elements of culture enrich the life of the 'masses' or the 'working classes' to the utmost extent possible. In a vast country like India with more than twice the population of

U.S.A. or the U.S.S.R., and with what is nearly equal to the population of Europe minus Russia, where is the harm if we have many languages, many religions, many kind of arts and crafts in order to beautify our lives ? Provided, of course, that we march hand in hand, and with an increasing degree of involvement in building up and sharing in common political system and economic order, whose aim is to end all exploitation and enrich human life; and all that though the original non-violent strength of the masses, both in peace and in war, both in the task of rebuilding out lives by common labour and also in resisting authority when abused ? For that was the definition which Gandhi gave of the meaning and content of Freedom." (Bose, 1967).

If the above is true for India as a whole it is more true for North-East India, where there is a greater variety of cultures and traditions. The solution of the political problem of the tribes of North-East India has very nicely been summed up by the late Prime Minister Jawaharlal Nehru in the following words:

"The problem of tribal areas is to make the people feel that they have perfect freedom to live their own lives and to develop according to their wishes and genious. India to them signifies not only a protecting force but a liberating one. Any conception that India is ruling them and that they are the ruled, or that customs and habits with which they are unfamiliar are going to be imposed on them, will alienate them."

Economic Problems

Our discussion above has shown that the political problem is more imaginary than real. Speaking about the political movements in North-East India, the late Prime Minister Nehru remarked : "There exists no political problem. The problem is economic and when the economic problem is solved, the solution of their problems will be easy."

In the beginning of this paper the scheduled tribes were categorized into two classes, the hill tribes and the valley-dwelling tribes. The economic problems of scheduled tribes also fall into two categories : the problems of the valley dwelling tribes and the problems of the hill tribes. The economic problems of the valley-dwelling tribes are not different from the economic problems of the Indian peasantry in general, that is to say, landlessness, land alienation, indebtedness, fiamentation of holdings, backward agricultural practices, so on and so forth. On the other hand, the economic problems of the hill tribes are entirely different. Tiil very recently, the tribes were in a primitive stage of economy, the basic principles of which are production for consumption, no capital investment, investment of excess wealth for enhancement of prestige, kin-oriented economic co-operation. Such primitive economy does not require a country-wide economic infrastructure. But in the recent past the hill tribes have suddenly become a part of the modern economy of the country, and the countrywide economic infrastructure has completely engulfed the tribes of North-East India. But because of the hangover of the traditional kin-based economic organization they have not yet been able to participate fully in the new economy and so enterpreneurs from comparatively advanced communities are taking advantage both of the economic infrastructure that has grown up in recent times and also of the simplicity of the tribal people in these areas, sooner or later this will certainly cause resentment in the minds of the tribal people when they will realize that others are taking advantage of the resources of their land.

As is the case with India as a whole, almost all the tribal people in North-East India are basically cultivators. So, the problem of economic development of the people of these areas is dependent on agricultural development. But the stumbling block in agricultural development in the hills is that most of the people in the hill areas are following a very primitive method of cultivation, known as shifting cultivation or jhumming. This method of cultivation involves cutting down of the jungle of a particular plot of land in the months of December and January and allowing the cut down trees and other vegetation to dry in the subsequent three or four dry months. Just before the monsoon the whole plot of dried up vegetation is burnt and seeds are shown, broadcast or dibbled. Just with the commencement of the rains the plants start growing and the ashes act as manure. Harvesting in the shifting plots starts from September and goes on till November-December, different crops being harvested at different times at the same plot. After harvesting in some areas the plot is utilized in the same manner for a second or even a third year. But anyway the plot is to be abandoned when it exhausts its fertility and such abandoned plot can be utilized again for cultivation when it is covered with jungle again after a period which may vary from 2 years to 4 or 5 years.

Shifting cultivation has its inherent defects. It can be considered to be adequate to satisfy the needs of a community in a primitive level of economy with undeveloped technology and very low density of population. According to an estimate (Tripura Government, 1966) made in soil and climatic conditions of Tripura, the net area required per consumption unit under shifting cultivation is 9.24 hectares, taking their existing standard of living and taking cultivation factor as 11 (i.e. fallow period of plots 10 years). In another estimate (Bose 1967) made in two villages of Mizoram, 0.75 and 0.97 acres respectively. The great difference between these two estimates is probably due to the variation of climatic and soil conditions. But from these estimates it is very clear that the carrying capacity of land under shifting cultivation is very much less than land under permanent cultivation. From the above estimates it is also clear that the problem of shifting cultivation is intimately linked with the rapid growth of population in the hill areas of North-East India. The phenominal growth of population in the hilly areas of North-East India can be judged from the following figures:

Period	*Percentage of increase in the whole of Assam.*	*Percentage of increase in the hills areas.*
1911-1921	13.2	8.2
1951-1961	35.0	35.9

Some British administrators, who had long experience in these regions, could foresee the situation as early as the first half of the present century, but unfortunately no corrective steps were taken either by them or by their successors. Recurrent famines in these regions were an ominous indication of the fact that the fertility of the soil under shifting cultivation was rapidly decreasing. In the Khasi Hills the effect manifested itself in the sudden upward trend of potato cultivation, which, in fact, came to dominate the whole economy within a short time. All over the hilly regions of North-East India, adopting of non-agricultural occupations by a gradually increasing number of people, particularly near the urban centres, is another indication of rapidly decreasing yield from the shifting plots. In shifting cultivation it is inevitable that with the increase of population plots become smaller and smaller and at the same time the fallow period becomes shorter and shorter. However, in many areas of North-East India the fallow period has remained 15 to 20 years. In such areas shifting cultivation has remained capable of satisfying the requirements of the population at their existing levels of economy. While in some other areas, due to heavy pressure on land utilized for shifting cultivation the yield has become insufficient even to fulfil the bare necessities. The population in such areas has tried to solve the problem in the following ways:

(i) By reclaiming land for settled agriculture.

(ii) By attempting to utilize plots more or less permanently by growing perennial fruit bearing plants like pineapple, betel, vines, arecanut, oranges, etc. In the Khasi Hills the Khasis have evolved an improved type of slash and burn cultivation for potato cultivation. It is an interesting fact that even in the areas where they have opened up land for permanent cultivation, shifting cultivation has persisted as a subsidiary method of cultivation for the following reasons:

(i) A number of traditional vegetables can be grown in shifting cultivation, while utilizing every inch of the permanent land for major crops like paddy and millet.

(ii) Some crops like ginger, cotton, hill jute, etc. are grown only in the plots of shifting cultivation and such crops give them a steady source of cash income.

(iii) As labour in the shifting plots is supplied both by males and females (rather, in some respects females work more) while in settled agriculture most of the work is done by males.

Women's labour can be fruitfully utilized if shifting cultivation is practised side by side with settled agriculture.

Social Problems

The tribes of North-East India are very much free from many of the social evils of the larger Indian society. They have no caste system and the associated evils like untouchability or social inequality, they do not have the dowry system as it prevails in the larger Indian society. Their womenfolk enjoy equal status with the males and both the sexes share the burden of life equally. However, the tribal societies are also changing very rapidly since there contact with the outside world. Many of the tribes are now living in urban areas and they have been able to utilize fully the benefits of modern science and technology. No one should now be surprised to see a member of a tribal community in the most interior area of North-East India possess a radio set, a TV or even a motor car.

The hills and plains division of the tribes of North-East India is also relevant in respect of the social change situation. The valley-dwelling tribes are in long contact with the Assamese society and culture. From very early times they became attracted towards Hinduism and all of them are now in different stages of Hinduization. However, very recently some trends of revivalism have developed among these tribes and in order to assert their identity they are trying to recreate their traditional cultures which were on the verge of extinction. On the other hand, the hill tribes remained more or less isolated and there was no remarkable change in their societies till the advent of Christianity, which has now become the major force of social change among all the tribal communities in the hills except those in Arunachal Pradesh. The origin of Christianity in North-East India can be traced back to 1793 when Dr. William Carey, a Baptist Missionary came to India. Dr. Carey in the beginning met with strong opposition from the East India Company's officials. In 1838 the American Baptist Mission took over the work of English Missionaries in Assam and the adjoining hill regions. With the change of the mission the British government's policy towards the Missionaries also changed, so much so that Captain Jenkins, the Commissioner of Assam, invited Missionaries to work among the hill tribes (Jaohn 1967). The Missionaries first tried to convert people in the valley areas, but their success was not encouraging. So, in 1867 there was a complete reversal of the policy of the Christian missions, namely, a change of emphasis from the plains to the hills (Sword 1935 : 31). It is interesting to note that the first converts in two major tribes were the achievements of two preachers work among the Nagas in 1872 (Philip, 1976 : 190) and Krishna Chandra Pal worked among the Khasis in 1813 (Pugh, 1967 b). Christianity achieved tremendous success in North-East India after an initial setback as will be seen from the following figures (Census of India, 1931) :

Year	*Number of Christians in Assam**	*Percentage variation from the previous decade*
1881	7,093	+137.2
1891	16,844	+113.5
1901	35,969	+ 85.1
1911	66,562	+ 98.5
1921	132,106	+ 88.7
1931	249,246	

Percentage variation from 1881 to 1931 +3,414.0%

The extent of Christianity among different tribes of North East India can be judged from the following figures from the Census of 1961.

Tribe	*Percentage of Christians in the total Population of the tribe*
Assam	
Garo	37.94
Khasi	47.54

(*Contd.*)

*In the Census of India 1931 the figures for Assam include figures for Assam, Meghalaya, Nagaland, Mizoram, Manipur.

Tribe	*Percentage of Christians in the total Population of the tribe*
Mikir	10.28
Mizo	96.95
Manipur	
Gangte	87.83
Kmar	99.21
Kabui	35.53
Kacha Naga	45.16
Mao	22.02
Paite	85.69
Tangkhul	88.09
Thadou	58.72
Nagaland	
Dimasa	0.21
Kuki	54.65
Naga tribes	55.12
Tripura	
Chakma	0.02
Hallam	1.55
Jamatia	*
Kuki	42.40
Lishai	98.73
Naga	0.06
Noatia	0.03
Riang	3.01
Tripuri	0.03
Arunacnal Pradesh	
Aka	—
Apatani	—
Ashing	—
Mishing	1.77
Galong	4.55
Khamti	—
Miju	0.93
Minyong	5.70

*Data not available.

Tribe	*Percentage of Christians in the total Population of the tribe*
Miri	2.37
Mishmi	0.48
Monpa	—
Nocte	1.51
Padam	23.61
Sherdukpen	—
Singpho	—
Tagin	0.88
Tangsa	1.21
Wancho	—

Thus it will be seen that Christianity has emerged as the religion of the hill people of North-East India (excepting those of Arunachal Pradesh and some parts of Tripura) and there is a feeling that has created some sort of a gap between the other populations and the hill tribes of North East India (Mankekar, 1972). But there are other opinions also which make other factors responsible for estrangement of the Hill tribes of North-East India from the mainstream of Indian nationalism (Srinivas and Sanwal, 1972). Even Christian leaders like B.M. Pugh feel indebted to Christian Missionaries for their contribution in uplifting the tribes. Pugh believes that Christianity will ultimately help in national integration:

"The Christianity will continue to spread among the tribes, there is no doubt in my mind. As Christianity is gracefully accepted by the majority community as one of the religions of India, and as its adherents are given full protection to practise their own religion, the loyalty of the tribal Christians to the great Indian society will grow and national integration will grow a pace converting the north-eastern region of India into a strong bulwark against any inroad from external enemies." (Pugh, 1967 : 242)

Christianity has not caused any serious imbalance in the social order of the tribes, because, Christianity has not disturbed in any way the traditional social framework. Only traditional values which stand in clash with Christian ethics were abandoned.

We cannot consider conversion to Christianity as a major problem in integrating the hill tribes in the mainstream of great Indian culture. Spread of education, development of communications, sharing of the common mass media, sharing of a common political system are some of the factors responsible for bringing the hill tribes of North-East India closer and closer to the greater Indian culture; rather, these factors have helped to build up a common culture for India as a whole.

CHAPTER IV

THE TRIBAL PEOPLE

Nature seems to have unfolded her bountiful art treasures in this eastern part of the Indian union. This region presents a picturesque landscape, a landscape of hills and ravines, steppes and slopes. Rich varieties of flora and fauna are found in the plateaux of the hills and the impenetrable forests. This eastern region, criss-crossed with rivers and mountains, has been aptly called "The Red River and the Blue Hill."

To the visitor from outside, this region has been a land of exceptional interest. Hemmed in on the north by the lofty chain of the Himalayas and on the south-east by the Patkai ranges, it is a picturesque country criss-crossed with hills and valleys that captivate the eye. The rich greenery is not the only attraction. The cultural heritage of the diverse people inhabiting the hills and the plains provides an equally inviting texture of ethnic interest.

The region with her diverse population speaking different languages and professing divergent faiths, may be regarded as an epitome of India. It is in this land that waves of immigrants from Tibeto-Burman and Mongoloid stock have met and woven with the aboriginals a pattern of common tradition and heritage. The people of the hills and the plains have lived long side by side and followed common pursuits of life undisturbed. They have the capacity of living and working together for common objectives.

Before the formation of five more states in greater Assam, it can boast of a happy synthesis of varied cultural streams. Up to the twelfth century, several tribal chieftaincies—Chutiya, Lalung, Mikir, Kachari, Miri, Garo and others—thrived in the region. And due to the close association between varied groups and their interdependence in socio-economic aspects, there has always been a mutual borrowing of cultural traits and religious values, especially when such exchanges were helped by territorial proximity.

The 13th century witnessed the Ahom invasion from the upper Irrawaddy valley. The Ahom had a tough time subduing the Chutiyas but succeeded finally in reaching the Brahmaputra valley. They later had to face a combined attack from other tribal people—the Kacharis, Mikirs and Lalungs of the plains. Even in the 16th century, the Ahom had to battle with the Koch tribe to establish their suzerainty. However the net outcome of the Ahom invasion was the establishment of a strong monarchy, introduction of a new land tenure system, importing Hindu faith from the western part of Assam. Gradually the small tribal estates were lost, though their vestiges are still to be seen. The Ahom however did not enter the Assam hills such as Khasi or Mizo and there the earlier political organization continued till the Britishers arrived in the nineteenth century. Varied caste groups entered the Brahmaputra valley from Bengal, Bihar, Uttar Pradesh, etc., to make a gradual impact on the tribal people of the plains. But the hills were left isolated and undisturbed (culturally) except for a few trade centres.

There is another point to be stressed in a review of the tribal culture of the plains of Assam. In the middle of the 15th century a new wave of religious faith was brought by Sankaradeva, who was born in the district of Nowgong. Sankaradeva visualised the fallacies in the ritual-laden Hinduism and initiated the Mahapurushiya faith based on simple prayer and discourses and absolute devotion to Krishna. His thought came up when this Eastern part of India was so much entangled with tantric cult. Sankaradeva tired to influence the then Ahom king but was driven away by the king's brahmin priest and took refuge in the jungles of Barpeta. Later, the king of Cooch Bihar got him patronage, his gospels were propagated through the length and breadth of Assam and Northern Bengal. Many of the tribal people of the Assam plains got them selves converted to the Mahapurushiya faith.

The whole of Assam has the pride of being the land of a number of lively tribal people who maintain cultural distinctiveness and yet display a certain amount of cohesion at different levels. There are the Mech, Rabha and Hajong of Goalpara, of Bodo origin. Some of the Kochs of the same areas have been so much Hinduised that they go for redesignating their tribal designation. Garo Hills are mainly inhabited by the Garo with their typical *nokna* system of inheritance. Then in the United North Cachar and Mikir Hills there are the Mikir, Dimasa and Semsa Kacharis, most of whom are Hinduised. Many Mikirs, living in close proximity with the Khasi, have taken Khasi wives and follow a combination of matriarchal—patriarchal system of social organisation. The district of Sibsagar is inhabited by the Morans, who are Assamese in culture and Burmese in physical features. Khamptis, the plain Daflas and Miris share much of the traits of neighbouring groups; yet each of the groups can be identified by its typical festivals, dances and ritual practices. The Chutiyas of Darrange and Lakhimpur hail the Ahom invasion. The Khasi, with the Pnar, Lyngamn, War and the Bhoi subgroups live in the Khasi and Jaintia Hills. The Mizo, Lakher and the Poi are to be seen in the Mizo Hills—and the tract where India meets with Burma and Bangladesh. Below, I delineate the life and culture of Assam's three important tribal groups—the Dimasa, the Lalung and the Khasi.

The Dimåsa, with their agnates the Semsa, form a predominating group of the eastern wing of the Bodo race and mainly dwell in the United North Cachar and Mikir Hills. 'Di' means water and 'Sa' is son and hence, the Dimasa claim that they are descended from the great river Brahmaputra. It was only when the Ahom came to power and organised themselves into a strong monarchy that the Dimasa were forced to push themselves back into the hilly terrain and jungle pockets of North Cachar hills, where they are to be seen now. Once they were also won over by the Koch king of Kamatapur and in spite of this unstable past, they have, even to this day, retained many of their traditional traits. Dimasa houses are arranged on high level and usually they are roofed by thatch, having a low mud plinth The rooms for keeping livestock are built on piles.

The Semsa have a separate structure, 'nodrung', to be used as a dormitory for bachelors.

The Dimasa houses built on highest levels are fitted with windbreakes—a device to check a strong gust of wind. They grow paddy on hill slopes through slash and burn method of cultivation and every housewife is adept in weaving beautiful scarfs, saris and wrappers. The combination of polychromatic flora and faunal designs speak of their keen sense of art. There are blacksmiths among them and the men also make baskets with square bases typical of Assam hills. Bihu is their chief festival and the whole village turn up mirthfully on the occasion.

The Khasis of the Khasi and Jaintia Hills represent a typical matriarchal community. The children take the clan name of the mother and the husband either settles in the wife's village or in her house. Of late, this system has been partially modified, in that the husband, in many instances, lives in a separate shed or apartment, constructed by himself, by the side of his maternal residence. Khasi boys cannot inherit any parcel of the property which is generally owned either by his mother or by his sisters. But the men are always the custodians of virtual power, because we see that "Siems" and "myntris" are always men, the Khasi clan durbars are patripotestal organisations and in running the family, the men have ample responsibilities to shoulder.

The central part of the Khasi hill is occupied by the main Khasi group, whereas the peripheries are occupied by the Khasi sub-groups among whom inter-marriages are permissible but not always possible. There are dialectical and cultural variations. Bordering the Garo Hills we have Lyngamns, bordering the Cachar district the Pnar Khasis and closer to the Sylhet plains there are the War Khasis, while adjacent to the Kamrup plains and Mikir hills live the Bhoi. Each group embraces people following Hindu, tribal or Christian faith, yet each has developed some distinctiveness. But the truth is that all are Khasis. All join and participate in the traditional festivals such as *Shad-Sukmynsiem, Beiding Khlam* and *Nongkrem* dance and all boast of the chivalry of the U Tirat Singh, the ex-Syiem of Nongkhom, who gave a good fight to the incoming Britishers when they were busy in spreading their tentacles over the Khasi hills.

The Khasis are primarily agriculturist. In the hills they practise slash and burn method of cultivation to produce maize, potato and paddy. In the valleys paddy is also grown through the wet method. But then there are Khasi craftsmen adept in basket-making, weaving, blacksmithery, brass-smithery and pottery. The crafts have developed and thrived in the Khasi and Jaintia hills backed by favourable ecological and cultural conditions. Thus the main Khasi area has abundant iron ore and so we have had there a number of villages with black-smiths; the art of brass-smithery could be imported to Pnar area; the potter's clay of the Sung valley has been able to collect the few Khasi potters in its vicinity and so on. Certain crafts involving heavy labour like brass work and black-smithery are always done by men; while the other crafts are performed by women. The women also give a hand, to their industries' parterns, in agricultural operations, in marketing commodities and on all other pertinent occassions.

The Lalung furnish us an example of a tribe which due to different ecological settings has been divided into two categories (1) the plains and (2) the hills. The latter group still possesses its antique *Chhamadi* or bachelor's dormitory house and other traditional festivals. The plains Lalung live in compact villages, having adopted many items of their neighbouring caste groups. The plains Lalung villages have at the central part a *Chhamadi* where the village council meetings are held. This is headed by a Sangdolui who also arranges their most prominent spring festival. Besides there are the harvesting festival (Washi rawne), Bihu festivals and *Jongkhong puja,* when Mahadeo, Lakhmi and other deities are invoked. There are different sets of priests for different rituals; and in a special festival they also expose their devotion for Sankaradeva, the great religious reformer of Assam. Though residing within a close range of the Hindus of the plains and being fully conscious of the caste order, they have not yet taken to the services of Hindu priest, probably due to their devotion for everything traditional.

Opinions differ as to the origin of the Lalungs. Some of them go as far to trace themselves from Tibet while there are some who call themselves akin to the Mikir. However, as the Lalung share Mikir culture and because even to this day among the plains Lalung marriage by capture of a Lalung girl with a

Mikir boy is acknowledged by society, a close traditional link of the Mikir and Lalung is suspected. If a Lalung girl is taken away by a Mikir boy, she must later come back to her father's house and only then a share of the property would go to her. The whole Lalung tribe is divided into a number of Khul or clans, with a Baijla or Khul-chief for each, but well organised in groups.

But, then working at Assam as a whole, one can justifiably say that this strategic state represents, in miniature form the whole of India. Assam is real laboratory for experimentation in achieving unity among people who speak in a myriad voices, belong to diverse faiths and live under varied conditions for the geo-politics of the region have tended, in recent times, to make some of the highlanders restive.

To the anthropologist, Assam is a rich field of study, with a polyglot population in all stages of civilization.

CHAPTER V

LIFE IN THE HILLS

The word *tribal* as used with reference to certain communities living in the plains of Assam is somewhat a misnomer. As a matter of fact we do not know definitely who the original inhabitants of India were. It is not certain whether the Dravidians or Austric speaking people, who peopled the country before the advent of the Aryans from Central Asia, were autocthons or immigrants. Whether the pre-Dravidians spread up to Assam or not is difficult to say: but some anthropologists have noticed pre-Dravidian physiognomical features amongst the people of lower Assam and also amongst certain communities.

All that we can say with certainty is that from about 2000 B.C. there was a movement of Mongoloid populations from the north to India through Assam and these people along with others who migrated from nothern Burma formed from the remote past the bulk of the population of Assam.

There were apparently wave after wave of these migrations and the invaders belonged to the Indo-Chinese linguistic family, of which the two most important sub-families are the Mon-Khmer and the Tibeto-Burman. The third, Siamese-Chinese, include Shan, which was spoken by the Ahoms, the last of these invaders.

The Mon-Khmer speakers appear to have come earlier than the others. They were subsequently driven by Tibeto-Burman horders into the Khasi Hills, which is the only part of Assam in which the sub-family now exists. Of the Tibeto-Burman sub-family, there were three groups, namely, Naga, Kukichin and Bodo. The Naga and Kuki speakers were driven to the hills and Bodo became the dominant language. It includes all the surviving non-Aryan languages of the plains, the Gara Hills and the North Cachar Hills, Kachari, Mech, Garo, Dimasa, Tipra, Lalung, Rabha and Chutiya are derivations of Bodo.

About the time the Mongolian horders were entering Assam through the north-east, the Aryan started spreading over the whole of northern India across the Gangetic plain, driving the indigeneous inhabitants to the south. Eventually some of the Aryans reached Assam in their eastward movement through Bihar and north Bengal.

A very significant fact about Assam is the fusion which took place here of Aryan and Mongolian cultures. We find here an example of how a dominant culture, although supported numerieally by few, can absorb and impose itself on weaker culture. Thus we find in Assam, a people by and large Mongolian, speaking at the present day, Assamese, which is an Aryan Sanskritic language. This happened not merely because of the superiority of an Aryan language over the rude tribal dialects but also because of the absorbing power and influence of Hinduism. The Brahmins from Northern India succeeded in absorbing into Hinduism all the tribal people of the plains including the powerful Ahoms who ruled over Assam for over six hundred years and who in course of time not only adopted the Hindu religion, discarding their own, but also forgot their own Ahom language and adopted Assamese. Now, Ahom language is dead, known only perhaps to almost half-a-dozen *deodhais* (Ahom priests) only. The same thing happened to all the languages of the Bodo group. The complete disappearance of such tongues like Rabha and Kachari, which are still spoken in the interior by old men and the womenfolk, is only a matter of time.

The bulk of the population of Assam is tribal or at least of tribal origin. Most of these tribal communities through assimilation have lost their tribal characteristics and similar assimilation of such communities as are called plains tribal is continuing. People who can still be regarded distinctly as tribals can be found now only in the hills.

The hill-tribals of Assam live in the districts of Garo Hills, United Khasi and Jaintia Hills, United Mikir and North Cachar Hills and the Mizo Hills. The North Cachar Hills are inhabited by several tribes such as the Dimasa, the Kukis and the Zemi-Nagas.

The first thing that strikes a visitor in any part of these hills is the magnificence of their natural scenery and the attractiveness of the people, because of their simplicity, cheerfulness, honesty, courtesy, hospitality, vitality, colourfulness and a perfectly democratic outlook.

In Mizoram, the scenery is different, rather, rugged as compared with that of the Khasi and Jaintias or the North Cachar Hills, but yet it has a sombre grandeur which one could not appreciate better from anywhere else than from the top of the Blue Mountain (7600 ft.) in the south-eastern corner of the district. On a clear day one can have from this point a view of the sun blazing the waters of the Bay of Bengal miles away.

No doubt surroundings influence our habits and character. The distinctive characteristics which are regarded as tribal are to a considerable extent shaped by climate, the nature of the soil, the terrain and the scenery of the land which they inhabit. Life in these hills are hard. One can hardly imagine the difficulty with which a Mizo or Zemi Naga has to eke a livelihood out of his little patch of land. From before day-break the womenfolk of a village march in processions, carrying a number of bamboo tubes in a cane or bamboo basket, hundreds of feet down to a spring or a stream to collect water for the day's use. The return journey up hill with the load of water on their back is strenuous. Immediately after their return they have to get busy preparing food for the family before they accompany their husbands to help them in their work in the Jhum (cultivation). About half-an-hour is spent at mid-day in eating the packlunch (consisting of rice, salt and chillies) they carry with them to the Jhum and then work goes on again till sun-down. In the evenings the menfolk snatch a few moments of leisure and relaxation which they devote to *Zu* (rice beer or spirit) drinking and singing while the women have to carry on with their household chores—cooking and attending to the pigs, the fowl and their own little ones. On special occasions, there is dancing both by men and women in addition to *Zu*-drinking and music. This is the normal routine of the average tribal's life in the hills which could not perhaps be better described than in the following lines of Thomas Gray composed in a different context :

> Far from the madding crowd's ignoble strife,
> Their sober wishes never learned to stray;
> Along the cool sequestered vale of life,
> They kept the noiseless tenur of their way.

In physical beauty the Khasi women excel their sisters both in the hills and the plains. Their complexion in a golden yellow and their soft smooth features have a Polynesian touch. As has already been indicated, ethnologically, the Khasis are different from the other hill-tribes of Assam. While the later are supposed to have migrated from the North-East, the Khasis came from the South-East. Their Mon-Khmer speech is still spoken in Cambodia and Pegu and anthropologists have noticed some common customs and habits among the Khasis and Malayasians.

The Garos belong to the stock called Tibeto-Burman and they have close affinities with the tribal races inhabiting the plains of Assam, North-Cachar Hills and part of Tripura, the Garos have the strongest resemblances, linguistically and physically, to the Kacharis. It is most probable that these two people originally constituted one, subsequently separating themselves, the Kacharis spreading over the north and the Garos over the south bank of the Brahmaputra.

The origin of the Mikir is obscure. Of the tribes of the North-Cachar Hills, the Zemis came from the Naga Hills. They are a sub-tribe of the Kachha-Nagas, who again are a branch of the Angamis, whose men are noted for their physical vigour and mainly beauty. The Dimasas are a branch of the Kacharis who ruled over Upper Assam until they were driven out by the Ahoms in the beginning of the sixteenth century. The Kukis came to the North-Cachar Hills in two waves from the Mizo Hills, from where they were ousted by the more vigorous Lushais. who in their turn had migrated from the Chin Hills of Burma.

As regards their domestic life, customs and beliefs, although a somewhat common pattern runs through all the hill-tribes, there are strong local variations. Apart from hard work in their fields and seeking relaxation and recreation in *Zu*-drinking, singing, dancing, feasting, hunting and fishing, which are habits common to all, each tribe has peculiarities which mark it out from the others. For example every Garo's life is spent in giving (or refusing) and demanding *dai* (compensation). A man's great grandfather was killed fifty years ago, he demands *dai* from the heir of the murderer, and if it is not paid his heir will still demand it in turn and so on until it is paid.

Marriage customs, law of inheritance, etc. also differ from tribe to tribe. The most distintive feature of Garo and Khasi societies is their matriarchate. Descent is claimed from a common ancestress and it goes down through the females. It is the husband who, after marriage, has to go and live in his wife's house and not *vice versa*. Property in inherited by the youngest daughter. Amongst the Garo, when the son-in-law comes to live in his wife's parents's house, he becomes his father-in-law's *NOKROM*, i.e. to say a kind of representative of the father's clan. After the death of the father-in-law, the NOKROM marries the widowed mother-in-law, thus becoming the husband of both mother and daughter. This custom is rather extraordinary and there is nothing comparable to it among the other tribes.

All the other hill tribes are patriarchal. The Lushais, Zemi-Nagas and Kukis have to buy their wives by paying a marriage price. The price is calculated in terms of a number of *mithans* (wild bulls or cows). If divorce takes place as a result of a lapse on the wife's part, her father has to return the marriage price. If on the other hand, it is the husband's fault which brings about a divorce, he loses the price. The custom of demanding marriage-price for girls among the partiarchal tribes is easy to appreciate when we take into account the fact that a woman's life in the hills is harder than a man's. While an unmarried buck, except for being compelled to put in his share of work in the fields, is allowed to go about freely hunting, fishing, drinking, singing, dancing and making love to his heart's content, a girl has to help her mother from dawn to dusk in running the household and catering to the needs of the menfolk. It is therefore, that an unmarried girl is looked upon by the family as a valuable asset which cannot be parted with except for reasonable price.

Divorce is easy to obtain amongst all the tribes. Among the Garos it is allowed almost automatically on payment of the customary *dai* of sixty rupees or so. Amongst the Khasis it is even easier. In the presence of witnesses, the husband gives five *cowries*, or pice in lieu, to the wife and the wife does the same. The husband then takes all the ten *cowries* and throws them on the ground and this completes the divorce.

Divorce amongst the Khasis and the Jaintias are so common an occurrence that children very often do not even know the identity of their fathers.

From the liberal nature of their marriage and divorce laws it would be seen that the hill people have a very scientific and liberal attitude to all matters concerning sex. Unmarried boys and girls are not interfered with in their love making and even the bearing of children out of wedlock before marriage is not strongly frowned upon. A different standard in sexual matters is, however, expected, particularly of the womenfolk, after marriage. This is specially true of the Zemi-Nagas and all other Naga tribes. Rape of a married woman is considered an offence more heinous than murder.

Besides hunting, fishing, etc., a popular pastime of the Garos and the Nagas till recent times was head-hunting. Human victims were required for sacrificial purposes also. But now there is no evidence of head hunting having been practised by any of the other tribes except perhaps the Kukis. The Lushais also raided the plains frequently before their land was occupied by the British, but they were satisfied with carrying off captives and were not after heads. Human sacrifices were, however, common in the Khasi and Jaintia Hills, especially among the Jaintias who might have borrowed the practice from Tantrik Hindus of the plains.

The practice of human sacrifice among the Khasis is an extra-ordinary institution. There is a superstition among the Khasis about a gigantic snake called '*U-Thlen*' which has to be appeased by the sacrifice of human victims.

The *thlen* attaches itself to property and brings prosperity and wealth to the owner, but on the condition that it is supplied with blood. Its craving comes on at uncertain intervals and manifests itself by sickness, by misadventure or by increasing poverty befalling the family that owns the property. It can only be appeased by the murder of a human being. The murderer cuts off tips of the hair of the victim with silver scissors, also the finger nails and extracts from the nostril a little blood caught in a bamboo tube and offers these to the *thlen*. The murderer who is called *u nongshohnoh*, literally 'the beater', before he sets out on his unholy mission, drinks a special kind of liquor called *ka iad tang-shi-snem* (liquor which has kept for a year). This liquor, it is thought, gives the murderer courage and the power of selecting suitable victims of the *thlen*. The *nongshohnoh* then sets out armed with a short club, with which to slay the victim; hence his name *nong-shohnoh*, i.e. one who beats. He also takes a pair of silver scissors above mentioned, a silver lancet to pierce the inside of the nostrils of the deceased and a small bomboo or cylinder to receive the blood drawn therefrom. The *nongshohnoh* also provides himself with rice called '*u khaw tyndep*', i.e. rice mixed with turmeric after certain incantation have taken place. The murderer throws a little of the rice over his intended victim, the effect of which is to stupefy the latter, who then falls on easy prey to the *nongshohnoh*.

It is always not possible to kill the victim outright, hence he resorts to the following subterfuge. He cuts off a little of the hair or the hem on the garments of a victim, and offers these up to the *thlen*. This is disastrous to the unfortunate victim, who soon falls ill and gradually wastes away and die.

Many families in these hills are known or suspected to be known keepers of a *thlen* and are dreaded or avoided in consequences. This superstition is deeply rooted amongst the people and even nowadays, in places like Shillong or Cherrapunji, Khasis are afraid to walk alone after dark for fear of being attacked by a *nongshohnoh*. The Khasis keep the snake *thlen* in a box called *bhut* (devil).

It may be stated that the greater number of the Khasis, especially in certain siemship, viz. Cherra, Nongkren and Mylliem, still regard the *thlen* and the persons who are thought to keep *thlen*, with the greatest awe and that they will not utter even the names of the latter for fear some ill may befall them. The superstition is probably of very ancient origin, and it is possible that the Khasi sacrifices to the *thlen* demon may be connected with the primaeval serpent god which characterised the religion of the Cambodians.

Such extraordinary local variations of religious practices notwithstanding, the animistic religion of the hill-tribes have the common feature of having strong affinity to Hinduism. They all believe in a Supreme Being (e.g. the Pathian of the Lushais and Tatara Rabunga of the Garos), subordinate to whom there are numerous gods and spirits who have to be propitiated with sacrifices of animals and birds for warding off evil spirits and calamities. From these beliefs and practices it would be safe to assume that the Tantrik form of Hinduism, which originated in the plains of Assam around the temple of Kamakhya, greatly influenced the tribal religions. In other words, this form of Hinduism contains features which are tribal and which were probably adopted by Brahmin priests for winning over their tribal neighbours, the most characteristic feature of Hinduism having been throughout the ages assimilation rather than conversion.

The most remarkable feature about tribal life in the hills of Assam is the fundamentally democratic basis of their social and administrative organisations. With minor exceptions, the land belongs to the community and not to any individual. Although in the Garo Hills the *Nokma* (the head of a clan or a village), in the Khasi and Jaintia Hills the *Siem* or the *Doloi* or the *Raja*, and in the Lushai Hills, till recently, the chief was the nominal proprietor of all lands within his jurisdiction, every villager could cultivate his plot of land anywhere as a matter of right. Wealth and income do not confer social privilages. The once powerful Lushai chief and the Khasi Siem, who were regarded by the neighbouring people as Raja or King, were as much commoners as the humblest of the humble. The Lushai chief who weilded enormous authority over his subjects, was the father of the villagers over whom he ruled. In times of scarcity, if the villagers committed robbery of grain from the chief's granary, they committed no offence.

This democratic spirit was strongly reflected in the indigenous tribal administrative organisations. The Khasi Siems were constitutional monarch. They can hardly ever give any decision independently. It is his *myntries* (ministers) who generally decide all matters for him. Thus, in spite of the chiefs and the Siems being chosen on the hereditary principle their administration was thoroughly democratic. Disputes are heard in open court where all the male members of the village take part In some areas even the women are allowed to be present at the trial of cases. The judgement passed on an offender, is regarded as a judgement of the whole village and not merely of the chief and his advisers. This system of administration suited the genius of the people and they were happy under it. The British with their experience of administration over half the world, were wise enough not to interfere with the indigenous administrative machineries.

Since independence, the tone and colour of administration in the hills have undergone a complete metamorphosis. The establishment of the District Councils under the sixth schedule of the Constitution suddenly brought party politics into the hills where it was unknown before. In addition, the creation of numerous new government departments, and as a result of the induction of hordes of officers from plains, with hardly any service to render to the people and with hardly any co-ordinating agency to regulate their activities, practically destroyed over night the old, strong, efficient administrative set up and disrupted the life of the people. The abolition of the institution of chiefs in the Lushai Hills was unfortunate step, the consequences of which are seen in the disturbances which are now shaking the once happy and smiling land of the Mizos.

The greatest harm caused to the hill people by the new set up, was the damage and degradation caused to their character. The outstanding characteristic of these people had always been their strong spirit of self-help and self-reliance. They made and maintained village paths, constructed school, church and hospitals, wells, water tank, play-grounds and did other work of public utility voluntarily, without remuneration. These were community projects. The establishment of development blocks without taking local conditions and temper of the people into account, and the liberal doing out of grants, loan and subsidies in the name of community development have now absoutely changed the picture. The people now not only refuse to perform any of the task mentioned above without payment, but these doles have affected their attitude to such an extent that they have stopped giving proper attention even to their rice fields, knowing that if crops fail, free or at least subsidised rice would be available by the government. Extracting something out of government for nothing has in fact become a practice with them. Hence these people have thus been so demoralised that they do not hesitate to resort to chicanery for obtaining gifts.

The *Deka-Changs* (youngmen's village club) are called *Nok-pates* in the Garo Hills, *Zawlbuks* in the Lushai Hills, *Morungs* in the Naga villages and the *Maro* by the Mikirs. These *Deka-Changs* are an excellent institution and a distinctive feature of every tribal village. In these clubs young boys have to serve and obey the older boys, besides being associated with agricultural, social and allmost all othera ctivities of the village community, instilled into the youth discipline, respect for and obedience to elders, a spirit of service to the community. It is a pity that these clubs are gradually becoming a thing of the past. The imposition of modern administrative set up has created a sense of frustration in them. A kind of mental unrest finds its expression in the tribal disturbances.

CHAPTER VI

THE ECONOMIC STRUCTURE

A study of the economic system of any area is a study of the combination of three economic structures-production, distribution, and consumption. Here, an attempt is made to have a look at these structures and find out whether they really fit in with the economy of the region. Generally speaking, the economic structure of North-East India is similar to the general economic structure of India, as a whole. It differs from the rest of India only in kind and not in degree. That is to say, the economy of the region is multi-structural as in the rest of India. But due to its physical geography as well as the social and political conditions prevailing in the region, North-East India has a relatively backward economy. While the region covers a bigger area of production than the national average, production per hectare is lower than that for India as a whole. Geographically, the area consists of hill and plains with different levels of economy. At the social and political plane, ethnic considerations sometimes come in the way of integrated economic development of the region. But since the economies of the hills and the plains are more or less complementary the whole region has been treated as single economic unit for the purpose of our present study.

Before the coming of the British, except in Assam where there was a relatively developed agricultural economy, in the hill areas there was only a subsistence economy; and in certain interior areas as in Western Meghalaya, the agricultural economy was so primitive that it hardly provided even subsistence to the inhabitants. While trade and commerce took place between the hills and the plains, there could not be any large scale exchange of items of trade due to lack of economic development, apart from the archaic social relations between the sub-regions.

The British after pushing up their administration to North-East India, did not help the region in bringing about economic development for the benefit of the area. Whatever industries they had set up, like tea plantation, oil and other mineral extractions, were done only to further their own interests. Hence, during the colonial period limited economic development took place, and that too was confined to the tea and oil producing are as of the Assam plains and in some mineral producing areasas in the Khasi Hills of Meghalaya. In the rest of the hill areas, barring a few pockets, the traditional "Tribal economy" of the primitive type of agricultural jhumming and pastoral economy, among others, persisted. This variation in the respective economies of the hills and the plains is the function of different physical features, different social relations, and the neglect and isolation of the region by the colonial masters. This in turn produced a multi-structural economy in the region which continued till India's independence. It constituted, therefore, a major challenge to the task of nation-building in free India. As a matter of fact, the Government of India had declared the whole of North-East India, except Assam, to be a "Backward region" for the porpose of industrial assistance. Despite the system of national planning, the economic structure of the region continued to remain multi-structural in nature with rural agriculture as the chief economy of the people of the region. For example, the percentage of agricultural workers of the total work-force in the region varies from 54.40% (Tripura) to 78.48% (Arunachal Pradesh). It is true that after independence, the "tribal economy" came to be exposed to money economy which had earlier penetrated only into certain district headquarters of the hill areas. But the effect has, so far, been marginal. Traditional "tribal economy" continues to be the essential feature of the economic structure of the hilly por tion of North-East India.

The agricultural economy consists of wet rice cultivation in the plains of Assam and Manipur, and terrace cultivation as practised by the Apa-Tanis of Arunachal Pradesh, the Aos of Naga and, and the Jaintias of Meghalaya. The single-crop agricultural economy of North-East India has resulted in low production and low living standards for the inhabitants of the region. In recent years the problems of agricultural economy, in Assam in particular, have assumed acute dimensions. Because of a rapidly increasing population, there has been heavy pressure on land, resulting decline in the size of landholding. Latterly, there has been study increase in the number of landless peasants as well as of small and marginal farmers.

In the case of agriculture in the hill areas, diminishing returns from low-yielding "destructive" jhum cultivation have become the dominant feature. Money economy as we have seen, has certainly penetrated the "Tribal economy" apparently through the developmental activities in the region. As a result the "tribal economies" have become increasingly exposed to a proto-capitalist economy since independence despite the Inner Line Regulation in certain areas. It is, however, the emerging middlemen among the hill people, who more than the pioneering tradesmen from the plains, are responsible for the main impact of money economy in the hill areas. In some urban areas the impact is quite disquieting where economic disequilibrium is the consequence.

A distinctive feature of the tribal economy is the controversial jhum cultivation. Jhumming has been regarded by many authorities to be destructive of the soil condition through denudation of the hill slopes and responsible for causing floods. The hill people are now convinced that there should be sedentary cultivation. But this view has not taken into consideration because the technological, sociological, and other problems which the hill people have to encounter. Quite naturally, those who are aware of these problems are categorical in the view that the jhumming as practised by the hill people is quite scientific. Contrary to popular opinion, it is not the practice of jhumming but it is the government contractors, traders, and sedentary cultivators who have actually destroyed the forests. The result is that the hill people have totally become confused as to which type of economy is best suited to them.

On the industrial economy of the region, the least said the better. As we have seen, the colonial power set up certain industries in the region for their own gain and not for the benefit of the region. Hence the industrial sector was very weak during the colonial period. Even now, industries on a large scale are yet to be started in the hill areas. All that exist are a few industries based on local raw materials set up in the small sector like the sugar industry in Nagaland, handloom industry in Manipur, cement and plywood industries in Meghalaya, and cement industry in Karbi Anglong of Anglong of Assam. But all these industries require either State or Central Assistance for their survival. In the Assam plains too, the paper and jute industry are surviving on the support of the State Government. And even the established tea industry is facing a crisis due to various factors such as competition from other tea producing countries, sick gardens and sheer mismanagement.

Despite the regions' substantial resource base with large proven reserves of oil, coal, silimanite, limestone, bamboo, and good quality timber distributed over a wide area, the empahasis has been on cottage industries. Some cottage industries have been set up in the region like sericulture, handloom and handicrafts in Assam, Meghalaya and Nagaland, handicrafts and Khadi in Tripura; handloom and handicrafts in Arunachal Pradesh and Mizoram; handloom, sericulture, bamboo, and cane articles in Manipur. This emphais on cottage industries welcome as far as it goes has in some cases induced intra-regional disparity through neglect of other potential industries of importance.

However, one would ascribe the lag in industrial development in the region to a multiplicity of other factors. The chief among these are lack of capital, problems of market labour scarcity, non-existence of entrepreneurship, the adverse topography of the hill areas, wide diversity in social relations among the people of the region, and not the least, lack of infrastructural facilities like communications, powers, skills and the related economic and credit institutions. Hence except raw materials, almost all other factors needed for industrial development are non-existent.

We have casually referred to the possibility of the market economy being developed in the region. However, due to lack of marketing facilities most of the products like horticultural produces go waste. The nature and soil of North-East India favour the growth of tropical and sub-tropical fruits like pineapple, banana, orange, lime and lemon. But lack of an organised marketing outlet for the surplus products at remunerative prices retards horticultural development.

The middlemen and other traders also take advantage of the lack of marketing and transport infrastructure. Growers of fruits, potatoes, and other horticultural products are increasingly dependent on these middlemen and associated traders. It is common knowledge that in places like Shillong, one can see in every post-harvest season local farmers making bee-line at the doors of certain class of traders to dispose of their perishable fruits, potatoes, and other horticultural products at very low prices. These growers hardly get ten percent of the retail prices.

For historical reasons, the hill people of the region used to turn towards Bengal, Burma, or China rather than Assam for marketing facilities. Since India's independence and the subsequent partition of the country, marketing routes have to pass through Assam rather than Bangladesh. During the last thirty years or so, despite the availability of administrative and communication facilities, Assam has not been able to take advantage of the rich hinterland of North-East India for the development of marketing or organisation. But for this, Guwahati could have emerged as the entrepot of North-East India.

The Guwahati Tea Auction Market is a pointer in this direction. Thus, though politically divided, North-East India has the potential to become a distinct and integrated economic unit with marketing and transport facilities of its own. Coming now to the emerging money in the region, except in the plains and certain urban areas in the hills, the economic exchange among the people of the region were, until recently, based on the barter system. The barter system may be unprofitable, but rural people used to prefer it to money exchange. Money has not been widely used among the tribal people as either a store of value or a medium of exchange. Hence money economy which is operating in the plains and other urban centres did not readily penetrate the rural areas of the hills. Since independenee, as already stated, due to extension of development activities money economy has penetrated the interior of North-East India.

Recently a number of rural banking institutions, have been set up in the area.

These banks are expected to cater to the needs of the rural people. But particularly in the hill areas they use these banks mainly for dealing with non-tribal groups or with administrative authorities. While the banking facilities have relatively ameliorated the economic conditions of the rural folk, the emerging local money-lenders who have mostly benefited from these new institutions are exploiting their own people. Generally, it is these private money-lenders, or merchants, or well-to-do people who really run the pecuniary economy that has entered the life of the rural people in modern times. Hence money economy has failed to improve the lot of the common people in North-East India, especially in the tribal areas.

The foregoing general discussion on the economic structure of North-East India suggests that with its multi-structural economy, the region should be allowed to plan the devolopment of its economic resources on the basis of the development of local entrepreneurship. Local entrepreneurship, however, cannot properly establish itself so long as local entrepreneurs do not come forward to develop the economy of the region at the level of planning from below. The present "lopsided modernisation" of the economy is precisely the result of the absence of a class of local entrepreneurs ready to take advantage of the possibilities of agro-based, forest-based, and mineral-based industries in the area.

Further, in areas like the plains of Assam where agricultural land has become limited, the emphasis should be on cropping intensity rather than on large scale farming and labour intensive technique. Similarly, in the hill areas because of mountainous contours and forests where large scale agriculture is not possible, the emphasis in approach should be on forest-based activities and on industries like the making of precision instruments wheres kills are more important than materials. Large-size production and labour intensive technique as applicable to the rest of India are thus not applicable to North-East India in general and to the hill areas in particular. Contrary to the appropriate technique for India, the region, particularly the hill area requires small-size units with capital-intensive technique. The technique may be further improved with the help of the hydel power which should be more freely available after the completion of the Loktak Project in Manipur, the Kopili Project in Assam-Meghalaya and the Gumti Project in Tripura. With the availability of power and the establishment of medium industries the setting up of ancillary industries in the region would also be a step in the right direction.

In addition to all this, the development of other infrastructural facilities like transport and communication, marketing organisations, credit and banking facilities among other are to be speeded up so that the area catches up with the rest of the country. Both the present national highways running through the region, and the existing broad gauge of the North-Eastern Frontier Railway are not enough. The number of National Highway must be increased and the broad gauge extended not only to Guwahati to develop the city as the Chief marketing Centre in the region but to Dibrugarh at the far end. The establishment of the North-Eastern Council may also help in fulfilling some of the economic aspirations of the region with its valuable advice to both the units of the region and the Union Government. But the Council will do will to confine itself to an advisory role and not assume executive functions unless so required by the units.

CHAPTER VII

AGRICULTURE

The North-Eastern Region comprising five states, namely Assam, Meghalaya, Manipur, Nagaland and Tripura and two union territories, Arunachal and Mizoram, has a total geographical area of a little over 2.5 lakh sq. km., inhabited by a population of about 20 million. Nearly 90% of the population live in the village. A sizeable percentage of the population is dependent on the most ancient system of agriculture known as 'jhuming' or shifting cultivation.

The north-eastern region again presents a unique geographical area in the sense that the altitude in the region varies from 100 metre to 4000 metre, the climate as also the temperature ranges from tropical plains to temperate hills. This region is well known for its high rainfall combined with very high humidity. All these factors affect the agriculture of the region.

For historical reasons, this region has remained a backward area, and as such, the agriculture of the region is also not at all well developed. The states and union territories of the area, except Assam have remained cut of from the mainstream of the country. Lack of research base, dearth of qualified technical personnel have also contributed to the backwardness of the area.

The area under cultivation as also under irrigation is not very high, particularly in the hill states and in the union territories. The level of production is also not high. The consumption of fertilizer per hectare of gross cropped area is about 12 kg. per hectare while the All-India average is over 30 kg. The rate in Meghalaya is about 9 kg. although most of it is primarily utilised for the potato crop only. Even in Assam, the rate is only over 3 kg. per hectare, similarly, the double cropped area is also absolutely negligible.

The major problems confronting agriculture of the region are discussed below :

The soil in the entire region is acidic in nature, the pH ranging from 4 to 5.5 on an average. This leads to low availability of phosphorus, which gets fixed, thus leading to low response of fertilizer. The soil again has high concentrate of iron leading sometimes to iron toxicity and sometimes to zinc deficiency. Proper technology for management of acidic soil and varieties of crops suited to such conditions need to be developed.

The high rainfall and humidity create favourable environment for wide range of pests, diseases and weeds, as also problems of their control through spraying. Similarly, the climate creates problems in storage of grains and hay making, etc.

Appropriate strategy for control of pests and diseases with lesser dependence on spraying needs to be worked out.

The high rainfall and cloudy sky again reduces the total sunshine hours so essential for food production. Even response to fertilizer is restricted by lesser sunshine hours.

The low temperature prevailing for a considerable period in winter limits the total period of time available during a year for crop production. Thus double cropping will be very much restricted unless crops and varieties are identified properly. Mixed or inter-cropping will also help to increase production. In some areas crop varieties, specifically of rice need to be developed with tolerance to cold.

The undulating topography, hill slopes and various altitudes also create problems of agriculture. In many cases varieties suited to low altitude areas will not perform well at high altitudes; separate varieties of the same crop are needed in such cases.

Four important but special problems of the region are (a) shifting cultivation, (b) citrus decline, (c) socio-economic constraints, and (d) floods.

As is well known, shifting cultivation has led to a wide range of adverse effects besides low production. Citrus decline has similarly been responsible for the elimination of nearly 75 per cent of the citrus orchards.

The agriculture of the region is very closely associated with many social and cultural customs, patterns and even habits. As such, a great deal of care in approaches is necessary to bring about the desired change in attitudes.

Dearth of proper technology as well as poor utilisation of technology have greatly limited agricultural production.

Technology to increase production taking care of the various problems cited above are still not fully available. Cropping pattern, and identification and development of appropriate varieties are only in the process of emergence. Similarly appropriate method of water harvesting, recycling of water used are yet to be developed.

The utilization of known technology is also poor. The area under high yielding varieties is extremely low in most areas of the region.

There is practically very little use of farm power or implements except in a small area. The drudgery of farm operations is mostly shared by the women, particularly in the hilly region. The only implements used in shifting cultivation are large knives, dibbling stick, weeding hoe and sometimes a sickle. In the terraces or plains also only a hoe is used in many areas, puddling of soil for rice being done by foot.

The difficult terrain of the area, difficult accessibility to some areas and the geographic isolation of the region as a whole creates hurdles in timely supply of inputs such as seeds and fertilizers. Inadequate arrangements for production of quality seeds add to these problems. Input in term of cash or loans is negligible even where facilities exist.

The area under irrigation is very meagre at present. Agricultural production cannot be greatly increased without assured irrigation.

Post-harvest facilities are absolutely lacking even in case of cash crops like fruits. Post-harvest technology appropriate to the region is not available in some cases.

Transport and communication system is absolutely poor in the whole region. Further, the prohibitive cost of transport to places outside the region hampers the transfer of technology, supply of inputs, etc.

Lack of marketing facilities is a major constraint, more particularly for commodities like pineapple, banana, orange, potato and ginger, etc. which have a sizeable surplus for marketing. The farmers of the areas bordering Bangladesh were very severely affected by the sudden closure of trade with the country.

The ownership of land by the community or the village chief and the land tenure system often act as a disincentive for proper development and maintenance of land.

Improper land use in many cases leads to poor returns from the soil. Land has not been used according to scientific land capability classifications or proper land use survey. For example, rice is grown even in areas in the hill slopes where it cannot give adequate returns. This is done primarily out of a false sense of insecurity attached to farming without this staple crop.

In-service training of extension personnel is very essential to keep them abreast of latest developments and to instil in them the desired confidence. The scope for such training is rather inadequate.

The potentialities of agriculture in the whole region are vast. Besides the present food and fibre crops, potentialities exist for growing a large number of other economic crops and plants. Rice, maize, wheat and ragi are important cereals while tuber crops, such as tapioca, yams and sweat potato are very important crops, particularly for the hills. Potato, oil seeds, primarily mustard and sesame, sugarcane, jute, mesta, ramie, cotton, pulse crops such as blackgram, greengram, pea, soyabean, arhar and lentil are other important crops of the region. Besides vegetables, all kinds of horticultural crops such as citrus, banana, pineapple, peach, plum, pears, apples, apricot and walnut can be successfully grown in different altitudes. Among the spice crops, ginger, turmeric, black pepper, cardamom and cinnamon hold great promise for development.

There are indigenous crops containing aromatic, medicinal and pesticidal properties in the region. Similarly, this region is also noted for the presence of various kinds of orchids. As a matter of fact, there are vast resources of plant material which are indigenous to this region. The region is known to be the primary source of origin of rice and may be the secondary source of origin of maize. It is also the source of origin of many other crops and plants, such as mandarin oranges. The genetic variability of the various crops existing in the region can be of immense value for improvement of crops all over the world.

The importance of plantation crops such as tea, coffee, rubber is well-known. Similarly forest trees of economic importance including fodder and fuel trees as well as canes and bamboos are of great relevance to the development of the region.

Prospects of animal husbandry are very good, especially in the hilly region. Pig is by far the most important livestock for the hilly areas. This region is again endowed with rare animal species such as mithun, yak and wild boar. The Himalyan sheep of Arunachal Pradesh is a very important animal. In aquaculture, indigenous fishes like Masheer and trout are considered to be very important.

From a review of the potentialities it would be evident that with proper development a wide scope could be opened up for agro-based industries. While available resources are vast, there is absolute inadequacy of investible resources, the difficult transport and communication and difficult marketing problems add to the lack of incentives for agro-based industries.

The agro-industrial potentialities of some crops have already been exploited. These include tea, jute, sugarcane, pineapple, orange and some other fruits. Recently, citronella, and aromatic crop, has emerged as an important crop with industrial potentiality. Similarly coffee and rubber are two other crops which have shown potentiality for large scale cultivation.

An important group of crops awaiting proper exploration are the spice crops. These include ginger, turmeric, black pepper, large cardamom and cinnamon. Southern states presently export most of the black pepper and turmeric. Both these crops grow here extremely well. The higher cucumin content of turmeric variety grown in Jowai district of Meghalaya is higher by one per cent than that of the varieties grown in the South, although the cucumin content is prepared by the importing countries. Similarly the north-eastern region is to be the primary source of cinnamon.

Yams, tapioca, sweet potato and maize are widely grown in the region. These plants are important sources of carbo-hydrate and starch and hence can be utilised for starch powder and as ingredient of livestock feed. Soyabean grows extremely well in the region. It is not only a source of oil but because of the high protein content, it can also be utilised as an ingredient of livestock feed. Livestock feed industry thus has a great scope for development.

A hitherto underutilized plant is ramie. This crop has a great prospect of being grown, more specially in Assam as a source of blendable fibre for the plyester complex proposed to be established there. Orchids growing will in the region have immense potentiality in the export market.

Agro-waste utilisation is another area that deserves consideration. About 22 per cent of arecanut produced in the country came from this region. Process for making high density hard boards from arecanut wastes has been developed by the Forest Research Institute, Dehradun. The Regional Research Laboratory at Jorhat has reported utilisation of paddy husk for production of molecular sieves, brick and cement. Similarly jute sticks, bagasse, paddy straw and decaffeinated tea waste have been utilised for making paper boards and building materials. Rice straw, paddy husk, jute stick and bagasse have also been used for production of an industrial chemical known as furfural. A start has already been made in the production of caffeine from tea waste.

Ethanol and its derivatives can be produced from sugarcane and tapioca. Countries like Brazil have gone ahead in a big way with their production.

The oil from Tezpatta (Cinnamomym tarnata), available in Meghalaya in large quantities, cotains 70-80 per cent engenol suitable for preparation of perfumary chemicals.

A large number of citrus species are available in the region. Analysis of juice volume and citric acid content of these species has indicated that some species contain very high percentage of citric acid and hence opens up potentiality for production of this important chemical. Prospects of production of enzymes such as bromelin from pineapple waste and papan from papaya also need to be exploited.

Weeds tike water hyacinth have been successfully utilised for production of biogas as a source of energy as well as for making paper board. Studies are required for hydro-carbon yielding plants.

There are several other medicinal, aromatic and insecticide yielding plants that await proper exploration. These include,

Coptis teeta (mishimi teeta), lemon grass, pyrethrum sp. etc.

The institutional set-up for development of agriculture in the region has come up only during the last decade. During this period, the development departments of the States and Union territorries have been adequately strengthened. The Assam Agricultural University, with its teaching, research and extension wings, has been helping the agricultural development of the region. Two more agricultural colleges, one in Nagaland and the other in Manipur have been started recently. In addition to the above, two major infrastructural developments are the establishment of the North Eastern Council and the involvement of the Indian Council of Agricultural Research in a major way in the development of agriculture in this region.

The Indian Council of Agricultural Research has sanctioned a large number of research schemes for the Assam Agricultural University. There are four other projects of the I.C.A.R. in the State of Assam. These are the station of Central Plantation Crop Research Institute at Kahikuchi, Gauhati, a centre on Ramie Research at Sorbhog under the Jute Agricultnral Research Institute, the units of Co-ordinated Research Projects in composite fish culture and air breathing fishes at Gauhati, and the Regional Centre of National Bureau of Land Use and Soil Survey at Jorhat. The I.C.A.R. also has a scheme on Human Resource Development for providing financial assistance to students for undergoing both under-graduate and post-graduate studies. However, the most important contribution of the I.C. A.R. is the establishment in 1975 of a full-fledged research institute, called the ICAR Research complex for North Eastern Hills Region with its main centre in Meghalaya and strong research centres in Manipur, Nagaland, Tripura, Mizoram, Arunachal Pradesh and Sikkim. The institute is promoting research in all fields of agriculture, animal sciences, fishery, soil and water conservation, agricultural engineering and agro-forestry. The institute also has four Krishi Vigyan Kendras and a Trainers' Training Centre attached to it. This institute, during the short span of its existence in the region has been able to make suitable innovations in technology for increasing production of field crops, horticultural crops, animals and fish in the region. The institute has through a detailed study found out the causes of a major malaise—the citrus decline, and is now involved in the rejuvenation of the declining orchards. Similarly, all aspects of shifting cultivation have been studied by the institute and it is advocating alternative farming system to replace jhuming. The findings of the institute have now started percolating down to the fields of the farmers through national demonstrations, lab-to-land programmes, training in the Krishi Vigyan Kendras of the institute, organisation of training at various levels including extension officers, farmers, etc. and through collaborations with the N.E.C. in its development projects.

From the foregoing discussion it should be evident that steps need to be taken to convert the natural endowments into income-yielding assets. There are three facets of such steps. These are a package of feasible technology, a package of service to the people involved in growing and utilising the technology to develop suitable enterprises, and finally a package of public policies to create the needed environment of growth. All these aspects deserve to be attended to with the desired zeal. The problems of transport, communication and marketing have already been referred to. Internal competition within the region for market will have to be avoided, and in many cases there will be need for co-ordinated or joint effort. Incentives in the form of subsidies, duties, etc. may have to be considered for providing the initial thrust since the region remains far behind the mainstream of the country in these areas.

Research and developmental efforts must be geared up. Investments in these fields need to be strengthened. Scientific land and water use system will have to be based on considerations of ecology, energy consumption, economics and employment generation.

The geographical barrier, market, etc. pose certain problems for large-scale industries. Moreover, organised industrial sector does not provide large-scale employment. Even now, agriculture and allied sectors provide employment to about 75 per cent of work-force. It has been estimated that by the end of the Sixth Five Year Plan, about 35 million people will join the work-force in the country and that only about 7 million of them will be able to get jobs in the organised industrial sector. This situation is more true of the N. E. Region because of its inherent constraints. Thus, major stress must be laid on the development of land and water-based enterprises which have full potentialities for development in the region. This will help to achieve the triple objectives of development, namely, to stabilise productivity, generate gainful employment and to increase the purchasing power of the rural population.

CHAPTER VIII

SERICULTURE

Sericulture is the north-east region's heritage for its production of eri, muga, mulberry and of late, oak tassar silk. The climatic conditions and environment are favourable for thriving of various silk producing insects and their food plants. In eri and muga culture Assam holds the exclusive monopoly in the world. Tassar rearing has recently been introduced in N.C. Hills and Karbi-Anglong District for favourable climatic conditions for rearing and availability of naturally grown oak tassar plants. Its prospects are yet to be ascertained. Sericulture has a great impact on the economy of the rural people of the North-East Region. Assam produces about two-thirds of the total production of non-mulberry silk in India. During the last three decades priority has been given to the development of non-mulberry sector and the State has lost its position as the premier producer of mulberry silk. Although it has its own merits as a cottage industry, because of its hazardous practice and uneconomic returns it has very little impact on production and employment. Rationalization is impossible. Only mulberry silk worm culture developed on modern lines can solve the problem of production and unemployment.

Eri Silk Industry

For topographical and meteriological factors the eri industry has widely spread over the north-east region. Plains and hill areas up to an altitude of 5000 ft. are proved to be suitable for sericulture and hence extensively practised. Eri culture is now a premier cottage industry. Two types of eri worms are mainly found in Assam. Philosomia cynthia and Philosomia ricini (known as Attcus ricini too). In the hills, Ricini is the domesticated variety with blue, green and yellow Larva producing white and brick-red open mouthed cocoons. Moreover, species like canningi, obscura lumuloides are found in Assam. Lumuloides is almost like vicini and found in Assam only whereas the others are distributed in different parts of the world.

Present Status of Eri Culture

In Arunachal Pradesh it is practised in foothills and plains areas since a long time and cocoons are utilised locally, as the people have special fascination for eri silk garments. In Manipur also some tradition is there for eri culture and the yarn is used locally. In Meghalaya, specially in Bhoi area, and in Garo hills eri culture is new, although some tribals have been practising it since a long time. In Nagaland eri culture is practised by plains tribals in Dimapur areas.

The spun silk mill at Jagiroad consumes about 40,000 kgs. of eri cocoons annually besides other silk wastes. The rest of the spinning is done by hand on takli (a wooden small instrument). A part of the cocoons is sold outside the region. Commercial spinning centres are organised by the State Khadi Board. The areas of West Gauhati, Rampur, Palasbari, Raha, Charaibahi are known for spinning and weaving. About 13,000 artisans are working under the Khadi Board. Hill people too spin and weave for their domestic needs. The surplus cocoons find a market in the plains. The eri cocoons are mainly purchased by the private weavers in the open market at a high price from the middle traders.

The requirement of eri seed in Assam is very large, and a large quantity of seed production is done by rearers themselves. The scheme taken by the Government of Assam during the Fifth Five-year Plan as sponsored by the N.E.C. was as below:

State	*Scheme*	*Place*	*Area in hectare*	*Year*	*Fifth Plan outlay*
Assam	Eri Pilot	6	Beloguri	75-76	2.17 Lakhs
	Tokenkata	6	Tokenkata	76-77	1.17 Lakhs

Problems and Remedial Measures

First of all, it is not a commercially organised activity as the rearing is done by stray castor plantation and other secondary food plants. The main difficulty in practising eri culture is the constraint in every stage from plantation to fabric production. The main food plant castor is expensive if planted simply for rearing. Leaves being plucked, new plantation is necessary involving recurrent expentiture. Large-scale castor plantation invites other caterpillars which devour the plants. Leaf plucking reduces seed quantity. Therefore, it is necessary to have plantation of high seed yeilding castor along with high tuber yeilding plants such as tapioca.

Because of lack of remunerative income no commercial motive enters in the entire operation. On an average not more than 10-15 kg. of cocoons are produced by a family in a year. One kg. of hand-spun yarn cost about Rs. 60/- to 80/-, the cocoons being purchased by the weavers at Rs. 40/- to Rs. 50/- per kg. in the open market. Whereas the mill yarn costs about Rs. 200/- kg. and the price paid for the cocoons is Rs. 20/- to 25/- per kg. A handloom wrapper is sold at Rs. 80/- to Rs. 100/- involving two months' labour. The per capita earning for weaving does not exceed more than Rs. 40/- per annum, in spite of the demand for the cloth. In absence of any marketing facility the weavers are constrained to sell their fabric at an uneconomic price to the traders. The rearer's or spinner's or weaver's earning annually is not more than a few hundred rupees inspite of all efforts. Now it becomes possible to spin Eri cocoons in an improved type of 'Ambar Charkha' where output of yarn is high and can be spun at the desired count. Cost of production is low and earning per spinner is increased considerably.

Muga Culture

The golden yellow muga silk is a prestigious production of Assam and not available anywhere in the world. Attempts to introduce it into other States resulted in failure either due to lack of suitable food plants or unfavourable climate. Muga silkworm is a semi-domesticated variety and widely distributed and cultured in the Brahamputra valley.

The Muga Silk Worm and Foodplants

The cultural operation is restricted to the Brahmaputra valley, the natural distribution of the Antheria species extends to the surrounding hills. Probably it originated at the foot of Naga hills and got distributed to the plains due to lack of food plants in its originating place. It is a multivoltine silk worm producing five broods in a year.

The main muga food plants are Som (Machilus bombycina), Soalu (Liseapolyantha), Digloti (Litsea slicifolia), Mezan-Kari (Lisea citrata), Chapa (Mach ilus oblonga) of the family Lauraceae. Antheria assama feeds on these plants. When it is fed by mezankari leaves with strong pungent taste, healthy worms can only survive giving creamy white thread. Digloti leaves result in darkish silk thread whereas Som and Soalu leaves fed worms give fine golden coloured yarn.

A sufficient quantity of Som in Upper Assam Forest and Soalu in Lower Assam and hill areas is found. Nothing is known of seed preparation and seed preservation in their cases. In recent years too much felling of forest trees has affected the muga plants. Therefore, to compensate the leaf loss, schemes have been taken to grow Som in village grazing reserves 35 to 40 feet apart from each other, Som, Soalu, Diglati can be propagated by seed but can be multiplied by cutting also. In Som plants after 4-5 years of plantation, cultural operation can be started continuing up to 20-25 years, whereas in Soalu upto 25-30 years. But for the benefit of rearers old trees should not be used if they are infested with moss and ant's nests.

Unlike other silk worm, rearing of muga worm is difficult and problematical as it is done outdoors exposing it to environmental hazards. The operation is to be started anew every year. Muga plantations take five years to grow and be ready for cultural operation and more land is required unlike mulberry plantation. Production per unit area is less and that too is unpredictable. With an uncertain economy the whole process is laborious and lacks rationalization. The private rearers in recent years have not taken up any muga plantation. Moreover, production of muga cocoons is found to be deteriorating due to want of healthy seed.

For lack of improved realing contraption of muga cocoons,

its silk production at village level by primitive contrivance of the bhir has limitations. Thus the situation is fully exploited in Land-locked areas like Sualkuchi by traders, who monopolise the market by procuring muga reeling cocoons mostly from Upper Assam. In Sualkuch (Population : 18,000) the bulk of reeling is done at nominal wage by the weaker sex. The reelers are dependent upon the cocoons of monopolising traders.

It is estimated that more than 10,000 families rear muga silk worm and their annual need of seed cocoons is about 50 lakh. Basic healthy muga seed cocoons are found at the foothills of Kamrup and Goalpara in Lower Assam which are known as seed zones. Upper Assam too produces cocoons. The villagers of Sualkuchi reel about 20,000 kg. annually showing a declining trend.

Muga Culture in Different States and Union Territories

Other than Assam and Meghalaya muga culture has been introduced in the contiguous areas only during the fifth five year plan period.

Muga culture in Arunachal Predesh is new and occasionally muga seed cocoons are produced from certain foothill areas. Similarly in Mizoram and Tripura muga culture is new to the State, whereas in Nagaland there is one muga sub-centre of 130 acres with cocoon production in the foothill.

Meghalaya is a good source of basic seed cocoon, specially from areas bordering Assam. Besides there are about 55 hectares of Government village Grazing Reserve plantation for increasing cocoon production. About 288 families are involved in basic seed cocoon production. There is one newly established basic seed farm in the Garo Hills. As muga culture is traditional in the Brahmaputra Valley, there are 7 (seven) basic farms, 2 (two) sub-centres for production of diseases-free healthy seed cocoons. But these establishments can meet only 10 per cent of the total demand.

The scheme taken by the Sericulture Department for plantation of muga food plants to produce seed and reeling cocoons, though it cannot be utilized fully due to acute shortage of seed cocoons, include 2237 hectares of village Grazing Reserve and 2466 hectares in homestead. Besides, under Social Forestry

programme N.E.C. sponsored a four hectare nursery at Boko at an estimated cost of Rs. 3.92 lakh far supplying planting material.

Problems and Remedies

In muga culture the main difficulties are non-availability of healthy seed, unpredictable harvest, uncertain rearing behaviour, natural enemies, race degeneration, difficulty in handling the large number of moths, large sex ratio for laying preparation, absence of hiberanating character in winter, absence of machinery and economic reeling, remoteness of areas of operation and above all, the middleman's interference in trade of cocoon yarn and fabric. Rearing is hazardous, cost of agrainage operation is high and the output of harvested cocoons is very low. Only in extreme cases the harvest proves good. Rearers thus have to take a long-range view for production of cocoons.

The reeling technology being inefficient, commercial reeling by improved machinery is yet to be a success. The nature of food plants makes cocoon un-uniform and in position of quality control bulk production is difficult.

With 20 or 30 cocoons harvest per laying effective rate of rearing is low and eggs per moth are less in comparison to eri and mulberry silk worm.

Moreover a few traders have monopolized the procurement of muga reeling cocoons, feeling them it off-season and paying uneconomics rate to reelers as only few rearers themselves are reelers and weavers. Private traders as organised co-operatives mostly manipulate the market price of muga yarn and muga cocoons. The study team set up by the Central Silk Board in 1979 made certain valuable recommendations for development of muga culture in this region, suggesting that rather than expanding the area of plantation, the existing one should be utilised efficiently and present infrastucture should be improved and upgraded.

Improvement of plantation in muga culture with sound agronomic practice may consist of utilization of clonal practice, as practised in tea plantation, planting these as bushy dwarfs trees in hedge at short distance with suitable pruning and pollarding and their expansion.

The most important thing in muga culture is however elimination of the middleman from operation by organisation of Raw Material Banks during the commercial season to introduce the reeling community side by side with reeling units at places of production. Thus with control and marketing facilities for the end products, the rearer, reeler, weaver will get their due share to plough back the profit margin to themselves for rationalisation of the industry.

Mulberry Silk Culture

Without interfering with the agricultural crop, with less space requirement, the mulberry plantation helps to supply leaves for 12 years at a stretch. Thus with effective high rate of rearing and less grainage expenditure mulberry silk worm culture is more convenient than others. This is the only rational agro-industry which can be easily handled by semi-skilled labourers with the highest earning per unit area and easier quality control of the end product.

The working group report on sericulture (1964) states that sericulture has a prominent place in Assam. By virtue of the favourable climatic conditions both mulberry and non-mulberry silk worms are reared and the industries are scattered all over the state. The report recommends that the rearing of mulberry worms required to be consolidated. The difficult terrain, problems, lack of research are the factors responsible for holding up the pace of development. The essential requirement of mulberry culture suitable climate, abundant gorwth of mulberry leaves, availability of agricultural and semi-agricultural labour.

Sualkuchi is the only village where silk weaving is traditionally prevalent with 8,000 looms in commercial activities. The present production of mulberry cocoons in Assam is estimated to be about 7,000 kg. annually, and 25,000 kg. of twisted mulberry yarn is brought from Karnataka at high price. The annual demand of mulberry silk of the State is estimated to be 50,000 kg.

Problems and Remedial Measures

In order to increase cocoon production, improvement of mulberry plantation in farms (9 Nos. with 103,09 acres), collective mulberry gardens (57 Nos. with 505,32 acres), rearer's homestead, with appropriate soil amendment and agronomic practice, introducing high-yielding mulberry varieties, with application of fertilizers and compost provision of irrigation facilities in winter, drainage in monsoon, are to be facilitated. Yarn quality effecting, agronomic baseless mixed varieties plantation practice in to be discarded and improved high yielding Berhampur varieties such as S2, S 799, or Knva 2, S 54, are to be introduced to get 15,000 kg. of leaves per hectare.

However their adaptability and yield potential should be tested prior to large-scale plantation. Construction of modern type rearing house at all levels, such as control of temperature, humidity and light, etc. in Government farms and collective mulberry gardens, with employment of selected rearers on fixed wages later linked with bank loan, can be introduced, Best bivoltine seed from Bivolting project centre of Bangalore and high yielding multi-volatiles, can be procured and rearers in potential cluster area should be organised. Farms like foreign seed station at Ummulung, Sangbar and other Government Sericultural farms of N.E. region, should acclimatize such races for adaptability in the area.

A fixed rearing target per family per year in half an acre of land, with at least 5,000 selected rearers, is to be organised to achieve production of good cocoons in reeling units.

Establishment of centralised reeling unit for production of quality silk, drying chamber, twisting plant, boiling plant, re-reeling machines with necessary adjuncts to reeling units, are necessary. To bring down the fabric price, together with organization of silk weaving in power loom, organization of dying, printing with efficient marketing system are necessary. Training of personnel in different branches of the establishment for all-round development of the industry is necessary.

CHAPTER IX

MINERAL RESOURCES

Of late, the north-eastern region of India has attracted the attention of the entire country for its varied natural resources, including mineral resources. Apart from petroleum endowed with major mineral resources as will be obvious from the following table :

Name of Minerals	*Quality*	*Reserve (in million tonnes)*
Coal	Low to medium ash and high sulphur	850
Limestone	Flux, chemical and cement grade	3400
Dolomite	Very good quality	380
Ceramic clay (of all categories)	Variable quality	90
Magnetite (Chromiferous and Nickeliferous)	—	5
Base metal (including nickel, cobalt, tin and tungsten)	—	Numerous occurrences under investigation

Apart from the above, there are deposits of sillimanite, graphite, apatite, glass sand, building material, etc.

The mineral resources of an area are relate to its geological set up. The north-eastern region is roughly a triangular land mass formed by the Himalayas in the north and east, the Meghalaya upland and the Mikir Hills in the South and the young mountains of Tirap District of Arunachal Pradesh, Nagaland, Manipur, Mizoram and Tripura (belonging to the Naga-

Patkoi-Lushai and Arakan Yoma ranges) in the south-east. The Brahmaputra valley constitutes the major plain area walled on the three sides by mountains. The Surma and Barak valleys in the Cachar district of Assam and adjoining area in Manipur and Imphal valley in Manipur constitute the other plains in the region. The Kopili river meanders througth the gap between the Meghalaya upland and the Mikir Hills.

Geologically the olden rocks, i.e. the Archaean ortho and para-metamorphites cover the Meghalaya upland and the Mikir Hills, constituting the shield area. These Archaean gneissess and pre-Cambrian metasediments are intruded by younger acid and basic intrusives and are covered along their southern flanks by younger Cretacaceous and Tertiary shelf sediments, which are overlain at places by Quaternaryand recent deposits. In the Himalyan region in the north and east (Arunachal Pradesh) various groups of metasediments and younger sedimentaries ranging in age from Plaeozoic to Tertiary and Quaternary are exposed. The geosynclinal facies of the Cretaceaous Tertiary sediments cover the Patkoi-Naga-Lushai-Tripura ranges flanked along parts of the river valleys by the Quaternary and younger sediments. Evidences of volcanic activity (Jurasaic period) are visible along the southern Khasi Hills, Meghalaya, Mikir Hills, Assam and Abor Hills, Arunachal Pradesh. An alkaline ultra-mafic carbonatite complex occurs in the Sung Valley at the border of Khasi and Jaintia Hills. Suspected carbonetite has recently been located in Mikir Hills at the junction of a meta-basic body against the gneissic complex. A series of lenses and bands of ultramafic rocks with minor basic volcanics occur in the states of Manipur-Nagaland along their eastern border of Burma comprising the "Ophiolite Belt", extending for about 200 km. The ultramafic rocks are partly to completely serpantinised.

In view of the occurrences of wide range of rock formations ranging from the oldest Archaeane to the youngest Quaternary, occurrences of variable type of mineral deposits have become possible, as indicated below:

1. Mineral resources in the oldest gneissic complexes of Meghalaya-Mikir Hills : Sillimanite-cornite-corndian

bodies, peg-metites and iron ore.

2. Mineral resources in the Cretaceous and Tertiary sediments overylying the geneissic complex: Oil and natural gas, Limestone, coal, clay, gypsum, phosphates.
3. Mineral resources associated with the palaeozoic metasedimentaties of the Himalayan area (Arunachal Pradesh) : Limestone, marble, dolomite, base metallic sulphides (with tin and tungsten).
4. Mineral resources associated with the Ophiolite Belt : Magnetite, chroite, niekel-cobalt and base metals.
5. Mineral resource associated with the carbonatite complex of Sung valley (Meghalaya) : Nickel-cobalt, base metals, apatite, etc.
6. Mineral resources associated with the Quaternary and recent formations: Glass sand, clay, gold-bearing placers.

Although this region is endowed with variable mineral resources, particularly vast potentiality of coal and limestone, major constraint in the development of the same is lack of communication in the rugged terrain of the hill areas and lack of infrastructure in most of the mineralised areas. In spite of such constraints, however, GSI is carrying out exploration in the mineralised area all over the region. Recently the North-Eastern Council has drawn up schemes to link the mineral deposit areas spread out in Nagaland, Manipur, Assam, Meghalaya and Arunachal Pradesh.

The mineral resources of the North-Eastern Region have been categorised as (1) energy resources, (2) raw materials for cement industry, (3) raw materials for refractory industry, (4) raw materials for glass and ceramics industry, (5) raw materials for fertilisers, (6) base metals and associated Energy resources.

Coal : The States of Assam, Meghalaya and adjoining areas of territories of Nagaland and Arunachal Pradesh are endowed with extensive coal-bearing formations, but these coalfields have not been properly developed owing to inaccessibility, complex geo-tectonic setting and inherent high sulphur content in the coal.

Oil and Natural Gas : This region is richly endowed with oil and natural gas. Indications of the same have been reported from all over the region and workable deposits have been established in upper Assam.

Raw Materials for Cement Factory

Mineral Raw materials for cement industry comprise limestone, coal gypsum and clay.

Limestone : For cement industry limestone is the principal raw material, of which this region has vast high grade potentiality in Meghalaya, Assam, Arunachal Pradesh and Nagaland. A small workable deposit also occurs in Manipur. The potentiality of the different states has been assessed by GSI by detailed mapping and regional exploration.

Gypsum : Except for minor occurrences in the Tuensang District, Nagaland and Badarpur, Haflong and Mahur, Assam, no deposit of economic significance has been found so far in the North-Eastern Region.

Raw Materials for Refractory Industry

Mineral raw material for refractory industry occurring in North-Eastern Region comprises sillimanite, dolomite, and fireclay. Sillimanite-Corrumdum deposit of Sonapahar, Nongstoin, Meghalaya deserves special mention, since it is reputed to contain the best quality sillimanite in the world.

Raw Material for Glass and Ceramic Industry

Abundant resources of mineral raw material for glass and ceramic industries occur in Assam, Meghalaya, Manipur, Tripura and Nagaland.

Raw Materials for Fertilizer Industry

Phosphorite and Apatite : Possibilities for phosphorite and apatite, comprising mineral raw material for fertilizer industry, have been revealed by recent exploration in the Garo-Khasi-Jaintia Hills and Sung Valley, Meghalaya. The grey shale at the base of the kipoli formation, overlying the prang limestone occurring along the southern flank of the Shillong plateau in Garo, Khasi and Jaintia hills area, shows intermittent development of nodules of phosphorite with average P 205 content 5 to 10 per cent. Apatite veins are located in the alkaline ultramafic intrusive complex occurring in the Sung Valley area at the border of Khasi and Jaintia Hills districts. The Department of Atomic Energy have established dissemination of low grade apatite in the soil covering the ultramafic of Sung Valley over a sizeable area. About 0.4 million tonnes of alluvial phosphate concentration (down to a depth of 6m) together with 10,000 tonnes of pyrochlore has been estimated. GSI proposes to follow up these findings by systematic exploration in the Garo-Khasi-Jaintia hills and Sung Valley. Search for phosphoric and apatite is also proposed to be extended in other states of North-Eastern Region.

Fuller's earth : An occurrence of fuller's earth has been reported from the north of Bhutan Khuti, Suvankhata area, Kamrup District, Assam. It comprises an area of about 9.2 sq. km. and its estimated inferred reserve is about 0.24 million tonnes. It is considered to be suitable for petroleum refining and manufacture of fertiliser.

Base Metals and Associated Ferrous Metals

Detailed geological mapping, followed at places by regional exploration has established base metal mineralisation in the metasedimentaries. (associated with granite gneiss) of Arunachal Pradesh, Shillong group of rocks of Meghalaya, pre-Cambrian Schists of Pancharatna hill, Assam, ultramafics of Sung Valley (Meghalaya) and the ophiolite belt of Nagaland-Manipur.

Polymetallic Sulphide Mineralisation of Umpyrtha, Meghalaya

Mineralisation in the form of massive lenses and disseminated grains of polymetallic sulphides has been established over a strike length of 105 m and average width of 10 m.

Reserves (inferred) up to depth of 54 M-0.12 million tonnes.
Grade-Zn 2.83%, Cu-1.35%, Pb-0.44%
Indications of molybdenim usually ranging from 150 to 300 ppm (occasionally going up to 1000 ppm) have been noticed in a few boreholes.

Sulphide Mineralisation in the Tyrsad-Barapani Area, Khasi Hills

Dissemination of sulphides in the Shillong group of rocks indicates the following base metal over an extensive area :

Cu : 20 to 530 ppm
Pb : 20 to 300 ppm
Ni : 20 to 150 ppm
Co : 20 to 95 ppm

Basemetal Mineralsiation in the Ultramafic Carbonatite Complex of Sung Valley, Jaintia Hills, Maghalaya

Sporadic sulphides, i.e., chalcopyrite, pyrite, etc., associated with magnetite (apatite bearing) and titaniferous magnetite occur in amphibolite and epidorites (altered basic/ultrabasic rock). Exploration by drilling was carried out in this area, but no economic deposit coal be established. However, promising indications of nickel, cobalt, niobium, uranium and apatite have been indicated. Base metal Mineralisation in and around Pancharatna village area and Goalpara District have also been found.

Low grade dissemination of chalcopyrite has been located in Pre-Cambrian Schists.

Mineralisation in the Ophiolite Belt

Preliminary work done by the GSI has deciphered the following mineralisation in the ophiolite belt.

Base Metals : Disseminations of copper sulphides (at place nickeliferous), chalcopyrite, chalcocite, cuprite, malachite, etc. are found within basic and ultrabasic rocks at a number of places in Nagaland and Manipur. So far no deposit of economic interest has been found.

Magnetite : Magnetite associated with serpantine occurs extensively within the ophiolite belt.

The occurrences are located in a very inaccessible terrain without any communication facility.

Nickel and Cobalt : Concentration of nickel and cobalt bas been recorded in the serpentine and geothits with magnetite and charomite deposits of Nagaland and Manipur. Besides, enrichment of nickel (with cobalt) has also been noticed in the serpantinites and the lateritic soil covering the serpentinite in a number of localities of Manipur.

Minor Mineral Deposits

Iron Ore : Apart from the large magnetite deposits, there are sporadic occurrences of small iron ore deposits.

Gold

Assam : Occurrences of native gold have been recorded from places of several Upper Assam rivers and the Subansiri river bed was the best gold producing area in Assam in early days. Small grains of native gold can be extracted by panning the alluvial sand. The placers have been presumably derived from auriferous quartz veins in the metamorphic rocks of the North-Eastern Himalayas (Arunachal Pradesh).

Meghalaya : An occurrence of gold has been spotted near Mawphlang in Khasi Hills. The gold-silver-tellutide mineralization along with pyrite and pyrrhotite together with carbonaceous quartz was found to occur within the sheer zone extending from Barapani to Tyrsad in Shillong series. Data from boreholes put down by the Directorate of Geology and Mining, Assam, reveal that the tenor is generally between 2 to 3 gm/tone, while in one case it is reported to be 6.8 gm/tonne, more investigation by drilling did not reveal any continuity of the gold occurrences.

Graphite : Graphite deposits occur in the high grade schists in the Subansiri, Siang and Lohit districts of Arunachal.

Salt and Brine Springs

Nagaland : Salt and brine springs are fairly common in Nagaland generally confined to the Disang Formation. They are located in Kohima, Tuensang and Phek districts. On chemical analysis, they have been found to contain 5.5″ dissolved salts and very low potassium. However, saline Girujaur clay has been found to contain 1.75% K2 and the same is likely to increase in depth.

There are a number of brine wells in Tsalsteko nala and are

used for manufacture of common salt by local people.

Manipur : A number of salt springs occur along the foot-hills in the eastern part of the Imphal valley. These springs appear to be located along a probable fault zone. Most of the springs are being tapped by local people by driving one metre diameter lined wells for manufacture of salt on a small scale. Exploratory drilling in the area is necessary to find out the yield of the springs.

Brine wells occur in Manipur East District. On analysis the brine samples were found to contain 0.840 to 0.87% Na and 18 to 20 ppm k. Evaporites including epsomite, halotrichite and anhydrous magnesium sulphate occur as encrustations, dissemination and thin layers around brine wells.

Arunachal Pradesh : Saline efflorescence (locally known as "Pung") has been observed in a number of localities within Tertiary Sandstones in Kameng, Subansiri and Tirap Districts.

Tripura : The occurrences of brine springs along the fault planes in the western flank of Sakhan range have been recorded to Sakhan village. The amounts of dissolved salt vary from 0.89" to 1.32% and the availability of salt has been estimated to be 5,000 kg. per day.

CHAPTER X

BELIEFS AND CHARACTERISTICS

The Nagas

The Nagas are the most singular race of Nagaland. They are of different classes, even though they have many characteristics in common. There are the Angami Nagas, the Ao Nagas, the Lhotas, the Regmas, Semas, the Nagas of the North-Eastern hills, and those of Cachar and Manipur, to mention only a few. The tribes are constantly forming new groups and associations, like the Chakhesangs, Zeliangs, Shamnyu-yungmangs and others. Thus the Nagas have quite a number of clans and affiliations.

The origin of the word 'Naga' is interpreted in different ways. One belief is that it is derived from the Assamese word 'naga' (Sanskrit 'nagna') meaning 'naked', for the reason that the Nagas were comparatively ill-clad. It could also be from the vernacular 'nag' which means a mountain. Or it may be the corrupted form of 'log' meaning 'people'. In fact some Naga tribes use the word 'nok' for people, which closely resembles the Hindi word 'log'.

The Nagas are a kind of Indo-Mongoloids whose presence was noted as early as the 10th Century before Christ, at the period of the Vedas. They were known as 'Kirata' or non-Aryans, and were described in ancient Sanskrit literature as subsisting on the flesh of the animals they hunted, roots and fruits of the forest, a warlike race, dressed in skins, and wielding formidable weapons. They are described as 'golden hued' in contrast to the dark complexioned people of the plains. It is also mentioned that they were rich, having exploited the plentiful minerals available in the hill regions and the forest produce of the mountain-sides. They were also expert weavers, a trait which exists amongst the race even now. It is mentioned in the Mahabharata that the great god Shiva took the form of a Kirata, with his consort Uma in the guise of a Kirata woman, and went in this form to meet the warrior Arjuna. Thus it is evident that the Nagas are not an alien race, but are a branch of the rich and varied tribes of India.

Nagaland is now split up into three districts viz, Kohima, Mokochung and Tuensang. These are administered from Kohima. The southern base in Manipur, with Burma on the east, Nefa to the north, and the Assam valley on the west side. The Naga country is covered largely with hill ranges having many spurs and ridges, and occasional gentle slopes. The height varies from four thousand to about ten thousand feet above sea level. The population is concentrated on the higher hills. Rainfall varies from 70 to 100 inches in the year. Numerous rivers and streams flow through Nagaland, but there is a marked absence of lakes and tanks.

Much of the forest has been cut down to make way for cultivation, and most of the wild game has already been exploited. Thus there are few wild animals left, like elephants, tigers, leopards and so forth. The Indian hornbill bird is greatly prized by the Naga inhabitants. It is used for decoration, and magic is also associated with it. The Naga State has a population of 6.18 lakhs and an area of 16,527 square kilometres according to the 1981 census.

The traditional belief is that the Naga tribes migrated from the south, except in the case of the/Kacha Nagas whose ancestors are said to have come from the mountains known as Japvo. There exists an isolating tendency amongst the race. One can almost categorise the type of Naga by a mere study of facial characteristics. In some villages the men are of tall stature, while others are marked out by the beauty of their women. Some are even distinguished by peculiar traits of character. For example, the villages of Kidima and Nerharma abound in men who are fond of litigation, and Tofima has the distinction of possessing a large number of liars:

Various tales are told about the origin of the Nagas. The Angamis, Aos, Lhotas and Semas are supposed to be descended from four brothers, and distinguished by the amount of clothing that they were authorised to wear. The eldest of these brothers was gentle and virtuous and so his parents gave him a picturesque dress to wear. The Angamis are his descendants. The second brother was troublesome and so he was given scantier clothing. He was the ancestor of the Aos. The third brother, from whom the Lhotas are said to have been descended, was much alike the second in conduct, and so he was clothed in much the same manner. The youngest brother, the ancestor of the Semas, was markedly wicked. When his parent sent him to scare away the birds from the field, he neglected his task and plucked off all the pumpkins. Fed up with his naughtiness, his parents tied a piece of cloth round his waist, and leaving him just like that, turned him out.

It is also said that the Naga tribes were all descended from one father, but he was the son of a second wife. The children of the first wife were given proper clothes, but the child of the second wife could get only a small piece of cloth which was sufficient only to wrap around the waist, and so his descendants still wear the kilt.

Yet another story of the origin of the Naga tribes is as follows: In the village of Kezakenoma there lived an old couple who had three sons. The sons used to take loads of paddy to spread out to dry on a huge stone. The heaps of paddy would multiply when laid on the stone due to the influence of a spirit living in it. One day the sons quarrelled among themselves about their precedence in spreading loads of paddy on the stone and fearing that there would be bloodshed, their parents broke some eggs on the stone, laid firewood on it, and set it afire. On being heated, the stone suddenly burst with a sound like thunder and the spirit inhabiting it went up to heaven in a cloud of smoke. The three sons thereupon separated and became the ancestors of the Angamis, Lhotas and Semas. It is said that the great stone, cracked when its spirit flew away, still exists opposite the house of the original founder of the village.

There are several legends concerning the origin of the Nagas of Manipur. According to the Tangkhul legend, one day a sow was tracked down a valley by the younger of two brothers. The sow littered by the banks of the Iril River, and the young man stayed behind to look after her. He found the country so fascinnating that he decided to stay there. He would send the produce of the plain country to his brother whom he had left behind in the hills, and get presents in turn from the latter. After some time the younger brother stopped sending gifts, which so enraged his elder brother, that he came down and forcefully obtained them. Subsequently, perhaps based on this legend, a curious custom came into existence according to which the Tangkhuls would swoop down on the day of the Naga sports and loot the women vendors, which made the Manipuris prohibit their women from frequenting the market.

Another legend concerns the Marring Nagas. It is said that they left the valley because of the heat and the mosquitoes, taking fire with them. The fire was extinguished when they reached a ridge between Hundung and Ukrul, but to make up for it the deity taught them to get fire from stone. The sacred stone, maibung, stands there till this day.

A legend concerning the Tangkhuls is given by themselves as follows: Some of the Tangkhuls were trapped in a cave, from which they emerged one by one. But a large tiger who was watching them, devoured each of them as soon as they emerged. Thereupon they took recourse to a stratagem. They dressed up an effigy to make it appear as a live man, and left it outside to distract the tiger's attention. Having done so they rushed out together, and the tiger was so greatly baffled by seeing the crowd, that he fled. To mark the occasion they set up a large stone on the hill-top, which is there to this day.

A story which features the Nagas, the Kukis and the Manipuris, is about a jumping contest held between the representatives of the three tribes. The Kuki leapt from the top of one range to the crest of another. The Naga, too, jumped across, but his foot slipped and touched the water of the stream. The Manipuri tumbled right into the river. For this reason the Naga bathes only now and then, the Kuki scrupulously avoids it, and the Manipuri, because of his dropping headlong into the river, is rather fond of bathing.

A legend about the origin of the Marams is also interesting. A flood came and destroyed everyone except a couple of the name of Medungasi and Simoting. The couple wondered if they should get married, but since there was no one to advice them, they went out into the forest. Here a god appeared to the man and told him that they could marry but their descendants were forbidden to eat the flesh of the pig. Therefore to this day the Marams do not eat pork.

The origin of the Marring Nagas is also curious. It is said that fourteen of them, seven men and seven women, emerged from the earth. At that time the men and the women wore the same clothes (the dhoti). But in order to make a distinction, the men tied up their hair into a knot in front, and the women behind. The women lengthened their waist-cloth while the men shortened theirs. Not finding themselves comfortable in the plains they migrated into the hills, where they are living to this day. Another legened about the Marrings is that while they emerged from a cave, horrible beast would devour them. The beast, however, was slain by a deity with two horns, and they could get out safely out of the cave.

A legend concerns the origin of the Vuites, another Naga clan. One day the head of the Thados clan of the name of Asian Ningthon found two eggs in a basket. He ate one and found it bitter. The other he put aside, so that it may become mature and nice to eat. From this egg, however, there emerged a lad who became chief of the Vuite clan.

Though constantly at war among themselves, the Nagas have a certain unity also. They intermarry only among their own clan, and not among tribes other than the Naga community. Though differing in build and complexion, they have common characteristics like a coarse and savage face, and a dull timid disposition. In the use of weapons, too, they have a similarity, for they all use only javelins and spears.

The Angami Naga is a particularly lithe and agile person. He is capable of a great deal of hard work and endurance, marches long distances and carries heavy loads. He has a curious way of bathing. The water from some stream is carried in a hollow bamboo, and the soap is made by pounding into pulp the fibrous stalk of a creeper which gives a lather like ordinary soap. A practice which has a smack of modernity is the wearing of wigs. The wigs were not worn by women, however, but by old men whose hair had greyed! They were made of bear's hair, with human hair hanging at the back.

The Angamis were very fond for weaing something as an ear-ornament. This was not necessarily a silver or gold earring, but anything which took their fancy, like plugs of black wool, pieces of red paper or cloth, and even the cog-wheel of a watch!

The men also wore cowries in rows of three or four. Originally these signified exploits in war, but gradually they became emblems of love, and the fourth line of cowries was worn by a man who had an intrigue with a married woman, with two girls of the same name, with two daughters of one father, or with a mother and her daughter at one and the same time!

The Nagas eat mostly rice and meat, preferring beef and pork. Though they have now started taking tea, and milk which was tabooed sometime ago, their favourite drink is rice beer of which they consume large quantities.

A word must be said about head-hunting. According to the Nagas themselves they got into this practice by seeing an ant and a lizard fight over a berry which a bird had dropped. The ant cut off the lizard's head! and thus provided the impetus to take heads. It is believed that the soul and its receptacle has its place in the head, so to bring home a head means capturing a great deal of spiritual power. Often it is the way to win the heart and hand of some lovely damsel in the tribe. Indeed at one time a Naga who had not won a head, could not get a decent girl in marriage. All these factors led to the Naga cult of head hunting. So much was the desire for heads that they were taken most cruelly and treacherously. A man would hide near a tank, and suddenly pounce upon and kill any woman or child who came to draw water. Or a group of Nagas would swoop down upon a hapless village, particularly when the men were out in the field, and behead as many old persons, women and children as they could, and be off before the men of the village returned. Davis records that when some men of Mozema went to Kohima, they killed one man, five women, and twenty young children, for their heads, and one of the onlookers told him 'that he never saw such a fine sport, for it was just like killing fowls'.[1] Fortunately all this is past history, and the last recorded case of head-hunting was in 1958.[2]

1. A. W. Davis, Census of India, 1891, Vol. I, pp. 237f.
2. Verrier Elwin, Nagaland.

The Khasis

The Khasis are found in the Khasi and Jaintia Hill districts of Assam in an area of about 6,157 square miles. A sub-division of the Khasis are the Syntengs (also called Pnars). While the Khasis inhabit mostly the Khasi Hills, the Syntengs are found in the Jaintia Hills. Apart from these two main tribes, the Lynngams inhabit the western portion of the Khasi Hills, the Bhois the hills to the north and north-east of the Kamrup and Sylhet districts, and the Wars are found in the south. Some Handem clans (sometimes called Kuki) are found in the extreme eastern portion of the Jaintia Hills.

The Khasis are brown in their complexion, varying from dark to light brown. The people living in the hills have a lighter complexion than those of the plains, and those dwelling in the village of Cherrapunji are particularly fair, while the Lynngams are the darkest of the Hill Khasis. The males cut their hair short, and keep a single lock at the back side which they call the 'grandmother's lock'.

The Khasis are short of stature with muscular bodies and highly developed calves. With such a body they can carry very heavy weights which they do by means of a band worn across the forehead. The women, too, are hardy and buxom, with greatly developed calves, which they pride in. The people are of a cheerful nature, fond of music, good humoured, good tempered, loving outdoor life, and attached to their families. The Khasis are in general an industrious race, capable of hard labour. They are enamoured of betels and betel-nuts, hard drinkers, and inveterate gamblers. McCosh describes them thus: They are a powerful, athletic race of men, rather below the middle size, with a manliness of gait and demeanour. They are fond of their mountains, and look down with contempt upon the degenerate race of the plains jealous of their power, brave in action.

The origin of the Khasis is very uncertain. According to one view they are connected with the Burmese, to whose king they used, in the ancient days, to send an axe as an annual tribute to signify their submission. According to another tradition they came from the north and spread upto Sylhet; but from there they were driven back by a huge flood during which the Khasi lost his book while swimming (while the Bengali managed to retain his!) which accounts for their having no written characters up to a long time. Yet another theory has it that they originally came into Assam from Burma via the Patkoi Range. It seems most probable however, that they moved into Assam from the east, and are possibly an off-shoot of the Mon-Anam family of eastern India.

The Khasis lay great stress on the potency of the egg. They use it for divination, for religious sacrifices, place it on the funeral pyre. This suggests an affinity to certain tribes of the Malay Archipelago whose medicine man, called gaji-guru, can see from the yolk of an egg which he breaks while counting from one to seven, the disease of a man who is ill. The Khasis also worship the serpent demon, and in this way appear to be akin to the people of Pagan who were originally 'Nagas' or or serpent worshippers. The Palaung women even now wear a dress which is like the skin of a snake. Another custom which is similar to the one which the Khasis observe at birth, is that of mixing placenta with ashes and placing it in a pot hung from a tree. This custom is observed as ancestor worship in Mandeling on the west coast of Sumatra. Thus there may be possible affinity between the Khasis and these Sumatra tribes.

The Khasis have now become modernised in respect of dress and men wear knicker-bockers, stockings and boots, coat, waist-coat, a collar without tie, and a cloth peaked cap. The women wear a chemise, a short coat of velvet, stockings, and shoes. But in the ancient days the dresses were quite different, and much more colourful ond picturesque. The male attire consisted of a sleeveless coat which left the arms bare, with a fringe at the bottom, and a row of tassels across the chest. The head wear consisted of a cup with ear-flaps, or a white turban. The women wore a number of garments, which made them look somewhat overdressed. Next to the skin was a piece of cloth called *ka jympien*, fastened to the loins by a cloth belt. Over this a long piece of cloth hanging loosely from the shoulders down to a little above the ankles, called *ka jainsem*. Over the jainsem there was a sort of cloak of a gay colour called *ka jain kup*. A wrapper, either white or of some bright hue, was cast around the head and shoulders. This was known as the *ka-tap-moh-khlieh.*

The Khasis also wear considerable jewellery. The women are fond of gold and coral bead necklaces, the beads being a hollow sphere filled with lac. A peculiar ornament is the silver or gold crown with tassels of the same metal hanging down the back, which is worn by young women at dances. Both men and women wear ear-rings and silver chains. The men wear the chains round their waist like a belt and the women hang them round their necks-dangling almost to their waists! The Lynngam men also wear cornelian bead necklaces called *pieng blei* or 'necklances of the gods'.

A peculiar ornament is the rupa-tylli or silver collar—a broad flat, silver collar, hanging down from the neck, and also worn. The Lynngam and Garo women wear so many brass ear-rings that their ear lobes are greatly distended. Their necklaces have a large number of blue beads of glass. After a Lynngam man has given a big feast he is entitled to wear silver armlets above the elbows and on his wrist.

The Khasis use swords, spears, bows and arrows as weapons, and carry shields for defence. They also knew about gunpowder and used the cannon. The swords they use are very heavy and cumbersome because they are forged, handle and blade, from wrought iron or occasionally, steel. The spear is about six and a half feet long with a wooden or bamboo handle. The bow (ka ryntieh) is the Khasi's favourite weapen. Two kinds of arrows are discharged from it—the one with a barbed head (ki-pling), used for hunting, and the other with a plain head (sop), used for archery, which is the Khasi's national game. The shield is circular, and is made of hide. It is studded with brass or silver. The Mikirs or Bhois use the spear and the bill-hook merely for cutting down jungle. They are the peaceful type of Khasis, quiet and hard working, and devoted to their work. Of them, Butler says : 'Unlike any other hill tribes cf whom we have knowledge, the Mikirs seem devoid of anything approaching to a martial spirit. They are a quiet industrious race of cultivators, and the only weapons used by them are the spear and the hand-bill for cutting down jungle. It is said, after an attempt to revolt from the Assamese rule they were made to forswear the use of arms, which is the cause of the present generation having no predilection for war.'

The Garos

The Garos are inhabitants of the hills known by that name, (about 3,140 square miles), which are bounded on the north and west by the district of Goalpara, on the south by Mymensingh, and on the east by the Khasi Hills. But they have also spread to the surrounding districts.

The Garos are darker than their neighbours, the Khasis, and have Mongolian features. They generally have wavy or curly hair, though sometimes they also wear it straight. Colonel Dalton's description of the Garos in his Descriptive Ethnology of Bengal is significant : 'Their faces are round and short. The forehead is not receding, but projects very little beyond the eye, which is small, on a level with the face, very dark and obliquely set. The want of prominence in the nose is remarkable. The whole face has the appearance of being flattened, the mouth sharing in the compressed appearance and not at all prognathous.'

The Garos are short in stature, and though hardy, they do not show the development of the lower limbs which is a marked characteristic of their neighbours, the Khasis. Those living on the higher ranges are somewhat healthier.. Some keep beards, but their moustaches usually have only a few hair because they pull out the rest. The hair styles are the same for both men and women. They keep the hair tied up in a knot behind, or wear a pugree. The women are buxom and healthy when young, though they loose their beauty quickly with age.

Their ears have to bear the weight of enormous earrings which quite often breaks their ear-lobes into two-and this is a great disfigurement.

The Garos are friendly and pleasant by nature, and straightforward, honest and tactful. They are very much taken up by litigation. They have few vices, and apart from their passion for drinking, they are an abstemious race, for they do not take any hemp or opium, abstain from gambling, and are not indebted. As regards personal cleanliness, the Garos leave much to be desired, for they seldom bathe. On the whole they are a peaceful, law abiding race, cheerful and light hearted, industrious and conscientious.

The principal garment worn by the Garos is the *gando*, which is a strip of blue cotton cloth with stripes of red. It passess between the legs and is then wound round the waist, and tucked in at the back. Sometimes the end of the flap has rows of white conch-shell beads. On his head the Garo wears a turban of dark blue or white cotton cloth, but for special occasions he dons one of red silk with an ornamented fringe. The turban is wound in many folds round and round, but leaves the top of the head bare. There is a strange belief to account for this. It is said that the huluk ape, when it sees the tangled hair on top of the head, calls out 'Huh ! Huh !' in derision as if to say 'what a miserable head of hair' and runs off into the branches of a tree. Thus, keeping the head bare drives off the ape ! when it is cold the Garo puts a cotton cloth or a blanket over his shoulders, otherwise the *gando* is all that he wears. At a dance the Garo man might wear a garment called *pandra*—a black cloth reaching to the waist, wound around the body and laced across with white cotton bands.

The women's main garment is the *riking*, which consists of a cloth just big enough to encircle the waist, like a petticoat. It is fastened on the top with two strings, and leaves the things bare. The women leave their bosom uncovered, except when it is cold, when they cover themselves with a shawl, generally of a blue and white cloth. On festive occasions the women wear a dress of coloured silk much of the kind worn by Khasi women, called a *marang-jasku*. The women sometimes go bare-headed, and at other times wear a turban like those of the men, or a folded turban called the *odoreka* or *salchak*, which is almost in the form of a cap.

As in other tribes, both men and women among the Garos wear ornaments. The mean wear two kinds of brass rings in their ears. Those worn in the lobe are called *nadogbi* or *atonga*, and as many as thirty or forty are worn in each ear ! In the upper part of the ear they wear a very small brass ring called *nadirong*, which is sometimes ornamented with four small brass discs attached to the outer and lower edge. Occasionally a semi-circular piece of brass, silver, or crystal, to which a string of beads is attached, is added to it.

Men and women both wear necklaces with barrel-shaped red beads. On festive occasions the *kadisil* is worn. This is a round circular ornament with brass studs, worn round the head. Another strange kind of ornament which only the village headman is entitled to wear is the *jacksil.* This is a particularly heavy ring, usually of iron, but sometimes of brass or silver, worn just above the elbow.

The women, like the men, also wear many varieties of ornaments. They too wear brass rings, called *shishas,* in their ears, but of a much larger size, and heavier, often more than fifty rings are worn in each ear, and the inevitable consequence is that the ear lobes can't bear the weight and get torn. Despite this the rings are not done away with. Instead, they are tied together by a strong string, and supported from the head ! The women of the Akawes and Chisak tribes wear an enormous necklace of many many rows of blue and white or red beads, which hangs very low over their bosoms.

When a man dies, his widow must take off her earrings. An adulterous woman was in old days punished by tearing off her earrings. But afterwards she was required only to take them off and not wear them till she was absolved of the charge of infidelity.

The women wear a kind of waist-band called *senki,* which has in it several rows of cylindrical shaped beads. Brass and bronze bracelets, too, are worn. A peculiar and spectacular head ornament, which is worn by women who take part in a dance, is the *pilni* or *salchak-maldong.* This is a bamboo comb which the woman sticks into the knot of her hair at the back. A strip of cloth, ornamented with cylindrical beads, is attached to the comb, and this hangs down the back of the head.

The weapons used by the Garos are the sword, spear, and occasionally the bow. They have, of course, the shield for defence. The swords are very ill-designed and cumbersome to use. The grip is curved and very thin, and ends in a sharp edge, so that the sword can be stuck on the ground by his side when a Garo halts. In fact the sword is more of use in clearing brushwood and jungle growth, than as a weapon. It is made from hilt to the point, of one piece of iron. The Garo spear is much better and more effective. Its blade is exceedingly sharp, and it is attached firmly to the bamboo shaft. Bears, and even tigers, can be killed by the spear, and it is used for slaughtering pigs for food. Unlike the Khasis, the Garos seldom use the bow.

The shields are of two kinds. The *sepi* is of wood. It consists of flat pieces of wood bound by thin cane strips. The other kind is the *danil*, made of bear-skin or cow-hide stretched on a wooden frame.

The Mikirs

The Mikirs are mostly found in the hills which bear their name. The origin of the name 'Mikir' is not known. They call themselves 'Arlengs', which means 'man'. Their complexion is a light yellow brown, and they are tall and muscular. Like the Khasis, they can carry heavy burdens upon their back. They wear a thin moustache, and their hair is gathered into a knot which hangs behind the head. The girls are often fair complexioned.

The Mikir dresses almost like the Khasi. He wears a dhoti of cotton, or if wealthy, of silk. His coat is a sleeveless striped jacket with a long fringe behind. A thick wrapper called *borkapor* is worn in the cold wheather. On the head there is a cap of black and red cloth, or a turban.

The women wear a petticoat of white cloth with red stripes, secured round the waist by an ornamental girdle. The upper garment is a wrapper drawn under the arms and tightly lacing the breasts. Normally they are bare-headed, but use a black scarf in funeral dances. Their hair is drawn back and tied into a knot. When a girl attains puberty it is usual for her to tattoo a vertical line with indigo down the middle of her forehead, her nose, upper lip and chin.

The ornaments are the usual ones. The ear ornament is a large silver tube inserted into the lobes of the ear. Ordinarily ear-rings of gold or silver are also worn. Necklaces of gold, silver, or coral beads are worn, and on festive occasions, feathers in the turban.

The weapons, too, are the usual ones—a long knife, a spear

and bow and arrows. The bow is made of bamboo with a string of strong bamboo fibre.

The Kacharis

The Kacharis are widely spread in Assam, but they are to be found outside also, in the north-east of Bengal, in Koch-Berar, and in the Tippera Hills. The branch of this race which became powerful was in the kingdom of Kamarupa (Koch). The earliest mention of the Eastern branch of the Kacharis is under the name of the Chutiyas, The Ahoms, with whom they had a long struggle, were ultimately victorious and drove the Kacharis to the foot of the Naga Hills. But the Ahoms pressed on their victory, and the Kachari Raja moved to Maibong, and then to Khaspur in Kachar. Here the Kacharis came under Hindu influence, and their kings, Krishna Chandra and his brother Govinda Chandra, professed Brahminism. It is said that they were place inside a huge copper replica of a cow, and on emerging were declared Kshatriyas, descendants of Bhima of the Mahabharata. Consequently the Darrag Kachiris consider themselves to be children of Bhima (Bhimani-fsa).

King Govinda Chandra's reign was short. The Burmese constantly oppressed him and finally drove him to Sylhet. He was reinstated in power with the help of the East India Company, but later he was murdered and his kingdom became part of the British dominion.

The Kacharis are distinctly separated into the Northern and Southern races. There is no intermarriage between the two, and the dialects also greatly differ. A story is related about the reason for this cleavage which has to do with the war of the tribe with the Ahoms. It is said that the Ahoms were pursuing the Kacharis, and their king, Dimasa, had to retreat when hard pressed. But the retreat was stopped by a deep river. Thus King Dimasa was in a fix, with the enemy on one side and the river on the other. In the night when he slept, he had a dream in which a god appeared and said that the king and his army should enter the river at a spot where they saw a heron standing in the water, but no one should look back. Next morning the king saw a heron, as the god had said, and led his men to the spot. They found that the river has turned mysteriously shallow there, and began to get across. But while some had mạnaged to get across, others were in the middle of the river, and yet others still this side of it, a man, wondering if his son was following or not, looked back. Immediately the waters deepened, and everyone had to cope with this unexpected turn of events. Some saved themselves by clutching rushes (khagris) and are consequently known as Khagrabarias. Others caught hold of of reeds (nals) and are called Narbarias. The Dimasas were those who could get across safely.

The Meitheis

The Meitheis are residents of Manipur State. The country given the name of Methei Leipak is their abode. On the west there lies the district of Cachar, the frontier touches Upper Burma, and towards the South there are the Chin and the Lushai Hills.

About their origin there is a legend according to which at the beginning of the Kaliyuga age was born one Pakhangba, who would assume the form of a god in the day and a man at night. It is said he could change shape at will and turn himself into a snake, but unfortunately his life was cut short by an unhappy accident in which his son, seeing him in the house and mistaking him for someone else, killed him with spear. Accoding to another story, the ancestry of the first ruling King of Manipur, Pakhangba, is traced to Brahma himself. According to Colonel McCulloch several tribes occupied Manipur, viz., the Koomuls, the Looangs Moirangs and the Meithei, and by degrees the last named subdued them all. It seems most likely that the Meitheis are descended from the surrounding hill tribes, and have close connection with the Nagas. The inhabitants of Manipur account for the name from the word 'mani' or jewel, which the Rajas of old possessed.

In appearance the Meitheis approach the Aryan type. Their girls are fair, sometimes with brownish-black hair, brown eyes, and rosy cheeks. The unmarried girls wear the hair behind their heads, combed back and tied into a knot, and left loose. The hair is combed forward in the front and cut, so as to reach a little above the eyebrow. Married women grow their hair long, comb it back from the forehead, and tie it into a knot behind.

The men are strong, well-built and muscular. Their stature varies, some being tall and others short. They have wide chests and well developed limbs. The men wear their hair long, combed back from the forehead and gathered into a coil behind. Beards and moustaches are uncommon.

As regards dress, there used to be many restrictions imposed by the old rules. For example, certain articles of dress could be worn only if permitted by the Raja, particularly in his presence. Thus a silk dhoti with purple patterns, or an orange coloured one, could be worn only by the princes and the sons-in-law of the Raja, and not by persons of inferior rank. A red or pink dhoti could be worn in the presence of the ruler only by privileged persons. Turbans with silk borders could not be worn in the royal presence. In the same way, women could not wear gold embroidered chadars in the presence of the Raja. The carrying of pieces of cloth of different colours, which the Meitheis used as rugs, also had a formal usage. Persons of high rank could carry a red woollen cloth, those of a lesser rank a green woollen one, and those of a rank lower, a cotton cloth.

In general, the men adopted the usual Indian dress, viz., the dhoti and kurta, and occasionally a chadar. In winter a padded coat with long sleeves and big collars is worn by those who can afford it. A short pugree forms the headgear.

The women wear a piece of cloth called a *fanek*, covering the lower body. This is hitched up to the knee and tucked in at the waist. It is of cotton or silk, with horizontal stripes. The bottom is stitched together, and has a colourful border. A thin white chadar is worn over the *fanek*, called the *in-na-phi*. In winters a short tight fitting jacket of satin, black, blue or green velvet may be worn. Girls below the age of puberty have the upper part of the body bare, wearing only *fanek* round the waist.

There are festive dresses for occasion like sports (boating and wrestling), and at dances or religious festivals women wear a very gay custume consisting of a small black velvet cap trimmed with pearls, a close fitting jacket of black cloth or velvet with gold trimming on the sleeves, a white cloth wound lightly round the waist and upto breast, and a green or red petticoat with a band of sequin ornamentation at the bottom of it. The costume, complete with decoration and ornaments, is very gay, and due to its prohibitive cost it is often obtained on hire.

Ornaments consists mainly of bracelets, necklaces and ear-ings. Ankle and toe ornaments are not worn. The women wear a small gold pin in each nostril. As in dress, there were ones of gold had to be obtained from the Raja, so far as ordinary classes were concerned. Men as well as women wore earrings, generally a thin plating of gold over lac. Women of the upper classes wore necklaces, quite often of pure unalloyed gold.

The weapons used by the Meitheis were the *dao*, the dart (*aramba*), and a catapult, which replaced the bow, firing pellets of hardened clay. Shields made of buffalo hide and studded by brass knobs, were carried mainly on ceremonial occasions. The dao was a blade from one to two feet in length, firmly fixed in a wooden or metal handle. The dart (*arama*) consisted of a heavy pointed piece of iron, attached to a bamboo rod and twelve long quills of peacock feathers. The handle was used to fling the iron piece with unerring accuracy. Gunpowder was known to the Meitheis, and they could make rough matchlocks and breachloading guns.

CHAPTER XI

ARTS AND CRAFTS

This part of India is a rich field for research, and almost in every place abounds in objects of historical and antiquarian interest. It was in April 1912 that the Kamarupa Anusandhan Samiti (Assam Research Society) was established at Gauhati to carry on research in matters relating to art, archaeology and history.

Assam is rich in ancient treasure and glories. She can be proud of her archaeological wealth. Old sculptures, stone and copper plate inscriptions, architectural remains, stone bridges, etc., have come to light. But it is unfortunate that no concrete numismatic evidence of the ancient kings, prior to the Ahom ruler Suklenmung (A.D. 1539-1552), has yet come to light. This does not however mean that the ancient kings of Assam did not have their own coins. If one goes back to the seventh century, one finds that Bhaskaravarman ruled over a vast eastern empirc. He was a friend and ally of Harshvardhana, the emperor of Northern India.

Bhaskaravarman was the most illustrious of the Kamrupa kings. Arts, crafts and industries reached their apogee during the rule of the Varman Kings of ancient Assam. The art of melting metals and impressing seals on clay or metal was known in Bhaskara's times, as is evinced by his Nalanda seal and copper plate inscriptions. Gold and copper were obtainable within his kingdom.

In the Silimpur stone slab inscription of the time of Jayapala (A.D. 1115-1125) the last king of the Brahmapala dynasty of Assam, it is mentioned that the king offened a large gift of gold equal to his own weight (tulapurusa) to a learned Brahmin, Prahasa by name. It numbered over 900 gold coins.

Although coins of Ahom kings prior to Suklenmung, as

stated above, have not yet been discovered, historical evidence are there that as early as the fourteenth century A.D. Sudangpha, alias Bamuni Kowar (1397-1407), struck coins in his own name on his accession to the throne. After this the practice became established with subsequent monarchs of issuing coins while ascending the coronation building known as the *Singharighar,* which contained a throne of gold for the new monarch.

The finest and oldest specimen of sculptural or plastic art in Assam is the stone door-frame at the Dah-Parvatia temple in Darrang district (Central Assam). The carvings, though characteristic of the early Gupta schools of sculpture, have an Assamese aroma. The goddesses Ganga and Yamuna stand, garlands in hand, in artistic and elegant posture. The door jambs are decorated with beautiful ornamental foliage. The artist's sense of proportion, the beautiful symmetry of the figure and ornamental devices and the excellence of execution tend to prove that this door-frame belongs to the same period as the great schools of sculpture which existed at Pataliputra and Varanasi in the fifth and sixth centuries A.D. What is known as the Umachala Rock Inscription of Surendravarman is the earliest epigraphic record so far discovered in Assam. It is in the north-eastern slope of the Kamakhya or Nilachala Hills near Gauhati.

On the Kamakhya Hill, about three miles from Gauhati, a number of sculptures of archaeological interest have been found. A special reference has to be made to the stone gateway dating back to the time of Naranarayana, the famous Koch king of the 16th century A.D. and rebuilder of the temple of Mother Goddess Kamakhya. The gateway, with heraldic looking lions on either side, has a pointed arch and the well surface is decorated with lotus medallions.

Pancharatna Paglatek is another remarkable site, where there are ruins of a Siva temple. It is well known in Goalpara District and dates back perhaps to the ninth century A.D.

The artistic beauty discovered in Darrang District, those of Bamuni Hill, Cole Park and the Missionary Compound are the remains which date back to the ninth and tenth centuries. The most striking specimens are the two massive ornamental stone pillars now adorning the gate of the Missionary Compound at

Tezpur. In Nowgong District, the Devaka finds of the Umalingana and the Suryamurti appear to be the finest and most artistic.

The Numaligarh ruins in Sibsagar District have a prominent place in the role of Assam sculpture.

Another sculpture in Sibsagar District is the famous Deopani Vishnu image, bearing an inscription in corrupt Samskrit verse.

The Ahoms came to Assam in A.D. 1228. They took some time to establish their rule. In the 17th and 18th centuries they erected palaces and lofty temples which attract the attention of a visitor. Among them the Sivadol (Siva temple), Devidol, Vishnudol, Ranghar (amphitheatre) and Karenghar (Palace) are the most important. They are brick-built and well decorated.

In Assam, neo-Vaishnavism brought in the practice of illuminating book with small illustrative paintings. Sankaradeva is also believed to have been a painter. On one occasion he is said to have painted on tulapat (ginned cotton paper) scenes of the Seven Vaikunthas (heavens). On another he painted in vermilion and yellow arsenic the likeness of an elephant and pasted it on to a wooden case to be presented to his royal patron, Naranarayana, Koch king of the 16th century.

The arts and crafts advanced at the time of Bhaskaravarman (Seventh Century A.D.), the most famous monarch of ancient Assam. There were various types of craftsmen in ancient Assam —weavers, spinners, potters, goldsmiths, workers in ivory, wood, bamboo, can, hide and so forth. From time immemorial Assam enjoyed the reputation of producing silk of a very high standard. The trusted envoy of Bhaskara, Hamsavega carried presents to Harshavardhana including silken cloths (*ksaumani*) pure as the moon's light, soft loin-cloths (*jatipattikali*) smooth as birch bark, sacks of woven silk, wrappers of white bark silk and various kinds of smooth figured textiles and other varieties of crafts.

Mat-makers, basket-maker, wood workers, painters throve and were skilful enough to be admired and extolled. Ivory work, mat-making and pottery are still recognised as important village crafts and cottage industries.

CHAPTER XII

THE ZEMI-NAGAS

The Nagas have come a long way since the British first came in contact with them in the middle of the 19th century and took defensive measures to protect British subjects and the tea plantations from raids by the hostile. The Nagas are now equal partners in the Union, with the formation of the Nagaland by joining the three hill districts of Kohima, Mokokchung and Tuengang into India's seventeenth State.

Mountaineous Tract

An expanse of forests, mountains and streams, the State, 6361 square miles in area with a population of about 4 lakhs, has more than 30 tribes with different customs, dialects and religious practices. Many of them are converts to Christianity.

Head Hunter

How did the Nagas get their reputation for headhunting? The custom springs from the belief in a soul force capable of bestowing vitality to an individual or community. Each community is said to possess a certain quantum of soul force which decreases with time, and has to be replenished if the tribes are to be healthy and prosperous and the harvests remain abundant. By keeping skulls in the house, the Nagas believe, this soul force is augmented. Some anthropologists, however, state that this scalp-hunting is a form of vendetta.

Marital Race

A martial race, the Nagas built their houses with defence possibilities in mind. The villages were sited on mountain spurs and surrounded by bamboo palisades or stone stockades. The eminence gave the Nagas a panoramic view of the countryside and kept them prepared for sudden attacks from other tribes.

Houses

The hearth is the centre of the Naga household and family and friends gather it to chat or partake of food. It is here that decisions are made. The chores are divided among men and women, the latter fetching water and attending to domestic duties. The men work in the fields on the hill slopes, where their women folk occasionally help them. There is a fair amount of rainfall, about 80 inches, and rice and vegetables are cultivated. In the plains sugarcane, papaya, pineapple and oranges are grown.

Jhoom

Agriculture is the mainstay of the economy. The traditional form of farming is known as Jhoom, a shifting system of cultivation. Every year trees in a part of the forest are cut, the area cleared, sown with seed and a bumper crop harvested This piece of land is allowed to lie fallow. It is cultivated again after a lapse of time. A fresh piece of forest land is farmed the following year.

The Nagas are now changing to other methods of agriculture. The Angamis of Kohima, for instance, have a terrace system of cultivation and make use of mountain rills to water their fields. Others have adopted modern farming tools and using high yielding seeds. Growing rice in built-up terraces has gained much publicity.

Usually a hut is constructed near the fields to store the produce. It also serves as a recreation centre. The tribals chat and sing at the end of the day's work. Their philosophy of living is a simple one—to work for their daily bread and relax completely when the chores are over. Dances are reserved for festive occasions.

Women Weavers

While the men work as potters or silversmiths, or fish for a living, the village women are experts in weaving artistically patterned shawls and fabrics for their personal use or for sale to tourists. Their clothes are always colourful, and they wear a profusion of ornaments made of silver or bone, and chains of coloured heads. Alcoholic drinks, made from rice, are popular both with the locals and visitors. Being mild drinks, women also partake of the brew especially during festivals which are frequently celebrated by the Nagas.

Festivals

One of the major festivals is the Sankarani Puja which coincides with Shivratri, single boys and girls join in the Sankarani Puja which lasts over a week. Chanting songs, they smoke, eat and drink to their hearts content. Contribution in money and kind is welcome from the participant families as well as visitors.

Smoking and Drink

Smoking seems to be a universal habit and the Nagas take to it even from the tender age of three. Men and women chew tobacco, smoke biris, and welcome the offer of a cigarette. Milk as a food—even for nursing mothers and children—is relatively unknown. Instead, rice gruel is taken frequently. Milch cattle are consequently few. The Nagas are fond of meat and are not averse to eating the flesh of any animal. They relish the flesh of snakes, field rats, pigs, cats, dogs and the mithun, a cross between a bull and the yak. Animals, brought by the Nagas from the plains of Assam, are herded into the villages for slaughter. They have a simple way of cooking meat, dispensing with spices and fat. This renders the flesh particularly rich in protein. Fish, whenever available, is popular among Nagas and is also dried and stored for use during lean periods. The food is washed down with liberal quantities of spirits-zau and Dekrizau.

Dormitories

Special dormitories for boys and girls known as morungs, and under the supervision of trustworthy old couples, still exist in some villages. The dormitory serves a dual purpose. It is a sort of cultural centre for the preservation of music, dance, and artistic expression of the tribes, for the youths learn the rudiments of the arts there. It is also a kind of military camp

Since the single men are located at one place with ready access to arms they can in an emergency be called upon to defend the village at any time of the night. The young men have their gayer moments too. They visit other morungs as far as ten miles away to seek the company of the opposite sex and engage in normal dalliance. Pre-maritial taboos are few and the children born of such liaisons are not frowned upon but accepted in society and are looked after, generally by the mother.

Democratic Practices

The Nagas are well disposed towards newly married couples. The bride and bridegroom are helped by the villagers in setting up a home built on a piece of land allotted to them and which incidentally, is owned by the village and not by individuals.

Indeed, the Nagas have certain democratic practices where the interest of the community is placed above that of the individual. The co-operative system functions at all levels and for practically every purpose, from building house to harvesting crops. The whole village gives a helping hand when a major chore has to be done and in return the workers receive free food and drink. Occasionally, the rich provide a feast for the villagers and are then entitled to a sort of status symbol displaying a sign outside their houses.

Game trophies and heads of the mithum are also prominently hung in the porch. The Nagas have a crude but effective way of curing heads, burying them for a period of time so that the flesh falls off leaving the heads fairly decent looking. The whole village takes part in the hunt, either as beaters or hunters whenever the summons for a chase is given. Though eager to possess guns, the Nagas make the best of their primitive weapons and are capable of killing even big game with spears, dahs or bows and arrows.

Their main sport being hunting, they are adept in trapping animals, wild bears, elephants and even tigers. All game meat is equally distributed among the poor and the better off. It is often smoked and set aside for future use. On festive occasions the killing of a fattened mithun which is tied to a post is almost a ritual—although a cruel one. Instead of shooting it outright the Nagas resort to disposing of it with a dah, one limb at a time, eventually severing the head.

Besides the tribes within state boundaries, there is an overflow to the neighbouring States of Manipur and the North Cachar Hills of Assam. They claim kinship with one another though their dialects differ. Predominant among the Naga tribes are the Angamis and the Rengma from Kohima, the Semas and the Aos from Mokokchung and the Phoms and the Changs of Tuensang.

All the tribes take pride in martial activities and tend to fight at the slightest provocation. Some of them have joined the Indian Army. Many members of the Ao tribe have taken to business. The Aos are generally more educated and advanced than other tribals. Ao girls wear modern, fashionable clothes and look smart.

There is much missionary activity among the Nagas. Christian priests of various denominations work there with American Baptists in a majority. There are also many Roman Catholic missionaries. Christianity has changed tribal marriage customs and the mode of life. Parents now prefer to keep their children at home rather than in the morungs, and send them to school.

The Sansaris, however, retain their customs and beliefs. The Phoms and the Changes in the interior of Tuensang dispense with clothes altogether. However, contact with the plains people obliges them to cover their nakedness but even so they wear the minimum number of clothes. The climate is pleasant so that there is no real necessity to wear clothes in summer; even the winters are mild.

Dress

Tribal dress and accessories are eye-catching. The red blanket, a symbol of office of the headmen (Gaon Burra) and a red jacket that of an interpreter (Do-Bhashi), are worn with pride though little or no monetary benefit accrues to the wearer, except possible signifying a position of authority and prestige.

In the interior, communications are still primitive though road building efforts are in full swing. Unlike other parts of India, the villagers can be entrusted with the responsibility of constructing and maintaining and if necessary, guarding the portions of road passing through their area.

But services only extend to the district headquarters. The

Nagas still covers long distances on foot despite the heavy loads they bear. Of course, they like to ride in a bus and their pleasure in this quick and comfortable form of transport is evident.

Doctor

The old witch-doctor with his sacrifice of chickens and practice of other rites still holds away over the country-side. Medical aids are primitive. The cure for sores consists in covering them with leaves. The Nagas, being hardy, shrug off minor ailments and often manage without modern drugs. Treatment of the sick, the old, and injured persons poses a problem. Young men, however, volunteer to carry the patients for miles and for days together to a hospital for treatment, provided they are convinced that the witch-doctor is helpless and the patient needs specialized medical care.

Scenic Beauty

The scenic beauty of the area strikes the visitor. He can never hope to see the place in one or two trips. It is a paradise for research scholars, anthropologists, botanists and tourists. It is worth a visit especially in the cold season when there is still a lot of greenery around.

A. ORIGIN AND HISTORY

Sub-Tribes of Kaccha Nagas

The Zemis are one of the sub-tribes of the so called Kaccha Naga Tribes according to the Zemis of the N.C. Hills. The word Kaccha Naga has been derived as follows. When the Britishers came to North Kachar Hills near about Dimapur they made Asalu as one of the headquarters of the British Army. The people living in the Asalu village were the Zemis themselves. From the Asalu headquarters, the district people started to move toward Kohing, but could not succeed due to thick forest. The people of the Asalu village stated that those who live there are all dacoits or Kahegami (meaning dacoits, a head hunters in the Zemi language). So the Britishers did not proceed further, but came down to Dimapur side and entered a village of the

Angamis near Kohima called Khonoma. When they entered Khonoma they called the people of Khonoma village as Angamis, (they derived this name from Kahegami, which they learnt from the people of the Asalu village). But the people of the Khonoma village (Angami) even today call themselves Thenemi. The British were enquired from the Angamis of the Khonoma village, as who are the people living to the western side of Kohima.

Kacchas

The Angamis said that nobody lives in that area but there are only Kacchas (Kacch is an Angami word meaning forest). That is in that area there are only jungles and no one lives there. But the Britishers moved and entered inside the western area, that is the Zeliang area at present, to their surprise they found some people living there. The Britishers mistook themselves at the Kacchas, (which they learned from the Angamis of the Khonoma village) and named them as the Kaccha Nagas. According to the available information the people living in those thick forests were the Zemi Nagas themselves, whom the Britishers mistook as the Kaccha Nagas.

Western District of Kohima

The Kaccha Nagas are the Zemis living in the Western district of Kohima, while the Zemi themselves are living in the North Cachar hills from a very early time. According to the Zemis of the N.C. Hills there are no marked difference in cultural and social activities of these two groups of Zemis.

The Term Zemi

The term Zemi means 'Southern' or the plain regions in comparison to the Naga Hills. 'Nzieme' is the name by which they call themselves. It is now an obsolete term previously used by the Zemi Nagas of Manipur to refer the Zemi Nagas of N.C. Hills. The word is pronounced with a slight nasal aspirant.

The word has been derived from the root word Zemina, meaning man.

First Inhabitant Started Back to 13th Century

According to the Zemis of the N.C. Hills of first inhabitants of the N.C. Hills were the Siami and Zeme and their settlement may be dated back to the 13th century. The Siamis were Zemis in general, but since they know the art of making 'Teluiteu', (Naga Necklace) out of the soft stones (conches), so the Zemis gave the name as 'Siami' 'Siame' (mean artisans), to those families which knew the art of making necklaces. Their artistic works and stone pillars are still to be found in Melangpeu. Boloson, Asalu, Impoi, and other Zeme villages of the North Cachar Hills.

Kechingpethka

According to them, since the 13th century Zemis were living on the Borail Hills, before the Geographical division of India. This North Cachar Hills was called 'Kechingpethka' (Borali-range). When the Ahoms and the Kacharis invaded this area, they asked the Zemes as to whom this land belong. The Zemes answered that this land belonged to 'Kachingpeka' (that is Boro, or Bara that is elder). They actually meant that this is the home-land which belonged to the eldest of the family of 8 sons. Since that time the name Borail (derived from Boro) came into use, which is still being used. During the 16th cenury there was another batch of Angami Naga migration into Borail Hills. The Zeme Nagas being the weaker groups went away and moved downward and westwards passing through the Borail range, and started colonizing beyond the hill areas.

Clanwise Migration

The Kaccha Naga as a tribe consists of three sub-tribes as follows, the Zemis, the Liangmes, and the Rongmes or the Kabuis. The first two groups speak the same language but little variation in accent and the last group speaks different one though there is a good number of words akin to the first two. According to the Zemi Nagas of N.C. Hills all these groups belong to the same stock but later some what clanwise migration had to take place to different parts in search of fertile lands for cultivation. In olden times the Angamies carried on raids against the Zemis who thus had to migrate further and further away from their original place of settlement till they came down to Borail range in North Cachar Hills. Thus scattered and separated by economical, political and social forces they had to live in different geographical units like N.C. Hills, Manipur and Nagaland.

Same Social Customs

Inspite of the different geographical situations in which they are placed, the social customs and manners of these three sub-tribes are almost the same.

The Zemis are the Kaccha Nagas who had been for a long time the virtual subject of the Angami people of Khonoma (Hutton, 1921, pp. 352).

Different Dialect

They resemble the ruling people in manners of dress though they speak a different dialect. It is difficult to say what customs and measures are originally of Kaccha Naga and what have been borrowed from the Angamis of Khonoma.

Their Origin according to Sir Grierson

How and from where the Kaccha Nagas come before reaching the present abode is still in mystery. The tradition goes that their ancestors came from the direction of Japro mountain in Nagaland (J.H. Hutton, *The Angami Nagas*, 1921, p. 352, p. 6) and spread towards the south. They have been connected with the head hunters of the Malay and the races of the Southern sea on the one hand and traced back to China on the other. (J.H. Hutton, The Angami Nagas, 1921, pp. 352, 6).

It has been stated (communication made to the Royal Anthropological Institute Quarterly from Man in India 1948, Vol. 48) that the Zemi Nagas apparently migrated to the present location from the neighbourhood of Mao and Kohima, by a route down the Borail range and reached North Cachar when the Kachari Kingdom at Maibong was well established.

On the basis of language, their origin is assigned by Sir G. Grierson (1903) to the second wave of immigration that of the Tibeto-Burma, from the traditional cradle of the Indo-Chinese race in North Western China between the Upper areas of the Yang-tse-kiang and the Ho-ang-ho rivers.

The Kaccha Nagas of the North Cachar Hills come into

contact with the Kacharis (Hutton, 1921, p. 13). The legends of the Kachari king Bhim are still current among the Kacharis. They believe that he is still sleeping in a cave among the hill immediately to the south of the Japro mountain when he will come out at sometime in the distant future to rule over all who eat from the wooden platter (Nagas in general).

The Zemi Nagas of N.C. Hills though know about such a legend which is current among the Kacharis yet do not accept the possibility of a Kachari king ruling over them.

Ahom King

The Kaccha Nagas (E.A. Gait, 1963, 1013) were also enlisted in the armies of the Ahom Kings who had relations inter-Manipur. During thirties of the eighteenth century a Manipuri raid was made into the Angami country (Gait 1963) as far as Kohima, which the Manipuris attacked and burnt and slaughtered large numbers of inhabitants. The Kaccha Nagas as neighbours and satellites of the Angamis suffered in the same way as the Angamis when the Manipuris raided into the Angami country as far as Kohima.

Angami Rule

The Kaccha Nagas were for a long time under the Angamis suzerainty and even they had migrated to the area in the North Cachar Hills the fluctuating suzerainty of the Angamis over the Kaccha Nagas was still maintained untiil the establishment of the British rule. The Kaccha Nagas owe alligence to the Angamis in that they had to pay a kind of tax during their subjugation which amounted to Rs. 2/- per household per annum.

Over and above, they had to assist them in their devastating raids on the plains. In some cases the Angamis made their settlements in the Kaccha Nagas' country and where each settlements were made, the Kaccha Nagas as their subjects had to accept allegiance to the ruling Angamis. But the villages were so made that the Kaccha Nagas were free to pursue their own pattern in matters of village organizations and administration. As a result to such settlements it is but natural that the Angamis would dominate them and hence superimpose on them their own customs, ornaments, etc. through the ages.

B. ECONOMY

North Cachar Hills

The Zemi Nagas are found mostly in North Cachar Hills (J.H. Hutton 1921, pp. 252, 6) and also in Manipur and Nagaland. Those found in the North Cachar Hills subdivision have been living together along with the other tribes like the Dimasa Kaccharis, the Kukis, the Hmars, etc. According to the Zemis of the N.C. Hills they come to this sub-division from the north-east and migrated down the Borail range and still farther to the west as far as to the bank of the Kopili river. Thus there is long continuous chain of villages, with few Kuki and Hmar at places from the bank of the villages Kopili on the west to the eastern border of the North Cachar Hills.

Population

There was no record of the tribe wise population in the 1951 census. The total population of the Zemi Nagas of North Cachar Hills according to 1981 census was 9478 out of which 4556 are males and 4922 are females.

Since there are no population of the Zemi Nagas separately in the earlier census, so it is not possible to give the population trend.

Physical Appearance

The Zemi Nagas in appearance are a mongoloid race. In most of the cases they have an epicanthic feature, which is unmistakably a characteristic of the Mongoloid group. They have mostly thick black hair, well built, strong and healthy body. (Journal of the Asiatic Society of Bengal, Part III, 1900, Vols. LXVIII, LXIX, and LXX).

Darker Skin

The Zemi Nagas who are living in the comparatively hot regions in the N.C. Hill district like Howraghat and Bokakajan ghat some what darker skin as compared to those living in the hills of Haflong sub-division. In general they are short to medium statured individuals with various shades of light brown to fair complexion. It has been seen that the Zemi immigrants intermarried with survivors of a jungle race exterminated by the Kacharis, and darkskinned, frizzly-haired individuals are found among the present day Zemi.

Land

Land, the most important property, can be held by the individual or clan. The waste land of the village, where no structure has been erected by any persons belong to the whole community of a particular village. Each village has also a small patch of forest land and rights to this land belongs to the whole community irrespective of clan. No individual person or clan or family can utilize such village land for the purpose of culti-vation or erecting a house. They only benefit enjoyed by them from such land is that any villager can utilize the building materials for constructing or repairing his house.

Clan Land

Clan land is allotted for cultivation by an agreement among the people of the clan. That is a person who wants to cultivate that land or a part of it will approach his clan's members who will sit together and give their consent. In case of disagreement, the person concerned will refer to the village council who would try their best to settle the dispute. Such cases generally ends with the interference of the Kadeipee and other members of the village council and it is seldom referred to the District Council for its final decision.

Kadeipee

Though the lands within the officially demarcated areas belong to the villages as a whole there are some patches here and there within the boundary which are socially regarded as owned by the Kadeipee at the time of the original settlement. These lands can be disposed of by the Kadeipeo in favour of any of his relatives or descendents. He may give a part or whole of the land to his daughter or daughters as a part of the dowry for their 'Chingrimiabam', meaning place for collection of fire wood; when they go to their father-in-laws' house. The land thus given will then be in possession of their family and it will be subject to a traditional leavy or tax called 'Mpua' which every non-Kadeipee must pay to Kedeipee in recognition of the latter's right over the land in case the land is cultivated (that too after consultation with him), 'Mpua' may be measured in terms of crops grown thereon, it may be a basket of cotton, Chillies, rice, etc.

Full Authority

The eldest member of a clan has full authority over the clan land. Allotment of land for cultivation may be made by himself as is the normal practice, after consultation with his immediate elders of the clan.

Livestock

Land and livestock are the only factor which play an important part in the economic life of these people. Since their economy is predominantly agricultural the entire social structure is dependent upon the ownership of land and cattle wealth like the buffalo or the mithun, is an important source of income. As a consumption it is good especially during ceremonious occasions. The price of the mithun usually varies from Rs.20 to Rs. 25 according to the size and thus is a source of income for the owner. The Zemi households in the village makes weaving and basketry for their own purposes. Though these traditional industries are not carried out in a large scale and do not find their way in the market but rather provide a utilitarian object to the producing household.

Blacksmithy

Blacksmithy as a profession among the Zemi Nagas is practised on a very small scale. It cannot be regarded even as part time industry in the village. There are no particular clan or clans who are attached to it. This is only when the cultivators want to improve their agricultural implements like spades, hoes, dao, etc. that they resort to this work, and that too, in their own houses, with the help of indigenous accessories. There is no tradition connected with the industry and there exists no class distinction among those who practise it and those who do not. The services of other tribes like Kacharis are obtained and in fact the implements like daos, spears, etc. are manufactured by Kacharis of Maibang in the olden days were considered to be one of the best quality available in N.C. Hills.

Shifting Cultivation

The principal basis of subsistence is shifting cultivation. As the Borail Hill is extremely steep and cliffs and crags abound, the spurs lie close to each other and gorges and deep ravines are in between, the land fit for jhum exists only in scattered patches while the greater part is rocky and impossible for cultivation. Moreover the land can be put to cultivation only for two or three consecutive seasons. It is then left to lie fallow for at least ten years when the land has recovered enough for jhumming. During the period when jhum field is left fallow, the cultivators shift their activities to another plot of land and resume jhumming in the old plot when it is again fit for cultivation.

Changing Pattern

Since as is generally the case, there is not enough land for shifting cultivation, it becomes necessary to change to permanent fields by which the same population could live as a fraction of the acreage needed for jhumming.

Wet Cultivation

Wet cultivation, even it is known to them, is impracticable for the simple reason that the land around the Borail hills is unsuited for the purpose. Even lands fit for jhumming are few and far between, being found only in small scattered patches.

Clearing of Jhumming Land

Usually the land to be jhummed is cleared with daos (heke) or axes (hrei) in the months of December-January and set on fire in March-April. The ashes are thoroughly mixed with the earth and holes are made with the help of the hoe (kepen). The holes are to be made in such a way that the soil is to be upturned, will generally depend on the nature of the soil and the kind of crops (paddy) to be grown. In stormy or sandy jhums the holes are usually made and in soft or laamy areas, the outer crest of the earth is upturned. There are certain kinds of paddy which are harvested late in November-December and requires sturdy growth and hence require deep roots for their proper growth. For these, holes are generally made even in soft soils otherwise the paddy plants will fall on the ground as they grow in cluster from the same one hole. But some kinds of paddy which are reaped early in September-October are broadcasted after the soil is upturned, for they are of stunted growth and do not usually need deep roots. At present broadcasting of seeds (after the soil is upturned) is the most popular practice perhaps because of poorer quality of soil and the need for early crops. The methods in practice seem to require less quantity of seeds also. This broadcasting method is possible only in plain or at least on very gentle slopes, while on hilly steep sides, holes are generally made, for the seeds if broadcasted will be washed away down the hill sides by the rains. Sowing begins usually after the first rains, i.e. during the months of April-May. Paddy is the main crop and chillies, pumpkins, millet, maize, etc. are sown as side crops along with paddy, each in a separate hole. The harvesting of paddy begins in November and lasts until December whereas in the case of maize, chillies, etc. the harvesting period starts in August and that of millet, in October-November. Sickles (sapinen) are used to out the ears of paddy and the sheaves so collected are beaten against a stone untill the ears are separated from the plant. Husking is done with the help of pestle (kemi) and mortar (gepa).

Cottage Industries

Though cottage industries like weaving, basketry and blacksmithy are practised by the community yet it may not be wise to include them as subsidiary occupations though, of course, they provide a source of income to the producing household. This is due to the fact that the industries are not carried on a large scale but are practised only when occasion arises, as has been mentioned before these products do not find their way to the market but are rather meant for personal use. Of the industries practised by them weaving is the most important and the clothes are meant only for personal use. Of the clothes woven by them the most important are 'Menipai', 'Hemi', 'dimdia', used by men and 'armiang', 'peingum' used by women.

Ngkum and Hemui

A small wooden machine called 'ngkum' is used to extract the cotton seed. After extracting the seeds, cotten 'Hemui' is available. The spindle is made of a strong piece of bamboo or wood pointed at the bottom and above it has a round flat stone with a hole in the middle through which the wooden stem passes from its upper end. The thread is put round the wooden stem as the latter spins. The loom (dekrain) is a simple ten loom. The warp of moderate length and breadth is made and fastened at the end to a wall while the other end of the warp is tied to the waist, of the weaver with a cotton leather belt. No reed is used and the shed is operated by a half healed process which is also operated by the hand. The weft year is inserted in the head by means of bamboo tube and a wooden string is used for beating up the weft. This kind of loom is common among them because of certain advantages it offers, such as the compact texture of clothes woven in a tension loom, the ease with which the loom can be erected in any place or rolled up when it is not in use and the simplicity of the loom which enables its parts to be replaced easily and practically without any cost.

C. LANGUAGE AND RELIGION

Well Defined Gods and Goddesses (Tingwang)

Although the Zemis believe in spiritual beings they cannot be rightly called animistic. They have well defined gods and goddesses who, they believe, take special interest in the life of the people. They believe, that there is a God known to them as 'Tingwang' who guides and controls the life of man and who is above all of the gods (hera) and spirits (herui). This Supreme God is omniscient, ominipotent and omnipresent. He is to be worshipped and prayed and he is to be feared and respected. He is the Supreme and dispenser of good and evil and it is He who makes man rich or poor, great and small. Besides this Almighty there is a good number of gods whom they fear and revere.

There are legends that eight of these gods are the children of a goddess called 'Hezale' and two of them, 'Chuprai' and 'Munsenieu' are the most important and due propitiations are to be given to them in times of sickness. The functions of the other goddesses are not known but they appear to be of less importance in their relations with the life of men. There are spirits good and evil, which manifests themselves in the jungles, the wood and trees, the valleys, the hills, the precipices, the rocks and rivers and the sky above. These spirits or herui are also to be propitiated and revered. The Zemis have no temple or shrine for the worship of gods and spirits, they are performed by 'tingkupeu', the priest. The 'ting-kupeu' directs all public ceremonies and fixes the day for them.

Tingkupeu

It may be noted that the office of the priest, or 'tingkupeu' is hereditary. The office while descending from generation to generation remains however in the hands of the old man of the family, the second brother succeeding the elder or the son, his father and so on. The priest also plays an important role in connection with the formation or shifting of a village to a new site. When a new village is to be built it is the duty of the 'tingkupeu' to go and select the site for the first house of the new village and in this connection the 'tingkupeu' performs a ceremony, before the construction of the first house in the new site. The ceremony being attended by the elders of the village.

Selection of House Plots

On the spot where the house is to be built, a cock is tied from the leg by a rope to a post. Early in the following morning when the sun is high the cock is killed and its blood is offered to tingwang, praying at the same time that the place so selected for the new village will be free from any misfortune and calamities. The flesh of the cock is then cooked and eaten by those present on the occasion. It may be pointed out that the sitting place in front of 'tingkupeu's' house usually contains the graves of the deceased 'tingkume' (plural of tingkupeu) and is regarded as a sacred place.

Sun and Moon

The sun (naimik) and the moon (hekeu) are not worshipped but are looked upon with reverence and respect. The hills, streams and rocks are believed to be the creations of Tingwang but solar eclipse (naimik nra) and lunar eclipse (hekeu' nra) are the cause of the devil (nra) who swallows them up at certain seasons of the year resulting in failure of their crops and famine following its terain. The thunder (hegikeube) is due to the quarrel between husband and wife living in heaven who turn all things upside down thus making the roar or noise in heaven. When sacrifices can not be strictly followed as instructed by the 'tingkupeu', hail stones (gesak) will fall down from heaven to undo the works of man especially that of his fields. Earthquake (kaketaibe) is caused by some spirits who shake the earth, which is usually followed by a poor harvest.

Life of Zemi

Life of Zemi is full of fears and horrors. The illness of a person is attributed to some wild spirits. In such case, therefore, the 'tingkupeu' the person who, they believe, has got spiritual insight and power is consulted. He is supposed to know the cause of the illness by the expedient of drawing lots and accordingly pronounces the cause which may be either due to the gods, goddesses or spirits inhabiting a particular precipice or rock etc. The 'tingkupeu' also declares the number of fowls or pigs to be sacrificed and offering to the gods is done according to his instruction.

When a person is suddenly attacked with unconsciousness and encounters fearful experiences or he meets with an unexpected death on the way or in the jungle, the cause of such misfortunes is attributed to the agency of wild spirits.

Herasiateuhe

In such cases an offering known as 'herasiateuhe' is performed and a dog, a pig or a fowl is sacrificed but their meat should not, however, be eaten. Also when a persons's health deteriorates, it is taken to be caused by the goddess 'Chuprai' or 'munsenieu' as the priest attributes it and a fowl is to be sacrificed to the goddess in order that she may leave the ailing person in good health. The flesh of the bird killed should be eaten only by the ailing person while the blood is offered to the goddess.

Nvuikereura

Every year in its beginning there is a sacrifice called 'nvuikereura' or 'sacrificed of ten hens'. This sacrifice is performed for the purpose of propitiating the Almighty God (Tingwang). The priest invokes the help of Tingwang to keep the people in good and sound health throughout the year. It may, however, be noted that there are two classes of sacrifice to the deities, viz., sacrifices to the family deities called 'kelakra' and sacrifices to the community deities called 'keluara'. If the ancestors of the past are not given adequate sacrificial articles at their death, their spirits may visit their descendents and trouble them. The number of animals to be offered depends upon the ability of the family or clan which performs the sacrifice. Sacrifice to the community deities is done when the general condition of the community is not good, that is, due to epidemic diseases like cholera, small pox, etc. On this occasion one or two white or black fowls are let loose and they are not to be caught by any body as these fowls are meant for the gods only. On this occasion no outsider or stranger is allowed to enter into the village and to prevent strangers from entering the village two boughs of trees are put on each side of village gate.

Dreams and Vision and Dogams

A word may be added regarding the interpretation of their dreams and vision. It is believed that when a person has a bad dream at night like falling from a tree or into the river or stream or encountering fearful experience that person must not leave his house on the following day. He is believed to have been caught by the evil spirits which are to be a propitiated by sacrificing a fowl. In this case the priest is consulted, who after killing the fowl on some plantain leaves, offers it to the spirits to free the person from their grip. When a person who, goes on a journey sees a black cat crossing the path he is to turn back home otherwise he will meet with some misfortunes on the way, when he sees a snake crossing the road he must either kill it or return home. When a dog howls at midnight it is considered as an ill omen and some one living in the village may die. The howling of the dog is taken to be a sign of the presence of evil spirits which pass through the village.

Christian Zemis

The Christian Zemis belong to the Presbyterian Church and follow the set pattern of the Presbyterian Church organisation.

The beliefs and practices discussed earlier are mainly applicable to the non-Christian Zemis. But these beliefs and practices still persist to a certain extent among the Christian Zemis, as illustrated by a case study.

Mr. John Jeme, who is Assistant Secretary, Executive Committee, N.C. Hills District Council, Haflong was staying at Bara Haflong. He told to his friend that one day his father was knocked off by a speeding jeep on the road. His father received injuries on the head and on the waist. Since the driver of the jeep knew him so he brought his father at home. At home his father remained unconscious for one night. Mr. John Jeme, though a graduate of Gauhati University, and with a responsible post, did not think of taking his father to the hospital. His father was laying on a cot in a smoky room by the side of the fire made for keeping the room temperature high. The room was not well ventilated. The relatives and friends were sitting surrounding his father. He was given only some tea when he gained his consciousness. The morning following the accident when he reached Mr. John Jeme's house, he learned that they are waiting for a man who wants to pray to God for the recovery of the patient. After some time the man came to his house. While he was praying all the persons sitting in that room lowered their head in regard to the prayer. That man (not the priest, but an elderly man) uttered few sentences in Zemi language, in a rhythmic tone for about 10-15 minutes. After the prayer was over the compounder of the hospital came at his house and saw the patient and asked them to take him to the hospital. They made a stretcher and he was taken to the hospital after about 3 hours. Later his friend learned from the doctor of the hospital that since he was an old man he got a shock, and the injury was not serious. Thus this case fairly indicates that such beliefs and practices of the non-Christian

Zemes still persists among the Christian Zemi to a certain extent.

Zemi Language

The Zemi Nagas of North Cachar Hills speak their own language which is known as the 'Zemi' language. The Liangmes who are the other sub-division of the Kaccha Nagas, speak the same language but with a little variation in accent or intonation and the Rongmes or Kabuis speak a different one though there are quite a good numbers of words akin to the Zemis and the Liangmes. Sir George Grierson (Linguistic Survey of India, Vol. III, Part II) classed the Kaccha Naga language in the Naga Bodo group. In the 1961 (Part III.C) census there were 185 male and 189 female Zemi speakers in the Assam Hills division. The same holds true for the united Mikir and North Cachar District. They have no script of their own instead use the Roman script with a few alternations in the alphabets. For example, A.I. (to be pronounced in high tone), 'm' (pronounced, 'im') 'n' (pronounced 'in'), 'ng' (pronounced 'ing'), 'ng' (pronounced 'eng') are added to the alphabets while C. F. Q. V. X. Y. are omitted. The Zemis, except the Christian Zemis have no literature of their own. There are songs, folk stories, legends, etc. which are never reduced to writing but are orally handed down from father to son through generations past.

Zeliangruoing Committee

The Zemi Christians have some written books, there is a Zeliangruoing Literature Committee which aims to bring about uniformity in text-books, script, etc. This has evolved common script so as to facilitate production of common standardized text books, for schools, hymn books, Bible extracts, etc. The District Council has not yet taken any steps to encourage their language. Though the District Council has provisions for the introduction of Zemi language in the primary stage and also for the preparation of text books in the Roman alphabet. The Council has taken over all the Government primary schools but the medium of instruction still used is either English or Bengali. The Zemi language has been introduced only in those primary schools which are run by the Presbyterian Mission to which the

Zemi Christians belong. The Zemi Primary text books which are prepared and published by the Mission are also in use.

Primary Schools

The villages which are nearer the town or have some access to the urban centres are having the primary school while the interior villages which are remote from the town are lacking even the primary schools. As a matter of fact, the idea of education is most readily appreciated by the Christian Zemis. In some villages the education is as old as the coming of Christianity.

Literate Persons

According to 1981 Census the number of literate persons in the North Cachar Hills are 437 out of the total population of 9478. This shows that the literate persons are very few among the Zemi Nagas. Most of them have not yet realized the value of education or are rather not yet willing to part with their children for education.

D. CEREMONIES AND BELIEFS

Sons most Welcome

A married couple always looks to the day when they will have children. To them sons are most welcome but daughters too are equally treated.

Heteu

There is no professional midwife or dhai among the community. Child delivery is taken by some old woman in the family and, in the absence of such a woman, any other old woman from the neighbourhood is summoned to help in delivering the child. The woman is not paid for their work but she is only entertained with food by the members of the family. An expectant mother about to deliver a child usually breaks the necklaces of beads (heteu) that she is wearing on her neck and at the same time takes off all her clothes except the one which she wraps over the body like a showl. She is kept separated from the rest of the household, her bed being separated and a separate hearth (hemibam) built for her though in the same room where the general hearth is situated. Zemis in the interior villages believe that if the father happens to be away from home, the child waits for its father and will not be born till he arrives. Regarding birth much of the old customs have been disregarded by the Christian Zemis. Among the Christian Zemis the expectant mother about to deliver a child need not break the necklaces of beads nor does she need to strip off her clothes. She is also not separated from the rest of the household as in the case of the non-Christian Zemis. The old methods of delivery, are still followed by them.

Genna

Among the Christian and the non-Christian Zemis, immediately after delivery the woman is given rice beer, rice and some chicken curry after the child and the mother are bathed and the naval cord is cut. The diet thus prepared is meant to compensate the stress and strain she bears during child birth. For five days or more the mother is fix exclusively on this diet and during this period, the husband as well as the members of the household observes genna among the non-Christian Zemis. That is they will not go to their work in others' fields. They must also live on the food which is available within the precinct of the house but not on the food which is brought from outside. If a male child is born then a cock is killed and if a female then a hen. There are some taboos connected with child birth in the family which are as follows.

Taboos connected with child birth

(a) The meat prepared for the mother should not be shared by the husband. Only the female members can share. Even small boys are not allowed as it is believed that when they grow up they will not succeed in sports like animal hunt, bird trapping, etc.

(b) The husband should not go out to the jungles, jhums etc. before the elapse of 5 days.

(c) The baby cannot be taken outside through the front side of the house i.e. the side facing the village street before 5 days are elapsed.

(d) The water used for washing and bathing the baby should not be scattered here and there but be collected in a pit specially made for the purpose at the back side of the house and the mouth of the pit be kept closed to prevent the demostic animals like dogs, pigs, etc. from licking the water. This is done because of the belief that any one who does not carefully observe these rules of hygeine is more prone to bodily injuries like cuts etc. while in the field or during sports like hunting, animal chase, etc.

(e) Formerly no outsider was allowed to enter the house before the elapse of 5 days after the child birth but now there is no such ban, this may be due to the urban influence and is more found among the Christian Zemis.

(f) After 5 days the child is taken outside and its hair shaved by one of the elders of the village. A fowl is sacrificed during the operation. Formerly the sacrificial meat could not be taken by anyone except the mother of the child and a very old man or woman of the village. Now there is no such restriction. After the ceremony the husband can go out freely performing his normal duty.

At the end of the 5 days the mother is allowed to go out but only through the back door of the house since no one should see her going out. While doing so she carries out all the cooking utensils, which have been used by her during the genna, and when no one sees her, she throws them away behind the house; while performing this act, her husband keeps watch so that no body can look at his wife, even himself, while she does so. It is believed that by doing so the wife and her child will be free from the grasp of evil spirits, but if any one sees her doing so, misfortunes would befall by her, which may result in her death and of the child. After the performance of all these, the mother resumes her normal life and eats and drinks from the same hearth and the same utensils which the family use.

Twin Child

Twins which are of rare occurrence are well received by the

members of the family. In case of the twins of the same sex the parents are congratulated and blessed. It is customary for the mother to cloth them in an identical manner, that is, the same variety and of the same pattern of design. But in cases where the twins are of opposite sexes wearing identical clothes is considered unlucky and it is believed that it may lead to the death of both the twins.

Tingwang

The birth of a child is dedicated to the Almighty God who is known as Tingwang. When a male child is born, a cock is killed and offered to Tingwang whereas in the case of a female child a hen is offered. The offering is made by the eldest male member of the family. The naming of the child take place usually after the ninth day of its birth.

Hezintak

After naming ceremony (hezintak) all relatives and friends are invited to a feast in which pork and zau are served. The name is given according to the wishes of the child's grandfather or relatives. Among the non-Christian Zemis the name given to a child is mostly considered from the point of view of the ancestral lines of the child's forefathers who were victorious in war or amassed wealth. The child is never given a name of a living relative as it is believed that the latter will die soon since a substitute bearing the same name has been provided for this earth. So the names of dead ancestors are very popular in the community.

Baptise

Among the Christian Zemis the child is Baptised after one or two months or more and no sacrifice to be observed in this respect. The Baptising ceremony which is done according to Christianity and consists of celebrating with rice beer and rice among the relatives and friends. Rice beer is not encouraged by the Christians but it cannot be given up by the converts who usually use it like others. The mother always carries her child on the back and continues to do so as she works.

Ear Boring

The ears of both boys and girls are pierced when they are about one year old. A sharp pointed iron is used for piercing the ear lobe. Earrings of metal are put on at the same times. When the parents have no means yet to procure earrings, small pieces of bamboo splits are inserted inside the lobe so that it may not disappear.

Pregnancy

Illicit pregnancy in the society is of rare occurrence but if there be a case, the elders of the village try to explore avenues to see if the boy, provided he is traced out, and the girl can be united in matrimony according to custom. If they cannot be united then the decision of the elders of the village going against the boy will be final. Sometimes fines are imposed. The girl is not turned out of her house. Sometimes the family of the boy invities the girl to their house to come and give birth to the child in their house. This invitation from the end of the boy's family is considered to be a good social behaviour and it results in either compromise or marriage. But if the boy denies his association with the girl despite the fact that it is through him that conception has taken place, then the girl after giving birth would go to the boy's family and hand over the child. The family of the boy will then take the whole responsibility of rearing the child at all costs. This practice is considered to be anything but honourable. Sometimes miscarriage or death of the girl takes place and this may amount to a very serious matter unless the elders of the village intervene. Sometimes the real culprit responsible for the pregnancy cannot be traced out by the girl because of her making associations with many youngmen. This is the case in which youngmen involve themselves with a girl of bad character, which is very rare.

The last of the persons making approach to her will then be responsible for the unwanted child. Possession of such child usually tells upon the future career of that man. In the village no case of illicit pregnancy was found.

Marriage

In the past marriage relationships outside the members of

the tribe was a taboo. But now this traditional ban has been relaxed perhaps owing to frequent contact with the members of other tribes. Among the Zemis a man may also marry his father's sister's daughter though such kinds of marriages are regarded as unfertile. However, marriage with mother's brothers, or father's sister's son is preferable as such kinds of marriages are conductive to the strengthening of family ties between the two parties concerned. In the Zemi society one can marry a girl whose clan is the same (one's mother or father). Again it is not considered to be socially expedient to marry a very close neighbour. The idea being that the family with whom they have had cordial relationships need not be explored for any help in times of danger or need he or they will come to help uncalled for. There seems to be another reason for this custom also. At the time of haggling over the bride's price the family of the bridegroom finds it hard to fix the price and to impose certain conditions and terms on the party. If the bride happens to be of different clan then the settlement of the price can be affected frankly and easily, it may be very high or very low. The higher the price, the dearer the value of their relationship and the lower the price will mean a psychological conquest of friendship for both parties.

To-day, the degree of marriage relationships, up to which marriage is prohibited among the zones is determined by the following social and other conditions.

No Sexual Intercourse in the Same Clan

(a) Sexual intercourse between persons of the same clan is regarded as incest, whether the intercourse take place before or after marriage. Such relations between persons of the same clan is against their social customs. One should not marry one's sister's daughter, aunt's daughter, Uncle's daughter, and so on. It is also restricted to contract marriage with one's sister-in-laws sister. The two brother's of a clan can marry two sisters of the same family belonging to another clan, but is believed that their married life will be marred by the premature death of the husband or wife.

(b) At present there is no traditional clan enemy but in the past, marriages were not contracted between two families if they were entertaining grudge, or having revengeful or inimical attitudes towards each other, left as legacy by the forefathers.

(c) It is prohibited to marry a member of a clan previously over taken by a unknown disease or who died by accident e.g. falling from a tree, or killed by a tiger, etc.

Consanguineous Marriage

The Zemis recognize the evils of consanguineous marriage which, according to them, may result in the child being born a more or less physically deformed.

Marriage Age

The usual age of marriage is between twenty and twentyfive among the boys and fifteen to twenty among the girls. However, the boys are often found to marry at the age of twenty-five and above and the girls at the minimum age of marriage.

Marriage by Consent

Marriage by consent and at the same time love marriage are the usual practice. The boy himself choses the bride and after making his final decision he informs his parents.

Initiative from the Boy's Parents

The boy's parents send word to the girl's parents with a view to ascertaining whether they will accept the proposal of marriage. After girl's parents agree to the proposal an answer to that effect is sent to the boy's parrents. As a rule, both the parties concerned take ancestry as a guide in making the decision. Usually before giving their consent the boy's parents first try to ascertain whether the ancestor of the bride has been victims of unknown diseases, and whether they had met with accidents of a serious nature etc. Similarly the parents of the girl will also trace the family history of the boy in the like manner as is done by the boy's parents.

Gachipai

After everything has been decided, the girl's parents pronounce their acceptance of the boy's marriage proposal. The boy then set off for the house of the prospective bride on the fixed day, accompanied by his party which includes one old man (gachipai) who is also one of his relatives. The party takes with them a small quantity of rice and two or three gourd of zau. The food and the drink are shared by the members of the party together with the bride's parents at the latter's house. On this occassion the dowry is also fixed for the bride.

Question of Payment

After settling the question of payment, the bride's price which may be either in cash or in kind is brought over from the bridegroom's house. The bride's price in terms of money usually ranges from Rs. 200/- to Rs. 400/- and that in kind includes necklaces, cattle, mithuns, etc. Sometimes even land is given as bride's price, but such practices are not found when a girl belong to a different village. It sometimes happens that the bridegroom's party cannot pay the whole amount of the bride's price at a time. In such cases the party pays or hands over the bride's parents whatever amount it can afford and the balance may be paid or given after sometime, generally after the harvest. When both the parties are satisfied, then a pig is brought by the bridegroom's party and it is killed and its meat is taken by them. The bridegroom's party then fixes the date when the marriage is to be solemnised. The marriage is, however, performed on the day fixed irrespective of the bride's price has been fully paid or not.

Mpaumei

On the appointed day a feast is given in the house of the bride on which relatives and friends are invited. The bridegroom comes to the house of the bride with his relatives and they all partake of the food and drink provided by the bride's party. This feast is known is 'mpaumei'. A day or two after the feast the bridegroom and his party accompanied by the bride and her party leaves for the former's house. Before doing so, the bride's father kills some fowls or pigs, the meat of which is to be taken to the house of the groom. An old woman (gechipai) acting as escort to the bridegroom acompanies the party to the house of the groom. On reaching his house and before the bride sets her foot in the house, the 'gechipai' makes the bride to step on a piece of iron placed just at the entrance of the house near the door. While doing so the 'gechipai' utters: "May the bond of your marriage be as strong as this piece of iron and may you both be happy and prosperous always". On this day a feast known as 'Kahegiapeu' is given in the house of the bridegroom.

Mpuimu

The bride usually makes a short stay at the house of her husband. During this period she is not allowed to use any of the articles she brought with her to her husband's house. Whatever she needs is provided from the husband's side. After some days the bride's father gives another feast known as 'mpuimu' in which the newly wedded couples are invited. On this occasion the wife receives the blessings of her parents, after which she and her husband go back to the latter's place and settle down. This completes the marriage rites and the wife can henceforth use any of her belongings which she has brought with her on the previous occasion.

Divorce

Though divorce is permissible it is rare to the community. When a man wants to divorce his wife within three years of their marriage all the property except the animals are divided equally between husband and wife. The wife must also return the bride's price to her divorced husband, children born of their marriage invariably belong to the husband. If a wife leaves her husband only a short time after marriage, say about a year or so, all the property including the animal like mithun, cattle, fowl, etc., together with the bride's price go to the husband or his parents. Where the wife seeks for divorce after two or three years of marriage the bride's price is not returned but only the personal belongings of the husband.

Adultery

If the divorce comes as a result of adultery committed by the wife, she or her parents must give one mithun if possible or else, at least a pig to the injured party, that is, the husband's relatives or part from the bride's price and either belongings of the husband. If a widow wishes to remarry after the death of her husband she is allowed to do so provided she receives permission from the late husband's relatives and provided also that she is still residing in her in-laws house at the time of her second marriage contract. When she remarries all the usual ceremonies and practices are performed. A widow can marry her late husband's younger brother but not the husband's elder brother.

Death

The death of a person is announced by a village crier and friends and relatives flock to the house of the bereaved family. The body is washed in warm water with 'heneu', the bark of a certain tree which makes the water. The body is washed by warm water by members of the family of either sex depending on the sex of the dead person. It is then placed on a bed and covered from head to foot with the deceased's clothes. If the dead person is a male, the deceased's ceremonial garments are placed over the body. The family of the dead person kills fowls or pigs or both and prepares feast. The feast is attended by the friends and relatives and those who engage themselves is making coffin and digging the grave. The dead is considered as one who goes on a long journey to the spiritual world. Hence provision of food is made for his use on the way. When preparation for the feast is ready, the watchman who is selected from those present, offers food and meat, especially the liver of animal killed on that occasion, to the dead. Rice and meat offered to the dead together with a gourd of zau is put in basket and the watchman will bid the dead to take it to his spiritual land and do according to his wish. The relatives bring rice, meat and 'zau' and all their food and drink are presented to the deceased's family who on that day can eat and drink only that which is brought by the relatives. A portion of his food and drink is placed over the deceased's head as a share. The dead body is generally kept in the house for two days and sometimes even more depending on the liking of the deceased's family. All this time the deceased's family remain in mourning. Meanwhile, some members engage themselves in making coffin (Kienga) and dig the grave (herau) either in the courtyard in front of the house or along the side of any one of the village paths. The coffin is made of wood and has no lid to cover it. When the dead person is a man his father-in-law or any of his elder male relatives stand on the left side of the body and spear is also placed on its left side. But if it is a woman a piece of black cloth is placed over the body. In both cases, however, a piece of hair is cut from the head of the deceased. When this preparation is complete the coffin is brought inside the house where the body covered with a piece cloth is placed. The dead body is duly wrapped with a piece of cloth and put inside the coffin and the household articles which has been used by the dead during his or her life time such as clothes, ornaments, spears, dao, hoe, etc. are first placed near the coffin and are later carried to the grave. Articles including grains, seeds, meat, chillies and other things like boxes, clothes, etc. used by the house hold are put on the graves but are not left there. They are taken back, after the burial, for use by the female relatives of the deceased. Beside these there are some other ceremonial articles though of no material value but are considered absolutely necessary to be put on the grave. These are the jaws of a pig which they believe would chase off the evil one who waits to devour the dead. Further they also place a little quantity of salt which they say the dead person will take to the new world, a piece of cloth which they think will deceive the evil one, some thorns to prick and kill the worms and a kind of umbrella made of leaves of plant to shelter him or her from the rain and sun. After the coffin is laid down in the grave, earth is heaped in and the grave is levelled. A memorial stone called 'herauchu' is raised over it and is also fenced with wooden poles. In respect of the burial of important persons like the head man or the priest, a bamboo shade is constructed over the grave of the dead. One wooden post with some notches on it is also raised. Each notch stands for some noble deed done by the dead person during his life time.

When everything is complete, fowl, pigs and sometimes mithuns are killed by the deceased's family and a feast is given to friends and relatives. The blood of the animals killed is offered to 'Tingwang', the Supreme Being, that he may guide the departed soul safely to the unknown. The skulls of the slaughtered animals are hung on top of the fence or some kind of structure erected for this purpose. At right angle to this fence and on the opposite side of the grave a bamboo rail is constructed over which clothes, ornaments, etc. of the deceased are placed and if it were a man, a spear is also struck into the ground. In the case of a woman a little bucket containing weaving implements, and also her ornaments like earrings etc. are placed on the grave. A flat stone structure (herauchu) is also raised over her grave.

Death Ceremonies of Christian Zemis

Among the Christian Zemis although the death ceremonies are performed according to the Christian rites there are some of the old practices which are also followed. Thus when a person dies, the corpse is washed, clothed, digging of the grave and the preparation of the coffin is done in the same way as the non-Christians. A kind of feast is also offered to those present and those who help in digging the grave and preparing the coffins. Before the burial would take place a ceremony consisting of Bible reading, songs, etc. is performed and the church elder and poster would conduct such ceremony. The coffin is taken to the grave for burial and before the coffin would be lowered down to the grave a simple ceremony of Bible reading and prayer is again performed. Over the grave a wooden cross bearing the name of the deceased and the date of death or sometimes a memorial stone (herauchu) is raised. After the burial is over, the church also organizes another ceremony in the death in which sermons, hymn songs and prayers are performed.

Spirit of the Dead Man

The spirit of the dead is believed to be lingering in the dead man's house until it is forced to go away and leave the house. This is the reason why they offer food and drink to the ghost (herui) at every meal. The offering ceases only after ceremonial separation of the deceased's spirit from the rest of the family is complete, therefore, on feast times (hengimai), usually held to commemorate the dead, big bowls containing 'Heneu' are placed outside the house so that the ghosts may bathe themselves like the living and join in the celebrations. During such times all the things that the dead may require which have not been placed in the grave at the time of the burial, such as gourds, seed, clothes, various tools, etc. are provided for the dead. When this is done the priest (tingkupeu) takes with him one fowl and proceeds to the top of the village where the fowl is sacrificed; after that he comes down the main footpath and in a loud voice asks the ghosts to take away their personal possessions and leave the place.

When the ghosts have gone through the gateway to the land of the dead, the 'tingkupeu' shuts the gate and returns to the village.

Unnatural Death

Persons killed by wild animals and those who die during childbirth as well as those who commit suicide, (though suicide is very rare among the community), are not allowed to be buried within the precinct of the village. Instead they are buried at some distance away from the village. However, the rites and ceremonies are nearly the same as those in the normal deaths. The difference lies in the fact that in accidental or suicidal deaths the flesh of the animals like fowl or pigs killed are offered to the evil spirits who are believed to be the cause of such misfortunes. The beads worn by the dead person can be taken off only by an old male relative of the deceased who at the same time buries the dead body. The flesh of animals killed in connection with such deaths is given to all youngmen and women. When a person dies from a fall, this cause is also taken as accidental and the rites and ceremonies are performed in the same manner as in the latter.

E. FAMILY AND COMMUNITY RELATIONSHIP

Hekiria

Generally in the Zemi villages the type of the family is simple and consists of husband, wife and the unmarried children. The term 'family' among Zemi means 'Hekiria, meaning 'Rows of houses' in broader sense thereby implying 'lineage' traced from the clan. In the narrower sense it may simply mean 'Kelak', i.e. House derived from the word 'Kelaktenbe' which means 'marriage'. When a man marries and sets up a house of his own, his house is called 'Kelak' or more correctly, 'Pekalak' meaning 'his home or his family'. Being patriarchal society the Zemi's trace their descent through their fathers or forefathers. It is the social ideal that parents live together with their married children and only when the married brothers fail to live together due to various reasons then they live sepatately and establish a new house of their own after a year or more of their marriage.

Head of the family

The father, being the head of the family, commands respect from all the members which the latter consider as a part of their duty. In the absence of the father the eldest son or in his absence the elder or younger one takes charge of the family and that too if the members agree and if he can win their affection and respect. Otherwise, a discord may lead to the split up of the family. But no such case was however found during the field study. The mother also commands much respect in the family and keeps good care for the children when they are young, looks after the needs and the requirements of the children.

In short, the family which is patriarchal in type is a well-knit unit and being patrilineal, the members are descended from the oldest male resident in the house, within the family men and women enjoy equal status, except in the property inheritance which goes to the eldest son.

Beside doing household duties, women render additional help to men in their work in the fields.

Clans and Marriage

The Zemis have the following clans namely Mpame, Nkuame, Henume, Nriame and Sogame, Ndaime and Hezanne. Of them Mpame and Nkuame are considered as belonging to the same clan. Marriage within the clan is not the rule and all the clans mentioned above are equal in status. The clans are believed to be descended from a common ancestor by whose name the clan is known. As stated earlier, Mpame and Nkuame belonged to the same clan. They did not intermarry and were socially regardedas belonging to the same family. According to the Zemis, it is said that there was a man belonging to this (i.e. Mpa-Nkua clan) group and was nicknamed as 'Nkua-mpeu' one who rolls and while competing in sports during festivals he uttered, as was his practice, a list of names of his grand fathers including his. Instead of uttering his own name he used his nickname (Nkuanepeu) to which the audeince took exception. It is said that from that time onwards his descendants came to be known as 'Nkuames', i.e., the members belonging to this clan. At present the members of these two clans, i.e. Mpame and Nkuame though originally regarded as one clan can intermarry but with a show of restraint or reservation Zemis believe that as the time passes the relatioshinp between the two clans become more and distant, and so they can inter-marry.

Low Exogamy

The clan is, however, sociologically of importance as the marriage unit and the low of exogamy obliges marriage outside the clan. It may be stated that there is no association of any clan with any occupation, as such the Zemi community is predominently an agricultural community.

Patriarchal

Being patriarchal, the father is the head of the family and on his death the eldest son assumes charge of his responsibility thereby inheriting the larger part of the property. This was in vogue in earlier times. Only males can inherit the property. If a men leaves no male issue at his death, the peoperty will be equally divided among the deceased's male cousins. The usual custom is for his father to divide the bulk of his property among his sons during his life time. When the sons marry, each son receives his portion of the acquired property from his father and on the death of the father, the eldest son, though he may already have been given his share, inherit rest of his father's property including the house which was in the father's possession at the time of his death. The property of any son who dies without leaving any male child during the father's life time reverts to the latter but after the father's death it goes to the youngest son, while in the case after the youngest son himself dies without a male issue, his elder brothers share his property equally. If there is no father, a brother or son living, paternal uncle or, in the absence of such, any nearest male relative on the father's side would inherit the property. The personal property of the mother including the cash and the ornaments, etc. goes to her daughters. Failing daughter, her property goes to her father's heirs who take all the property including ornaments, even if she has a son. But presently it is found that though in the Zemi society only male members have the right to inherit yet it is not correct to say that the eldest son gets the largest share. When the grown up sons get married and establish their own new homes, they leave their parents and live independently. It is customary on the part of the parent to ask the youngest son (even after his marriage) to remain with him. The idea is, that the parents now being old, should be looked after and attended by one of his sons. In such cases the normal procedure is to leave the entire property at the hand of the youngest son at the time of his (parent's) death and some amount of property also goes to other sons as willed by the dying father. The quantity of property to be shared among the sons may be less for one and more for others as warranted by their circumstances in which they are placed.

Property

If a man has only daughters and therefore leaves no male inheritor the property will go to the nearest and eldest relative of his family who in turn will be charged with the responsibility of looking after his (dead man's) widow and daughters, whether married or unmarried. And in case, the man dies living no issue, his property will go to his nearest and eldest relative who will take charge of the property as well as the widow thus left behind. The widow to be cared for and maintained must remain under the roof of that family but if she prefers to leave the family and go to her own family, the responsibility of her husband's relatives ceases. But such action of the widow leaving the family of her husband is rare and is socially and morally denounced.

Relation among the Different Segments of the Community

The real unit of the society are the clans. In the past relation between the clans were not always in amity (J.H. Hutton,

1921, p. 109) and this antagonism or rivalry coloured the Zemi life. The jealousy and suspicion of one clan for another had been a source of weakness. If there were disputes between two persons of different clans, then the clansmen on each side appear as partisans and foment the discord. However, only in cases of a breach of social code and religious observances the clans would unite.

Clan Enmity

At present there are no traditional clan enmity. The clans are strictly exogamous and on no account can a clan marry within the clan. The clan is also recognized as a unit for genna purposes (T.C. Hodson, 1911, p. 73) and what is genna to a clan, say for the death of one of their members, may not be genna for other clans. Except for the gennas for the religious and ceremonial purposes for the tribe as a whole. All these still hold true among the present day Zemi society. Each village possesses a well defined area of territory not only of cultivated land but of waste and forest land as well. The village is a unit of socially organized community, acting as a whole and participating in the ritual associated with and intended to assist the cultivation of the community. Members of the same clan are found in different villages situated at long distances from one another. Since the villages are situated at long distances from one another and are not easily accessable so as the time passes, the kinship among the persons belonging to the same clan becomes remote, but sometime such relationships among persons belonging to the same clan of different villages are traceable as told by the Zemis themselves.

Women from other clans

In the exogamous community the male element is the permanent element of the society and the women are only brought in from some other clan while the unmarried girls are destined to leave their clan of origin on marriage. This is one factor which keeps the various elements of the community rigidly apart.

F. INTER-COMMUNITY RELATIONSHIPS

Homogeneity

The Zemi Nagas are distinguished from other Naga tribes by its remarkable homogeneity and specially localized in the Borail hills (D.A. Waddel, 1900) and so are in contact with the Kukis, the Dimasa Kacharis and the Hmars rather than with the Naga tribes. With the Dimasa Kacharis they have been in contact long after they came into this part of the Borail hills, the contact was rather peaceful. But they have not always been on good terms with the Kukis, boundary disputes and trespasses are the problems which can in no way be solved. The cause of the enmity has been inherent in the two communities, since British days (U. Grahn Baver, 1946, pp. 50-57). Both the two rival communities practised shifting cuitivation and when the Zemis first came to these hills they claimed a large tract of land for cultivation. Since they follow cycle migration and come back after about 10 years to the former site only when it has fully recovered. The properties are buried on the old site to mark the place for reoccupation. In course of time the Kuki immigrants appeared and were in search of new lands to replace the one which was exhausted. The British Government in order to check onward a certain tract of land which certainly had been old Zemi sites and presumed to have been abandoned. Thus the Zemis were ultimately left with only that part of their land which was in cultivation when the boundaries were demarcated. As a matter of fact much of the good land was lost to the Kukis, which the Zemis could not forget easily. Excepting the Kukis, whom they look on with distrust and suspicion, their relation with other communities as Dimasa Kacharis and Hmars has been peaceful. The fact of the dispute between the Zemis and the Kukis has been accepted by the Zemis, but the enquiries regarding the dispute is yet to be made from the other.

G. STRCTURE OF SOCIAL CONTROL, PRESTIGE AND LEADERSHIP

District Council

In spite of the present day political administration the ancient system of social organization of the Zemis is still in vogue. The District Council recognizes the functions and duties of their organizations as well as the members of office bearers. Each village has its own headman known as 'Kadeipeo' whose office is hereditary and who is assisted by a council known as 'Samkakibe' which is always held in the bachelors' house or morung (hangseoki). The 'Kadeipeo' convenes the village council (samakakibe). He, with the help of village priest (Tingkupeu) choses elders to sit in the council. As a matter of fact all adult male persons above 30 years old are members of the 'Samakakibe'. Among the members of the council there is, besides, the headman, an assistant headman who performs the duties, of the headman in his absence. Then there is the 'tingkupeu' who is responsible for the public sacrifices and who conducts the religious life of the village. He is also empowered to fix the date of the gennas on which people abstain from work as well as the dates of festivals. Over and above there is a village crier (sabepen) whose duty is to proclaim to the villagers the decision of the village council on matters that accept the common weal as directed by the 'kadeipeo'. The council decides nearly all matters relating to the village and has jurisprudence over minor disputes, while complicated disputes normally go to the District Council Court at Haflong. Disputes concerning land, theft, inheritance of property, adultery, divorce, etc. are disposed of by the 'Samkakibe' in accordance with their own tribal law and a dispute which cannot be settled by the council is referred to the higher court of the District Council.

Morung

The most notable feature of the social structure of the Zemis is the institution of the morung or the bachelor's houses. Their morungs has always become their pride and joy and the very life-veins of their social and cultural activities. In every village there must invariably be a morung and if a big village, two morungs for the comfort and convenience of village lands. In the Laisong villages there are two such morungs. The boys' dormitory is known as 'hangseoki', while the one used by the girls is called 'leoseoki'. However, members of both the dormitories are collectively known as 'Kienga'. The girls have no such 'leoseoki' of their own but usually use the house of each member by turn.

Compulsory Membership

Every male member in the village should be a member of either of the two morungs, if there are two morungs in the village. The morung has members of all the clans and is not confined to one clan only. From the same house or family there can be members belonging to different morungs. It is not necessary to divide the number of houses for the purpose of membership but usually there is an approximate, if not equal, balance in the strength of the membership in the two morungs.

Admission to Morung

The method of admission to the Morung is a simple one. If a male child is born in a family, and a member of either of the morungs informs the father of the child that he should become a member of his (informer's) morung and that settles the question of the child's membership. As soon as a boy or a girl reaches the age of eight or nine he/she ceased to sleep in the respective dormitory. Girls work at home during the day and use the dormitory only at night. In the dormitory they learn spinning, weaving, music and songs. No married man, not even the parents in whose house the club is held for the night, ever enters it and only the village headman may drop in for a fatherly visit. If there is any other visit at all it is from a young man who comes stealthily at night to see his own sweetheart. Unlike the girls the boys spend the whole of their time in the hangseoki and go home only for meals or when they are ill. Sometimes, some of the boys exempt themselves from work in the fields and do nothing except to drink zau, gossip or do a little basketry work, play music, bathe and groom their youthful body for the favour of young girls. Indeed, it is a grand life, to which a married man looks back wishfully and with regret, for the day a boy marries he ceases to be member of the hangseoki and therefore he ceases to sleep in it. It should be noted that the kienga have their own leader known as 'kezeipeu' whom they themselves elect from amongst the village elders and who teaches the youths by precept and examples. They are taught to make themselves perfect in hunting, fishing, fighting and other namely arts. It is in the morung that the village young men are given training for their future. It is here that they learn to make baskets of different designs, learn musical instruments, reherse folktales, learn the art of using spears, shield, etc. The most important thing they learn here is the spirit of co-operation and unity and the realization that one must place the community's interests above one self in order to succeed in life.

Resident Leader

Every morung has a resident leader or guide who lives in the morung itself, usually at the back side of the building specially alloted for him. He is appointed by the village elders. He should be an elderly person with specific views on matter common to the villagers and also be a man adopt in the art of compromise and reconciliation. He should be expert in basketry, cane works, music, folk tales, etc. and lastly be very sociable for obvious reasons. He is appointed for indefinite periods. If he wants to quit the office he may informs the elders of the village who will in turn select some one of his type for the purpose. Lower in rank than the leader, there are two young men or youth leaders called herangmepeu selected from among the members of the morung by all the other members. Their function is to enforce the order or direction of the morungs leader. They are to see to the daily needs of the morung in matters like provision of firewood, water etc. and also to enforce discipline in the morung life. They may hold office indefinitely.

Hangseoki

The 'hangseoki' as a corporate body organizes dances repairs, the village pipe line, makes new water troughs, cleans the village paths, and constructs and repairs the existing paths. They may also be hired by a rich man to bring the harvest home or construct a new house and the payment either in cash or kind received, usually goes to the hangseoki's fund for feast during festivals. The payment depends on the volume of work which usually ranges between Rs. 20/- to Rs. 30/- in cash and ten to twenty baskets of paddy in kind. This corporate body also helps each member in turn to work in the fields which is ready for weeding or harvest.

No Class Distinction

Though there is no class distinction in the society yet women do not enjoy the same status as that of a man. Women have no part to play in public activities and it is only young girls who make only brief and formal appearance and that also with their club members (kienga). They never appear in a village durbar in person but are represented by a male relative. They cannot enter the meeting and it is immodest to see them in the boy's dormitory. Women have no legal rights at all and man are paramount in society. No man will eat a game killed by a woman for it is unclean and unnatural. Hunting is a man's job and no woman participates in it. All works which require physical strength are men's responsibility, while works like cooking, drawing water, cleaning the house, etc. are always women's job.

Even at present in the non-Christian Zemi villages the hangseokip lays the same important part as it was in the ancient days particularly in those villages which are far away from the urban centres. Among the Christian Zemis, particularly those living in the Haflong area have clubs for the male and the female members, where boys and girls in their respective clubs learn songs, dances and games, etc., and other activities from the elders. It is more in the nature of clubs in the urban area. In the interior Christian village, the morung system prevails particularly among the newly converts, who have recently accepted the new faith.

F. DRESS DWELLING AND FOOD

Dwellings

Villages are generally built on the slopes of hills and as such there cannot be much space to accommodate many houses. There is no clanwise clustering of houses. It should be noted that though the United Mikir and North Cachar Hills District Council passed a resolution regarding the regrouping of villages so that existing small villages may by replaced by bigger villages with a large number of people living side by side, the resolution is still not applicable to the Zemi villages where the average number of households are very small comprising only about 50 households in each village. All these villages look more of a hamlet and Laisong is the biggest village among the Zemi villages consisting of 124 households (according to 1961 census) and even in this village, houses are added together on the slope of the hill. From very early times Zemis adopted a system of cycle migration, when the villages were temporarily abandoned in the course of the cycle. Then at that time the boundaries or monuments were marked or memorized, and the jumping places where major sacrifices were performed and when heads taken in war were buried, was marked by an upright monolith. (Communication, Man in India, 1941, Vol. 48, No. 102).

Bamboo houses

The houses are single storeyed and stand on bare ground roughly levelled to form the floor after building. The roof is thatched, the sides almost touching the ground. This kind of roofing prevents the houses from being blown off by strong winds. The houses are arranged in two rooms which lie on either side of the footpath facing each other. Each house has a small clearing in the front where their dead relatives are buried. Small uneven paths or sometimes steps connect the houses in the village. In most households where there is enough open space the little patches of maize or mustard are frequently found in the homestead ground. The house rest either on bamboo or wooden supports. The walls of the buildings are of split bamboo frames. Generally the house has only two rooms. One which forms the front room Kungduaki is meant for outsiders or strangers. This is also used as a storeroom where paddy is placed inside great baskets (keluang) which are placed against the walls of the rooms. In this room pigs and fowl and the agricultural implements such as mortar (gepa), pestle (kemai), baskets (keluang), hoes (kepeu), daos (heka), etc. are kept. The second compartment is separated from the first by a plank wall on which there is an opening or door way. In this compartment there is the hearth (hemibam) which is made of three upright stones embedded in the earth forming a kind of a stand for the cooking place. Generally by the side of the hearth there are some two or three beadsteads (zeira) made of split bamboo and raised about two feet from the ground. There are no windows and the doors are the only ventilation of the home. The home has usually three doors one at the front which serves as the main entrance, another at the back of the house and the third at either side of the walls. The doors usually measuring 5′ 6″ by 4′ are made of either wood or plank. Each house has the space in front of it surrounded with a low wall of slab of stones marking off its compounds. As there are no chimney so the smoke has to find its own way out of the house. The result is that the walls look black and dismal.

Kemarumbe

It is customary that a person who builds a new house receives every assistance he needs from his fellow villagers who are never paid for their labour but are entertained with rice beer and sometimes with food also. The owner of the house, on its completion, entertains those who helped to a feast known as "Kemarumbe" literally meaning, 'trimming the front part of the roof'. This is so called because the grass on the front portion of the roof of the house is made to suspend or hang down low. The edge is then neatly cut or trimmed with sickles by young men of the village. With the assistance of neighbours, friends or relatives and the availability of the materials the construction of an average type of house does not require more than one or two days. On the day when work is completed the villagers are invited to a feast and the owner's friends and relatives join in the revelry and partake of pork and rice beer (zou or zu) which are served together with rice.

Utensils

The household utensils include among other indigenous ones such things as enamel mugs, bowls and plates, aluminium cooking post and occasionally brass dishes. These are the result of contact with the urban people. The principle indigenous household utensil s are earthen pots for cooking (hegamli), wooden spoon (terui), wooden platters (ching kuak), cups or drinking vessels of bamboo (hepaipiak) drinking vessels made of mithun's horn (buikepick), gourds for storing and carrying liquor (nrau), baskets, for storing and mixing liquor and vats, troughs and jars for fermenting liquor. Besides, there are inside the porch and the front rooms, the skulls of animals killed by the households in the chase or slaughtered by him on festive occasions. Brightly coloured insects and the plumage of birds are placed upon one of the cross beams to adorn the house. The houses are devoid of any piece of furniture or lavish decoration and thus are simple in both construction and design.

Modern Furniture

The Zemis living in Haflong town and working in the government offices and who are better economically than the Zemi Nagas living in distant villages from the town are found to be having furniture like tables, curtains, etc. as found in the urban areas.

Hongseoke

The 'hongseoke' or the morung of the Zemi village consists of a big house as shown in the photographs. The methods of construction and the materials are essentially the same as the other houses, the only difference being the largeness of the building. From the ceilling of the Hongseoke number of households materials like baskets, pots, etc. are suspended. In the centre of the morung is the hearth around which there are wooden planks on which the boys sit.

Dress and Ornaments

The Zemi Nagas show not much interest in the modern types of dress with the exception of those living in town and in plains who generally put on European dresses. They still love to wear their traditional dress. Their clothes are richly coloured with beautiful and elaborate design woven on them according to their fancy and skill.

Henipai

The male dress consists of a garment (henipai) which hangs down from the left shoulder, the front end reaching below the knee. Another piece of cloth known as 'peni' is fastened round he waist and the upper portion is secured to the body with a strip of a cloth called 'dindia'. Women's dress are not so very different from that of men. A piece of cloth called 'aringmang' is worn round the upper portion of the body effectively covering the breasts. A kind of shawl called 'peingum' hangs down from the shoulders. It is to be noted that their traditional dress which they put on, especially the designs on their garments are not in any way related to status in the society at present. In earlier times the elaborate design on the garments were related to the status in the society attained through participation in war, success in love-making, etc. The Zemis who are living in the towns wear shoes and chappals, this is also observed among the Zemi's livinge, particularly the menfolk, than as compared to the females.

Male Ornaments

Among the men it is observed that a silver ring is worn on each ear and sometimes rings of metal specially made for the purpose are suspended from the earlobes. Sometimes a feather or a flower (mapa) is also worn along with the earrings. Necklaces of beads (heteuba) are also worn around the neck. The non-Christian Zemis who can afford to wear 'Teleiteu' (made out of counch shell) generally do so.

Female Ornaments

The women are fond to wear earrings (kumchie) and necklace of beads (hetu), elephant tusk (teuba), piece of bone (telvil) or corn of mithan (buisangke) round the neck. They put on brass bracelets (heta) on their hands. The Zemis do not practice tatooing, the hair is nicely cut and in such a way that it covers both the ears while on the front side of the head, the hair is cut short. The hair styles of the Zemis differ from one individual to another depending on one's own choice. There are three types of styles observed among men.

Hair Style

1. Telap-pei : The hair is cropped very short only about half an inch in length so that it reveals the forehead as well as the ears and portion of the head at the back.

2. Pei-Suk : About half an inch above the ear the hair is

cut at equal length all around the head so that it looks somewhat like a hat. The end of the hair is curled with the tips facing inward touching the exposed protion of the skin.

3. Nagga peit : This type of hair style closely resembles the Angamis. It is like the 'pei-suk' style with the difference that the ends of the cropped hair are not coiled. In the centre of the head a small bunch of hair is grown long for the purpose of tying a white cotton ball (Kelang Kua).

Married Female

The unmarried females crop their hair short in the front just above the eye brows, then across the forehead more or less in a slightly semi-circular manner ending abruptly some distance behind the eye brows and thence trailing in thick, long strands round the head thereby concealing part of the face and the ear. This type of hair style is known as 'peibide'. Among the married women the hair at the back of the head is left as long as it would grow and it is plaited into two equal from the centre of the head. These braids are made into a knot at the back of the head. This type of the hair style is known as 'kakeibe'.

Primitive method

The primitive method of cutting the hair with a dao is still in vogue among the Zemis of the interior village and also the combs (timrau) of fine strips of bamboo are used by them.

The Zemis who are living in town or near the town are much influenced by the urban way of life and thus they use the scissors, combs, etc. for the hair do.

Food and Drink

Rice is their staple food and some vegetables either raw or cooked and meat are also taken along with rice. Vegetables includes leaves of certain plants and also tree roots and tubers. They eat the flesh of both wild and domesticated animals. Among them the most important are the cows, pigs, mithuns, goats, fowl and fish, especially dried fish and some species of wild animals as well as birds. Pork is their favourite delicacy, mithun meat features well during festivals. The animals' fat is used as an eatable and also for preparing curry. Fats of animals (panan), after being boiled, is kept in a bamboo pipe which is placed above the hearth for some days until the fat decomposes and give off pungent smell, and later they are collected and stored. Dry fish (katiam) is also placed above the hearth as stored food. It has been stated that the intestines and blood of animals are boiled in water and eaten deliciously. This is in vogue only in interior villages, and not in towns or in villages influenced by urban life. Just above the hearth a line is hung where large pieces of meat and fish are smoked and dried. These are usually preserved for a long time and when required, pieces are cut off and boiled or roasted on the fire for consumption.

Milk

Previously it was in vogue that women especially young girls, should not take milk and mutton (J.H. Hutton, 1921, pp. 95) for it was believed that milk and mutton greatly increased sensuality and eroticism. Men should not take the head of a fowl for they fear that if they do so they would fall down from the top of the trees. They also believed that eating the young shoots of the palm trees, which is sometimes used as vegetables, will make the eaters' hair curly. These beliefs are not prevalent among the Zemis of the present day.

Meal Time

Meals are generally taken three times a day, in the morning, at midday and in the evening. Morning meals are taken just before going to the field. When going to work the midday meal is taken along with, wrapped up in plaintain leaf and eaten in the fields. Evening meals are taken after returning home from the field. Tea is not much favoured in the villages, instead rice beer is a favourite drink, it is almost the staple article of consumption. There are three varieties of rice beer or 'zau'. The mildest is 'dekrizau' which is prepared from millet, 'nduzan' is of medium strength and is prepared from rice fermented with yeast made of wild leaves or roots, the third variety is known as 'nehiakne' which is a kind of liquor prepared by distilling rice or millet and is the strongest one. The first variety is a common family drink while the second and third are used only in festivals and by men only. Each family brews its own rice-t beer which is made almost daily to keep pace with an increasing consumption.

System of Recording time, space and weight

In the interior villages the time is reckoned by looking at the sun. The day begins with the first cockcrow and with the rising of the sun.

With the rise of the sun, the people become active and start for their respective work, and go to the fields. As the sun lowers down to the west they start returning from the field and just before sunset they all return to homes and the night begins with the setting of the darkness, thus in the villages the days come and pass away and the people are not much bothered about the hours. The Zemis living in the town and in nearby villages reckon the time as the town people.

Generation time scale

The long periods of time are usually measured in generations. The term of office of each set of Kadeipo or village headman is a generation and which is usually a period of 25 years or so. The two main divisions of the year are the cold and the hot seasons. The cold season begins when dew is first seen and when the days are growing shorter. When the days are growing longer and when the voice of the cuckoo is heard. the hot season begins and it is time to sow the fields. The months are reckoned successively by the appearance of the new moon. The months are of course a lunar month although no one can say how many of such are there in a year. Only a few months have names and other things are reckoned according to the agricultural operation, carried on during those times. They usually recognize the following months.

Kezing is the month when sowing begins. It is equivalent to the month of March of the English calendar.

Gepi is the month in which sowing is complete and is equivalent to the month of May of the English calendar.

Habai is the month when the grains are ripened and the harvesting starts. It is equivalent to the month of October.

Heru is the month when all the fields are harvested and it is equivalent to the month of November.

Ndui is the month of taking the stock of the year's labour and it is equivalent to December.

Directions can be vaguely expressed as towards sunrise and towards sunset, that is, east and west. There is no way of accurately, indicating north, south and so on.

The Zemis who are living in and near about the urban centres expresse the distances in miles.

But those who are living in villages often expresse the distance in miles vaguely. Invariably their guess about the distance comes out to be wrong. Usually, long distances are described in terms of the numbers of pipes which a traveller would smoke while covering the distance and generally one tobacco pipe is consumed while covering a distance of 2 or 3 miles. For shorter lengths. such as dimensions of a house, the length of the out stretched arm is the standard. The depth of water is reckoned by a man's height, while the height of a tree is spoken of as so many ladder steps.

Rice, maize and other food cereals are usually measured in a basket (keluang) which is the standard either for loan or for sale. While repaying the rice it is measured out in the same basket used at the time of borrowing. Rice is the only thing which is usually lent or sold and every one keeps such a standard basket in his house which generally holds about 5 seers of rice.

G. VILLAGE LIFE AND RECREATION

Fond of Dance

The Zemis of North Cachar Hills are very fond of dances. Dances have a place in their festivals and also on ordinary occasion forming a part of their recreation. There are a number of dances and each with a different name. They are named after the manner in which hands and feet are executed to resemble the movements of a bird or an insect or an animal. For example, 'nruirelians', known as 'cock dance', that is, the dance which resembles the trait of a cock; 'gethinglim' or 'cricket' dance that is, a dance in which hands are moved to and fro, some what resembling the movement of the insect, 'temangnetin' or the fly dance 'hetateulee' or the Bare dance which was usually done by men when defeating enemies. All these dances are performed with the accompaniment of songs and music. Drums and cymbals are beaten at regular intervals while the singers arrange themselves on one side or form a circle so as to allow space for the dancers in the centre. As dances have got different meanings and functions so also their songs. Songs which are generally and commonly sung by both young and old alike may be classified as follows:

Songs

1. Heliamleu or dancing songs—they are composed and sung by young and old alike and are usually romantic.
2. Hereileu or war songs—composed by old people about the pride of their life, their bygone days, usually sung in memory of the victory or defeat in war.
3. 'Nduleu' or legendry songs—composed by old men to commemorate any significant event in old days or that of a person who had done something notable during his life time.
4. 'Hekialeu' or songs about self—these songs are composed by old men of their eventful career while they were young and strong.
5. 'Hekialeu' or a duet—composed by both young and old and is sung by young boys and girls together.

Games

Besides dances and songs, there are also various games played by both young and old for their recreation. Games are generally played during their festivals and sometimes also on ordinary occasions. Among the games usually played by the Zemis the most important are the following:

1. 'Hezua' or long jump : There is a mound of earth measuring about 4 feet in width and 30 feet in length usually in the centre of a village. A slab of stone is laid at one end of the mound. The jumper runs toward it from some distance, pause for an instant on the stone for balancing the body and then jump. The distance is usually measured by the marks made by the feet where the jumpers land on the mound.
2. 'Teri' : It is a race run along the slope of a hill outside

the villages, the destination being the centre of a village where a crowd awaits to receive the winner.

3. 'Hetung' : In this game a strong bamboo pole about 5 feet long is used and two or more combatants hold both ends of the pole and push the opponents backward untill they fall down on the ground.

4. 'Hepua' : It is a wrestling competition between two persons, where one tries to lift the other by the waist and throw him to the ground.

5. 'Mapei Kambe' : A big pole about 8 feet high well greased with fat is raised on the ground. On top of it is hung the head of a pig and the competitors try to climb up the pole and take away the pig's head.

Riddles also constitute some pastimes of both young boys and girls. Riddles are varied and are laden with meaning. As for example, to open the door of winds means to take fun; to give water for curry; to fish 'to hide hands' is to set traps for birds and animals or to hide some valuables, 'to lose teeth' is to build one's own house ; to spread wings 'to build one's house with the help of friends and neighbours', 'to sit on the top of a tree but on the ground' is to pluck some branches of a tree for sitting on and rest on the ground, 'to put one's legs' is to delay work; to throw stone at the wooddecker but miss it and hit the wood' to make an honest man scape goat. Sometime an enigmatic description of an object is given by a member of the party and the other member are asked to name that particular object.

The descriptions given under leisure and recreation are based, on field studies. Due to the impact of Christianity and urbanization, the modern games and sports like playing with balls-badminton, etc. are finding way into the Zemi society parti cularly among the school going children.

Sanitation Absent

Sanitation, in the real sense of the term, is totally absent in Zemi villages. There is no drainage system in and around the houses and foul water finds its way out in to village streets. In the interior villages there are no pit latrines or any lavatories the nearby jungle is used for such purposes where pigs perform the task of sweepers. The Zemi villages which are nearby the urban centres are sometimes found to have the pit latrine system in some houses. As there is no dustbin all waste matters are seattered around the houses and rubbish is thrown carelessly along the village footpaths. Thus the village paths become filthy and stinky especially during the rains, emitting foul smell.

As far as the persons are ceoncerned they are clean and wash themselves frequently. Near every village washing places are always to be found where men and women stop to wash their hands and feet on their way to and from the fields. The teeth are cleaned by brushing with a small stick, usually the bark of a wild plant and rinsing with water. Soap is now in use in those villages which are nearer to town while in interior villages the bark of the tree which produces a foam like a soap is used.

Before taking meals people usually rinse their hands with water. Wooden and earthen dishes are usually, though not thoroughly, washed after use. But earthen cooking pots and vessels do not receive such hygenic treatment. These are generally rinsed with only a small quantity of water, since the villagers fear that too much washing of cooking pots and pans may cause the article to break too early.

SOCIAL WELFARE

No Urban Influence

The life of the Zemis remains much the same is to be expected of a community which has not been influenced by the urban ways of life, particularly those who are living near the urban centres, but even in such cases the rules of the traditional customs and manners still hunt them and are not therefore easily forgotten by them. Their tribal religion has undergone a slight change. This is due to the adverse economic conditions and other calamities which ruin their economy. Since their religion is mostly concerned with the performance of sacrifices of animals so it entails much expenditure. In the face of proverty and unavoidable hardships, it becomes easier if the restrictions and barriers imposed by their religion were removed as early as possible. So after such realization they are now gradually making some changes in their social customs and manners. They are now believe that sacrifices to the gods should be limited to the bare minimum and that festivals which involve too much outlay of money be abandoned.

Outdated Agricultural Implements

With their outdated and worn out agricultural implements and tools they are forced to till the unfriendly and unyielding soil. Improvement in their method of cultivation is necessary and better seeds, better manure and improved implements are all the more necessary to better their economy. There is neither any co-operative society where the cultivator can offer his products for sale at a reasonable rate and avail the facilities of improving his lot, nor does the community have any idea of it. Community development blocks which are meant to better the life of the rural people in every respect of their social and economic structure do not throw light on their community particularly in the interior villages. Education which is an important factor to raise the standard of the rural community seem to have little value to the community as is seen from the percentage of literacy. Hence one of primary needs of the community at present is a really efficient and cheap system of education that may give them a chance to get themselves acquainted with the world of knowledge and learning, particularly in the interior villages. There are some welfare agencies run by the Presbyterian Mission like free distribution of some medicines, and schools, etc. at Haflong.

H. COMMUNITY FESTIVALS

Community Festivals

The festivals observed by the community are all connected with cultivation. Each of these festivals does not seem to be obligatory for any one to perform, and is in fact usually performed only by one who can affored. The following tables gives the names of festivals with the dates of their performance and their underlying significance.

Name of festival	*Corresponding month*	*English Equivalent*	*Significance*	*Remarks*
Heleikanebe	**Kezing-Keram**	**March April**	**After harvesting is performed at the beginning of the sowing season.**	**All these festivals are performed in connection with cultivation.**
Nehangbam	**Gepei**	**May**	**The completion of sowing season.**	
Puakpat	**Hebai, Heru**	**October Nov.**	**Before harvest begins i.e. when the grains are ripened.**	
Nsiamngi	Heru-Ndui	Nov. Dec.	When all fields are harvested.	
Hega or Ngidi	Nudi	Dec.	Taking stock of the years labour.	

Heleikanebe : This festival is usually performed by every household in honour of Tingwang who is supposed to be responsible for the success in cultivation. It merely entitle the killing of an animal, except goat and the feasting of friends on the meat of the animal killed. The priest (tingkupeu) prays to Tingwang to bring good harvest. The tingkupeu will then take little grain of seeds which he sows at the village gate. The offshoots of the seeds will indicate prosperity or otherwise.

Nehangbam : During 'Nehangbam' festival no wood is cut and paddy is neither husked nor spread to dry in the sun, as it is believed that if it is done the seeds sown in the fields will not thrive but may dry up like the wood cut. Pigs, or fowl are killed by the priest as an offering to Tingwang as the one who pours this blessings to the seeds. The blood and intenstine of the animals killed are offered to Tingwang while the meat is taken by friends and relatives.

Puakpat : It is celebrated when the grains are ripe and marks the beginning of the harvest. On this occasion all male folks must obtain rice and beef and also the flesh of buffalos but may only drink zau and eat the flesh of other animals. On this day all males wash themselves in the nearby stream and bring fresh water in new 'hepiak' (Bamboo pipes) and would not use the old water that has been stored in house. They must collect the fermented rice contributed by each one among the adult male folks in the village to make zau with the new water which they have brought and then they eat and drink on that day. On this occasion women are not allowed to eat together with men (Hodson 1911, p. 171) which still holds true, and do not take part with men in the feast.

The meal and the zau which cannot be consumed during the day is to be buried in a pit. On the following day the whole village abstains from working in their fields and stay at home. No sacrifice is offered to Tingwang on their occasion. On the next day reaping begins.

'Nsiamngi' : This festival is celebrated when all fields are harvested and all the grain reaped by every one is carried home. In this festivals men eat together with women but sleep apart from them at night. On this occasion also men go to fetch fresh water in new 'hepiak' and wash themselves. The water is used only by men for washing and cooking. The village folk do not go to work on that day and no one goes anywhere. The whole village makes merriment and eats and drink in their respective clubs. It may be noted that the feast on this occasion is held by voluntary contributions in kind which each of the members brings, namely, a basket of rice or fowl. The adult males also join and contribute liberally in kind.

Hega or Ngidi : This is the most important of all the festivals observed by the Zemis. 'Nnduikeu' means 'fathering month' it generally takes place at the end of December. This festival marks the end of the year's labour and they turn their grateful eyes to Tingwang to thank him for his blessings and guidance throughout the year. In this occasion they eat, drink and make merriment. On this day the Tingkupeau takes a fowl to the village gate where it is killed and its blood offered to Tingwang. Meanwhile Tingkupeu prays to Tingwang to accept his humble offering and at the same time implores him to continue to pour his blessings in the coming year. The flesh of the sacrificial fow is genna to both men and women as it is meant only for Tingwang.

Mithun Hunting

The most notable feature on this occassion is the traditional mithun hunt (Kabui'nsa) which is performed on the same day. In this hunt a competition is held between the members of the hangseoki (morung) to capture the mithun, and any one who wins the game gets the head of the mithun. The flesh of the animal is cooked and eaten by all the members together. It may be noted that in this 'hega' or 'negidi' festival no genna is observed except by the household where parents have died sometime during the year. In the hunt generally a big buffalo or mithun having large horns is chosen for the chase. Its horns are closely wrapped and coiled with thick creepers to prevent any fatal injury to the chaser. The chase is, by tradition a stern test of nerve and stamina. The men who take part in this chase wear nothing except the kilt. Before the chase the participants take rice beer which acts as a stimulant. On the day fixed for the hunt, all women, children and the disabled are shut in doors and every house front is tightly closed. The animal is taken to the morung's porch where it is firmly tied to a post. The Tingkupeu takes a stout stick and one elder man cuts the rope with a dao with which the animal is tied. At the same time when the rope is cut, the Tingkupeu gives a strong blow with his stick on the horns of the animal. The infuriated beast on finding itself free rushes down the village street with the young leaping wildly on its heels. The chasers stumble and fall and again rise on their feet, scramble, and keep on chasing the beast until it rushes to the nearby jungle. The real game is played in the jungle. The chasers make loud shouts and when one of them gets a tight hold of its tail, he shouts for his friends and all of them rush towards the spot for the animal in its track. The animal is securely bound the thrown against the ground. The chasers will not be considered victorious, unless they fell the animal once during the chase, though, any one of them may get hold of its horns. Sometimes the infuriated beast, instead of running away tries to attack them instead picking up the scent of its enemies who by that time seek safety on the branches of trees. When the animal misses its enemies it invariably rushes towards the thick undergrowth of the jungle and immediately the chasers run towards the animal and scramble and overpower the animal. The person who first catches hold of the mithun's horns is the winner, he twists the head of the animal, grabbing it by its horns, and forces the animal to sink down on the ground. The captured animal is then tied and brought to the 'hangseoke', where it is killed and feasted. The head of the animal is awarded as a prize to the winner who first catches hold of the mithun's horns.

Herakuabe

There is another important ceremony observed by the community which is not connected with cultivation. It is known as 'herakuabe'; meaning driving away the evil spirits and is performed once a year. The Tingkupeu invokes the help of Tingwang to drive away the diseases from the village. On this day all male members go to the nearby stream and wash themselves. After their return the priest kills a cock. The cock killed is cooked and eaten by the priest himself.

The villagers eat pork and beef and drink zau. On this occassion the men live apart from the women and they refrain from drawing any water. The whole village is prohibited from going to work and going out and coming to the village is strictly prohibited. On the following day the Tingkupeu takes a dog with him which is fastened with a leash and he goes up and down the village shouting in a raucous voice that no person should leave his house as the evil spirits are proceeding to their habitation. The dog is then killed outside the village and the priest returns home after which the life returns to normalacy.

Christmas

Among the Christian Zemis, Christmas is celebrated on the 25th while the Christmas feast accompanying it is performed sometimes on the 25th or sometimes on the 26th or 27th December according to convenience. Whenever it may be, the birth of Christ is observed on the midnight of the 24th December. Just at midnight at 12 o'clock the Church bells toll announcing the birth anniversary of Christ and people come to the Church to offer their prayers and song. The Church elder or pastor conducts the ceremony and gives a sermon relating to the birth of Christ. The next day the Church organizes a meeting in which a ceremony consisting of songs, Bible reading, sermons and prayers are performed in the Church. On the same day or on the following day the Church members will have a feast in which rice and meat are served. The Church members make contribution whatever they can afford which ranges between Rs. 0.50 to Rs. 3.00. Young and old alike take part in the feast. On the New Year day, similar meetings are organized by the church at 12 o'clock at midnight i.e. on the 31st of December. On the following day or any day convenient to them they will organize a feast. Sometimes non-Christians also take part in this feast. The rate of contribution is similar as on the Christmas feast and young and old alike take part.

CHAPTER XIII

THE MIKIRS

The Mikir

The origin of the word 'Mikir' is not known. Some eminent writers[1] wrote that the name 'Mikir' is given to the race by the Assamese. The Mikirs call themselves 'Arleng' meaning 'Man' in general. Not warlike and rather peaceful in character, they are also extremely homogeneous. Whether in the North Cachar Hills, the Mikir Hills, the Jaintia Hills or Nowgong, their tribal institutions, their language and their national character are all identical. They practise jhuming in the same manner as their forefathers who raised in ordinary years hardly sufficient food even for their bare subsistence.

Dr. Grierson in his 'Linguistic Survey of India' Vol. III, part II, classed them as intermediate between the Boros and the Western Nagas, but Dr. S.K. Chatterjee in his Indo-Mongoloids, 1951, classed them with those tribes which form the connecting link between the Nagas and the Kuki clans. The preponderance of their affinities lies with the latter.

The Mikirs[2] had once settled in strength in North Cachar to the immediate north of Borail range. The oppression of the Kachari kings compelled them to migrate westward to the territory of the Jaintia Raja for protection.[3] Although in this region, north of the Borail, no more Mikir villages are now found, local names belonging to their language indicate their former existence. But while living there they must have been in contact with tribes belonging to the Kuki-Chin stock who have

1 L.A. Waddell, *Tribes of the Brahmaputra Valley*, 1900, p. 29; Edward Stack, *The Mikirs*, 1908, p. 4.

2 Edward Stack, *The Mikirs*, 1908, p. 151-53.

3 C.J. Lyall, *Report on the Census of Assam*, 1881, Ch. VI, p. 78.

for centuries occupied the hill ranges to the south of the valley of Cachar and the mountains between that valley and Manipur. Colonel Dalton[4] also supported this view and said that the original home of the Mikirs was in North Cachar but they were afterwards driven into the Jaintia territory by the Kacharis. But there they were dissatisfied with the treatment accorded to them by the Jaintias also, and so they sent an embassy to the Ahom governor at Baha offering to place themselves under his protection. As their envoys could not make themselves understood, they were buried alive in a tank. Hostilities ensued and the Mikirs were soon suppressed. Henceforth they settled in the hills that now bear their name although a good number of them are still found in Nowgong and the Jaintia Hills.

Divided into Sub-Tribes

The Mikirs are divided into four sub-tribes, namely, Chintong, Ronghang, Amri and Dumrali and these sub-tribes are again sub-divided into various exogamous groups. Chintong and Ronghang rank higher than Amri simply for the fact that the Amris excused themselves from sending a representative on the fatal mission to the Ahom Raja in Sibsagar (Raha) when a representative was required from each tribe. The Amri sub-tribe; is therefore excluded from sharing the liquor drunk at sacrifices; they were looked down upon especially by the Western Mikirs. Dumaralis acted as interpreters to the embassy and were therefore allowed to have a share of the liquor. Hence it may be presumed that they had lived in the Assam Valley for a pretty long time until they were driven to the hills they inhabit at present.

Ethnic Composition

Different authorities like C.J. Lyall in his "The Report on the Census of Assam, 1881"; Dalton in the Journal of Asiatic Society of Bengal, 1845, and L.A. Waddell in the "Tribes of the Brahmaputra Valley, 1900" have given different opinions regarding the classification of the Mikir Tribe into Kurs of

4 Colonel Dalton, *Journal of Asiatic Society of Bengal*, Vol. 14, Part 1, 1845.

exogamous groups. These 'Kurs' are further classified into sub-kurs or sub-groups. The following table (p. 170) shows the names of persons belonging to the group or sub-group.

From the table (p. 170) it is seen that the people are divided into five exogamous groups or kurs, viz,, Terang, Ingti, Ranghang, Teron and Timung and these are sub-divided into sub-groups or sub-kurs. There is no class system among the Mikirs and there is no such distinction as high and low classes.

Settlement

The settlement is not a compact one and houses appear on top of six low hills and they are all connected by footpaths. The nature of the family looks like the joint type, that is, all members of a family occupy a single house. The house is, as a rule, divided lengthwise by a partition into two or three rooms with one portico on one side. Generally the house is divided into a 'kam' or a room for outsiders or guests which is always on the right side where the only door into the house leads to, and another which is known as a 'kut' is meant only for the family. In the 'kut' a platform or chang about 2 ft. high called 'tibung' and raised above the floor runs along the wall and is used as sleeping apartments for the members of the family, that is, for the young, and unmarried sons, or in some cases, for the married couple and in that case the unmarried sons have to sleep along with their parents in the Damthak. Outside the wall of the 'kut' but attached to the house is a place called 'biroi' in which fowl and goats are kept. There is a fire place called 'mehip' lying at the back of the 'kut' and by the side of the fireplace is the 'damthak' where the heads of the family, i.e., the father and the mother sleep. Here also stands a paddy receptacle (ingkro) made of bamboo. Behind the fireplace there is a place called 'dambuk' which is attached to the 'damthak', where the young and unmarried girls sleep. The front verandah is known as 'hong-kup' in which are kept the loin loom, baskets, firewood, mortar and pestle, vegetables, etc.

The floor of the house is usually raised about four feet or more above the ground and is supported by strong posts on all sides. The whole structure of the house including the side walls is made of split bamboo finely woven and knitted together so firmly that no mud plastering or anything of the sort is necessary. The roof of the house which always consists of two sloping parts is thatched with sun grass which is generally replaced after a lapse of four or five years. The floor of the house is covered with knitted bamboos arranged as above and fastened at each end to the posts which support the roof of the house. The inside of the house is rather dark except for the scanty light that filtrates through the openings in the split bamboo walls. There is no window or chimney—the main door and the tiny slits in the bamboo walls act as sources of ventilation.

Staple Food

So far food is concerned rice is the staple food of the Mikirs, but they also eat all kinds of flesh including beef. But there is not a single household in the village which keeps a cow or any draught cattle. This is due to the fact that cattle cannot be kept in confinement and when they are allowed to roam they may be killed by wild animals especially tigers. Fowl, goats and pigs are kept for their meat and are used specially at sacrifices. Eggs are eaten and the flesh of various wild animals and birds is also taken. Meat is eaten either roasted or cooked or after it is thoroughly dried over the fire in the 'chang'. Sometimes meat is also dried in the sun. The villagers prefer dried fish which they store in small baskets which are placed by the fireside. Vegetables (han) of all kinds including wild vegetables and also roots of trees and plants are taken by them.

Drinks

The Mikirs are all addicted to strong drink which is known to them as 'Hor'. This is a rice beer prepared by each household for its own needs. Women and children do not indulge in this drink. There are different kinds of rice beer prepared by them, viz. 'arak' which is the strongest variety, 'thap' a medium-strength liquor and 'hor' which is mild and ideal for a common family drink. Gourds are used for keeping rice beer as well as for carrying it about for outside use. 'Hor' figures prominently in the observance of their ceremonies and festivals. Tobacco is also widely in use by the grown-up males and small tobacco pipe (thenghong) is used for smoking. Opium and tobacco are grown by them though in small quantities. Betelnut (kove) together with pan leaf (bikon) and lime purchased from the market is heavily consumed by both sexes, an indulgence which is common among all people of Assam. Reckoning of time and measuring of distances during journeys are made on the basis of the number of betel pieces chewed at intervals.

Mikir Dress

The Mikirs commonly put on a piece of cloth known as 'rikong' which is wrapped round the loin and on their heads they wear turbans called 'poho' which is similar to that used by the male Khasis. Males also use a waistcoat called 'choi' with a long fringe which covers the buttocks and comes around in front. An end cloth called 'peinki' is used by them during the cold season. Women put on a petticoat known as 'peni' which is fastened round the waist with an ornamental girdle of old silver coins called 'vankok'. Another cloth known as 'pekok' is used to cover the upper part of the body. This cloth is tied under the arms and drawn tight over the breasts. The hair is combed straight and tied in a knot (chubi) on the head. No footwear is used by them. The Mikirs are fond of ornaments too.

A characteristic ornament is a large silver tube which is inserted into a hole pierced in the lobe of the ear known as 'nothangpi'. Males wear 'Norik' or earring of gold suspended from the lobe of the ear. Necklaces called 'lek' of coral beads are worm by women. Rings or 'urnam' and bracelets or 'roi' of gold and silver respectively are worn by women while the former are worn by men also.

Monogamy

Monogamy is the rule in the Mikir and polygamy, though permissible, is rare. The Mikirs are also divided into a number of clans and therefore marriage within one's own clan is not permissible. One of the important sequences of this tribe into a number of clans is to avoid taboo (laisnem) such as is laid down by their traditional customs. Cross-cousin marriage is generally preferred by the villagers. But while one can marry his father's sister's, daughter or his mother's brother's daughter, it is taboo to marry his father's or mother's sister or father's daughter or mother's sister's daughter belonging to a different clan.

Child Marriage

Child marriage is not in practice. If a young man fancies a girl, he informs his parents who go to her parent's house and make their offer of marriage of their son with the girl. If the girl's parents agree to the proposal, the boy's parents give a betrothal ring or bracelet to the girl. This is known a 'simkeba' or formal engagement.

Seduction

Seduction is rare, and when it occurs, the girl's parents have to give their girl away in marriage to the boy. Illegitimate birth in the village is nil. Adultery, even if it exists, is as general rule very rare and such a case is tried by the Village Council. The guilty pair are tried publicly thus subjecting them to the jeers and scorn of their neighbours. They are released only after the fine imposed by the Council is paid. Capital punishment in such eases is never inflicted. The husband of the erring wife may take her back; he may also refuse to do so except when the wife has borne him children. Remarriage of widows is allowed. Divorce (kachati) is rare though it is allowed provided there has been no offspring. Divorce can also be granted when the girl runs to her home after marriage and refuses to go back to her husband.

Funeral Rites

The Mikirs do not normally bury their dead. Cremation is the usual method of disposing the dead and is done after the performance of some ceremonies. The body of a still-born child, a child who dies soon after birth, or of a mother who dies during child birth, is buried without any ceremony. Victims of smallpox or cholera are buried shortly after death, but the funeral rites for the deceased are performed later, the dead body or bones being dug up and cremated according to custom. In the case of a person killed by a tiger, the body or his clothes, if found, are buried at some distance from the village because the tiger is supposed to visit the burial place.

TABLE

Name of group	*TERANG*						*INGTI*						*RONGHANG*				*TERON*				*TIMUNG*							
Name of sub-group	Beh		Kro		Returns as Tarang		Hanse		Ingleng		Returns as Ingti		Tiso		Returns as Ronghang		Not Classified		Tokbi		Rongpher		Phongcho		Dero		Returns as Timung	
Number of persons	M	F	M	F	M	E	M	F	M	F	M	F	M	F	M	F	M	F	M	F	M	F	M	F	M	F	M	F
1	2	3	4	5	6	7	8	9	10	11	12	13	14	15	16	17	18	19	20	21	22	23	24	25	26	27	28	29
277	19	15	4	3	5	9	1	1	12	7	23	19	6	4	15	20	14	21	2	1	7	7	10	6	1	3	19	23

Economic Life

The economic life of the Mikirs is simple and the whole lot of them depend for their livelihood mainly on cultivation. Paddy is the most important crop and the villagers attach more importance to the growth of paddy than to that of any other crop. Next to paddy, maize, gourds sesame, cotton, etc., are grown as side-lines in the jhum fields along with paddy. Livestock occupies the next important place in respect of the sources of wealth of the village. The rearing of livestock such as pigs, goats and fowl is also important for both ceremonial and religious reasons apart from their economic value. Though weaving, bamboo and cane works which require such skill and labour are followed by them, the people do not depend for their subsistence either mainly or partially on any of them with the result that these minor but important industries receive no particular attention. This apathy is mainly due to the availability of factory product in the markets at a reasonable rate. These industries are considered only as part-time jobs and that also not for marketing purposes, but only for their personal use. The village is rich in forest resources; hence firewood and building materials are easily and abundantly available. The forests are owned by the community and any person can use the timber free of cost, but clearing the forest for jhumming without the permission of the Village Council (Mei) is prohibited.

Occupations

Weaving occupies the position of a very important household industry among the Mikirs. A crude wooden loom called 'petherange' or loin-loom is employed in weaving. The spinning wheel by which cotton raised in their fields is spun into thread is known as 'mithongrang'. Weaving is done mainly by women which art has been their skill and pride from time immemorial.

Hunting

The Mikirs are very fond of hunting and fishing, especially the latter, in which both men and women generally take part. There is no recognized functionary who takes initiative or who plays some special role in either hunting or fishing. The hunting season is usually during the winter months whenall ae not occupied with cultivation although only male folks take part in hunting. The chief implements use in hunting are the spear (chir), bow (thai) and arrow (thai aso), while dogs are used to track down animals. No gun is used by the villagers because none can afford to buy one or none gets a licence for possessing one.

Fishing

Fishing is also practised with as much interest as hunting and both men and women take part. A fishing party is also sometimes organised and every member carrying and fishing baskets (hak) and traps set out for the nearby stream. A trap (ru) is placed at one end of the flowing water and both men and women wade into the stream and beat the water with sticks which they carry in their hands thus frightening away the fishes and driving them straight into the 'ru'. Another method of catching fish is by placing a basket under the water for sometime until the fishes have gathered there when it is lifted up. But this method needs energy, time and patience and is generally practised by women. Rods, lines and hooks are also used and are common with the young boys. Another common method is by poisoning the river or stream with a certain kind of wild plant. The plant is boiled first and the juice thus obtained from it is used to poison the fish.

Progress and Welfare

While development measures relating to communication, improvement in agriculture, poultry and livestock, water supply etc. have been spread over and proved beneficial to most of the villagers within the jurisdiction of the Block, but it is still backward. Agriculture is still practised according to age-old methods with primitive daos and kodalis and the villagers have to toil hard to earn their living. Though wet cultivation has been taken up by the villagers, there is not much scope for development as most of the tract is hilly. Only in small valleys intercepted by hills could the land be put to wet cultivation, but the extent of such lands is insignificant. There is no dispensary either for persons or for animals in or around the village except the one which is far away hence villagers take recourse to self-trained medicinemen who provide sacrifice and herbal medicines to every person in the village. They have witch doctors to perform sacrifices for the cure of ailments. But as man is what he believes, they are not worse off despite all their drawbacks.

A. ORIGIN AND HISTORY

The Word Mikir

The Mikir is one of the Scheduled Tribes of Assam as given in the Scheduled Castes and Scheduled Tribes Lists Modification Order, 1956.

The non-Mikirs in general call this tribe as Mikirs, while they call themselves as Karbi or Arleng of which the former that is Karbi is more common in use. The Mikirs call non-Mikirs particularly the Dimasa Kachari, Bodo Kachari and Assamese as Parok: this has been derived from the Mikir word 'Parok-Jangphong' (Parok of the non-Mikirs); jangphong fruit; that is fruit of the non-Mikirs, implying jackfruit). The etymological significance of the name 'Karbi' as the legned tells that the name 'Karbi' comes from the latter half of the word 'Thakar-kabi', meaning offering of sacrifices at the beginning of worship of god, marriage ceremony, harvesting of corps and birth of a child, which is called 'Thakar kibi'. The word ultimately got transformed into 'karbi', thus omitting 'tha' and 'ki' of the word.

There is another legend which tells us that once upon a time a 'Mikir' man left a flaming fire at his own home while his wife asked him "Me askar chenghoi bi kangkok" meaning why he left the flaming fire, these somehow got transformed into 'karbi' and so the later generations were known as 'karbi'.

According to Lyall (1908, p. 4-5), Arleng properly means a Mikir man and not a man in general who would, according to him, be called 'monit'-'munit'. Further, according to him the etymological significance of the name Arleng came from the fact that their forefathers generally used to dwell on the hill slopes and so they were known as Arleng or hill dwellers or hillman.

According to Gemini Paul (1956, p. 152) the word 'Mikir' is a combination of 'Mikiri', meaning 'hill people'. But according to the Mikir this has been wrongly expressed by the other. Instead of Mi-Kiri it should be Mengkiri (Meng-cat; kiri-to search) and according to the Mikirs there is a legened behind this which is as follows:

History

Once long, long back a few Mikirs were in search of the pet cat which they lost sight of in the jungle while they were hunting. Then those Mikirs roamed through the jungle in the search of the cat. During the search for the cat they met a non-Mikir person (could not say the community with certainty Dimasa Kachari or Assamese) in the jungle. The non-Mikir asked the Mikirs what they were searching for but the Mikirs could not follow his language but only answered Meng-kiri, that is, searching for a cat, searching for a cat. Since then the Mikirs are known as Meng-kiri which later got transformed into Mikir by the non-Mikirs.

The Mikirs do not claim any relationship with any other community. According to Edward Stack (1908, p. 4-5) the Mikirs belong undoubtedly to the great Tibeto-Burmese stock while Gemini Paul (1956) stated "though originally of Austric origin, probably the latest migration, they are now overwhelmingly a mixture of the 'Austric' and 'Bodo' with the latter as the predominant strain." Sir George Grierson (1904-1928) classed them as intermediate between the Bodo and Western Nagas on linguistic grounds.

According to Dalton (1872, p. 54), "they were driven by Kacharis from what is called Tolaram's country between Nowgong and Kachar, and sought refuge in Jaintia, but not being satisfied with their reception, they placed themselves under the Rajas of Assam, and have ever since peacefully occupied the hill country in which they are now settled. It is said, they were disarmed or made to forswear the use of arms by the Assam Government, and this is assigned as the cause of their unwarlike disposition, which makes them good subjects, but exposes them to the attacks of their more warlike neighbours." The Tularam country possibly imply the area under the rule of the Dimasa Kachari King whose general or 'Senapati' was Tularam.

According to Lyall (c.f. Assam Census Report 1881; p. 78-81)......"there are sufficient indications to warn us in declaring Mikir to be the Kinsman of Bodo rathei than of Khasi..... ...On the whole, until we know more about the Nagas dialects bordering on the Mikir country. I think we may conclude that this language is an outliner of the Bodo or Kachari group though perhaps widely separated from the general stock than other members of the family."

Tibeto-Burman Stock

Edward Stack (1908) claimed that the Mikirs belong to the great Tibeto-Burman stock, while Gemini Paul (1956) stated that of Austric origin, probably of the latest migration, thay are now overwhelmingly a mixture of the 'Austric' and 'Bodo' with the latter as the predominant strain. According to Sir George Grierson (1904-28), Mikirs were classed on Linguistics grounds as intermediate between Bodo and the Western Nagas and Lyall (Census of Assam, 1881) supported the fact from linguistic grounds and classed them as kinsmen of Bodo.

In Robinson's Account of Assam (cf. Assam Census Report, 1881: p. 77-78) it is stated, "......the Mikirs have tradition that their ancestors originally came from the Jaintia Hills. Colonel Dalton's verson of the legend is that they only went to Jaintia on their expulsion from Tularam's country by the Kachari, and that not being satisfied with their new quarters, they eventually placed themselves under the protection of the Rajas of Assam. The story that I have been told of first appearance in Assam is that driven out of the Jaintia Hills into what is now the Nowgong district, they sent emissaries to claim protection from the Ahom province of Raha. These luckless persons being unable to make themselves understood were straight away buried alive in a tank which that officer was then engaged in excavating. The hostilities which ensued were concluded by an embassy to the king himself in Sibsagar, and the Mikir have been living peacefully eversince in the territory assigned them."

Progeny of Valmiki

According to Pakrashi (1954), Arlengs or Mikirs have a vague idea that they are the progeny of Valmiki of Mahabharat. Sometime in the distant past, the ancestors of the present day Arlengs had settled on the eastern slopes of the Khasi and Jaintia Hills, bordering on the Kopili River (Nihang). The following account has been collected by Pakrashi (1954) about the traditional story of Arleng or Mikir migration.

When descendents of Valmiki were living peacefully in Nihang, as the legened runs, they were troubled by occasional raids by Khasi invaders. Gradually they had to withdraw from their original settlements and move into the kingdom of some Kachari king of ancient Hirimbapur (present day Dimapur) and settled down as revenue payers (ryots) of the Kachari King. The common Kacharis as well as the King were naturally suspicious about these new settlers. In the pretext of 'testing' their intelligence the ministers and the King decided to give them adequate punishment. The king then proclaimed that all Arlengs of his kingdom assemble before him. When they come to the court they were asked to straighten a buffalo horn without causing and damage to it. They were also told that if they failed, the king would seize their movable and immovable properties and that they would lose their 'status of ryots'. Apparently this task was impossible but fortunately a group of friendly cow boys come to their help, and they could straighten the horn by applying liberally wax on it. By their amicable behaviour, and unfailing allegiance to the king, the Mikirs won the friendship of the Kacharis, and gradually became the most favourite subjects of the Kachari king. But some of the court ministers could not tolerate the popularity and prosperity of the new settlers and they tried to convince the king that the Arlengs might dethrone him. The intrigues proved successful and the loyalty and industriousness of these settlers appeared to the king to be some subtle move to overthrow the Kachari rule. The Arlengs now tried to test the intelligence of the Kachari and asked them to flatten a curved gourd. The King himself accepted the gourd, but in his attempt to straighten it he broke the neck of the gourd, others also tried but failed. This convinced the king and the common Kacharis that the Arlengs were really intelligent. But a section of the ministers being jealous tried to poison the ears of the King with falicious allegations. They again appealed to the King to test the intelligence of the Mikirs by asking them to make a garland of sand and paddy flowers, they also requested the King to take severe action against them, if they fail, so that they may not live in this kingdom.

The King then asked the Mikirs to get this thing done. They again sought the help of the cowboy and with amazing ingenuity the cowboys did what was impossible for the Mikirs. The King was so delighted with the garland that he at once proposed to hold a royal hunt to test the skill of the Arleng ryots. The party was not successful because no game was found. On his way back, the King however, found a tiger which he brought home.

The crafty ministers advised the King to feed the cub on cow's milk, but secret instructions were given by them to spread the false rumour that the King wanted the Mikirs to feed his tiger cub upon human milk. Men were accordingly, sent to collect milk from the Arleng women. The spell of torture and molestation that followed compelled the Arlengs to flee from the Kachari Kingdom and search for a new homeland where they could live in peace. When the King's men visited the Arleng settlement for a fresh supply of milk then a solitary and brave girl Rongpharpi who stayed behind in the village asked them to come inside the dark cottage one by one to collect the milk. As the King's men entered the dark cottage, came the axe from Rongpharpi and the man was severed in two. Thus many Kacharis lost their lives in the hand of the gallant girl Rongpharpi. The rest fled in panic to the King.

On getting this information, the King with his troops followed the trail of the fleeing Arlengs in the deep jungles but the pursuit appeared to be fruitless. So the King sent spies who entered deep into the forest and came across the fugitive Arlengs, mixed and stayed with them. But one night, the Arlengs discovered that their Kachari 'friend' had disappeared. So, immediately they moved forward towards remote forests and came to Barpani (near Chaparmukh railway junction) where a big river obstructed their path which they crossed and settled on a clearing reaching the bank. On getting this information the King moved to Barpani with his troops to punish the Arlengs.

The Kacharis

The Kacharis tried to cross the river by a wooden bridge, but when the kingsmen reached the middle, the bridge collapsed drowning a good many of them. The Arlengs thanked God for the rout of their enemies. The King then gave up the pursuit because he came to believe that God was protecting the Arlenges.

One night Rongpharpi dreamt that God was asking her to come and visit his kingdom next morning, Rongpharpi found a white elephant hitherto unknown to the Arlengs, and was desiged with joy, for God had sent this elephant to show the path to his kindom. Other Arlengs came and saw this miracle. They also found a big tiger roaming about in the clearing made by the white elephant. Rongpharpi then spoke about her dream and told the Arlengs that God had ordained that she should lead the Arlengs to his abode. So Rongpharpi trailed the foot prints of the tiger and the Arlengs followed her down the clearing in the jungle. During their trailing Rongpharpi chanced upon a full granary with a few beautiful nuts nestling nearby, this she considered to be the kingdom of God, and the Arlengs settled down on the site. Years passed by and the Arlengs lived in peace and prosperity.

Meanwhile, Chintong, who lived in God's company fell in love with Rongpharpi and she too could not resist him. This made Arnamkethe angry with Chintong and Rongpharpi. She dreamt that God was very much displeased with her conduct and ordered her folk to leave his kingdom. The Arlengs had then to leave the kingdom of God. Chintong proposed marriage to her, Rongpharpi accepted him, and they lived as man and wife. The Arlengs too accepted this union in their society.

In time a boy was born to Chintong and was named Thong, who gradually grew up to a handsome youngman. But Arlengs could not enjoy their prosperity for long, because the Khasi and Jaintia people destroyed their houses and friends. When the Arlengs began to resist the invaders, the Khasi king proposed that the Arlengs sould co-operate with the Khasi in clearing jungles and making road. One evening the Khasi and the Arleng working parties assembled in a rest house, there the Khasi gang leader wished to count the Arlengs who were working. The counting was done by marking every tenth man on the forehead with a dao-blade. Thong came to learn about the incident and after taking blessings of his mother he appealed to the Arlengs to muster courage and fight back.

The next time when the Khasis and the Arlengs again assembled in the rest house, the Khasis proposed that heads should be counted as before. Thong this time took the opportunity and suggested that the Arlengs should now take their turn in counting the Khasis. The Khasis agreed and Thong now took the revenge, he began to chop off the head of every tenth man, and in a short time many Khasi heads were severed. Then the Khasis tried to run away, but the Arlengs pounced upon them and killed many of them.

When the King learned of this he became enraged and sent his best warriors to teach a lesson to Thong and the Arlengs. Thong fought gallently and killed one and gouged the eyes of the other and then sent the heads of the warriors back to the Khasi Kings.

To make peace the Khasi King welcomed Thong to his court, where he felt proud and boasted that even wild elephants would be less than his match, what to speak of man. The Khasi King now proposed that Thong should demonstrate his might in a tug-of-war with thousand elephants. Thong accepted and when the elephants were brought, they raised their trunks and saluted the hero in respect and thus he won the challenge. The Khasis were amazed and they all immediately acclaimed him a super-human hero and warrior.

The Khasi King next time ordered his men to let loose venomous cobras upon him by surprise. When Thong found that he was about to be encircled by the snakes, he clamped battle sheilds tight over the mouth of the pits and dropped off their fangs. So the Khasi King was finally convinced that, Thong was no ordinary mortal. So he declared before his people that he would adopt Thong as his eldest son in order to succeed him and ordered his subjects to pay respect to Thong as the eldest son of their king. Thong was greeted with cheers by the Khasis, except a few who could not feel happy over it.

When the Khasi King learned that the Arlengs suffered at the hands of the Kacharis, then he asked Thong to take out an expedition against the Kacharis.

Thong and his soldiers successfully subdued the Kacharis in due course. On their way back the Khasi soldiers encamped in a banana grove where some of the Khasi soldiers made a plot to kill Thong. They requested Thong to pluck a few mangoes, since they could not climb the tall trees. When Thong was innocently plucking mangoes unaware of such a plot, the plotters sent swarms of arrows and Thong who was unarmed now met his tragic end. His head was chopped off. The rebels told the King a fabricated story of a bandit falling upon them on their way home. The King immediately ordered them to fetch the severed head, which proved to be that of Thong, for Thong had a tooth set with gold.

This was a shock to the King, the common Khasis and the Arlengs. Thong's mother Rongpharpi was driven mad with grief. In revenge, the King ordered live crucifications for those who murdered Thong. Thus Khasis and Arlengs lost their great friend and warrior whose memory live forever in their hearts. From that day the Arlengs and Khasis lived together in peace until the Arlengs migrated, many years later to their present home.

Descendants of Thong Nokbe

The belief still exists among the Mikirs of today that they are the descendants of a great Raja called Thong Nokbe (not Phongnogbi as reported in the Census of Assam, 1891, p. 255). Nobody knows where this Raja came from but he was known to have married many women of the country where he finally settled in the far west and that his descendants worked their way eastward towards the present district of Cachar in Assam. This claim is perhaps true to the extent that some of the villages in the North Cachar Hill bears the names belonging to their language, indicating their former presence. They had once been settled in strength in North Cachar to the immediate north of the Barail range and had been in contact with the Angami, the Kaccha and the Kabui Nagas. Due to the oppression of the Kachari Kings, they migrated westwards to Jaintia Hills in search for protection from the Jaintia Raja, but while migrating to the Jaintia territory they were dissatisfied with the treatment given out to them by the Jaintia chiefs. They, therefore, resolved to move into Ahom territory and sent an embassy to the Ahom Governor at Raha (Nowgong) offering to place themselves under his protection. As their envoys could not make themselves understand, they were buried alive in a tank. The hostilities which thus ensued were concluded by an embassy to the King himself in Sibsagar. Since then the Mikirs have been living peacefully in the territory assigned to them (Census of Assam, 1891).

B. THE LAND AND PEOPLE

Distribution of Population

Regarding the geographical distribution of the Mikirs, Lyall (cf. Assam Census Report 1881, p. 78) stated that, in the isolated mountainous block which fills the tringle between the Brahmaputra on the North, the Dhansiri valley on the East, and Kapil and Kalang Valleys on the West, the characteristic elements of Mikir topographical nomenclature as Lang, river water; Langso, small stream; Inglong, mountains; Long stone; Rong, village; Sar, chiefs are found everywhere, as well as in the southern part, now inhabited by the Rengma Nagas, from the Hills across the Dhansiri as in the northern portion included in the Nowgong district and more particularly as the Mikir Hills. They are also found in considerable numbers to the south of the Langkher valley, in the mountains now inhabited by Kukis, Kutcha Nagas (Kaccha Nagas) and Kacharis, as far south as the courses of the Jhiri and Jhinam. In the centre of North Kachar they are rare; but there is a considerable group of Mikir names again to the west of this tract about the head water of Kopili and on the southern face of the hills north of Badarpur, Mikir terms also abound, mixed with Lalungs, on the northern face of the Khasi and Jaintia Hills; and along the courses of the Kopili and Umkher rivers. Across the Brahmaputra the topographical nomenclature shows no trace of them, though there are a few colonies of them in Darrange.

People of the Lower Hills

"They are thus essentially a people of the lower hills and

adjoining lowlands of the central portion of the range stretching from the Garo Hills to the Patkoi. Their neighbours are (1) the Santengs of Jaintia on the west ; (2) Bodos or Kacharis on the south ; and (3) Assamese on the north and east where the country is inhabited at all; and intermixed with them, are recent colonies of Kukis and Rengma Nagas and older ones of Lallungs and Rengma Nagas and older ones of Lalungs and Hill-Kacharis." (cf. Assam Census Report 1881, p. 78).

Robinson Distribution

The distribution of Mikir as given by Robinson (cf. Assam Census Report, 1881, p. 78) is as follows, "...their present seat is chiefly in the Mikir Hills, low mountain tract in Nowgong, cut off by the valleys of the Kopili and Dhansiri from the mountain range of the Naga Hills, but with Naga population in its southern half, while large numbers again are to be found still in their original settlements along the foot of the Jaintia Hills, both in Nowgong and Kamrup. A few communities have immigrated into Upper Assam and across the river into Darrange."

Population Trend

The following table shows the population of Mikirs in the State of Assam from 1901 to 1961:

Year	*Total Population*	*Males*	*Females*
1901	87,335	44,256	43,079
1911	106,259	54,257	52,002
1921	111,629	57,383	54,246
1931	129,797	66,045	63,752
1941	149,746	77,108	72,638
1951	152,537	80,373	72,164
1961	121,082	62,827	58,255

The above table shows a sudden fall of the Mikir population in the 1961 Census. This may be due to the fact that during 1961 Census only those Mikirs residing in the four Autonomous

Hill Districts of Assam were enumerated while those in the plain districts were accounted with the general population. According to the Scheduled Castes and Scheduled Tribes Lists Modification Order, 1956, notified under the Government of India, Ministry of Home Affairs, Notification No. SRO 2477A, dated 29th October, 1956, (Census of India 1961, Vol. I, Part V.A(ii) (p. 11) the scheduled areas are regarded as such throughout the state of Assam, but the Scheduled Tribes are confined to certain scheduled areas within the state. A Scheduled Tribe of the Autonomous District can be regarded as such anywhere within the four autonomous districts of Assam, but cannot be regarded as a Scheduled Tribe if he goes outside the precincts of the Autonomous Districts. Thus a Mikir residing in Sibsagar District cannot be regarded as a Scheduled Tribe.

Geographical Distribution

The Arlengs or Mikirs are found only in the hill areas of Assam, particularly in the United Mikir and North Cachar Hills and Khasi and Jaintia Hills districts, and an insignificant number of them are found in Garo Hills and Mizo Hills as evidenced from the Table on next page.

It is evidenced from the table that the Mikir population is predominantly concentrated in the rural area of the United Mikir and North Cachar Hills District and in the Khasi and Jaintia Hills District. They are also found in great numbers in their original settlement along the foot of the Jaintia Hills, as has already been stated earlier, they had once settled in great strength in the Jaintia Hills, but were driven away from this area by the Jaintia Rajas. Possibly this may be the reason for the lesser concentration of the Mikirs in the Khasi and Jaintia Hills today.

In the State of Assam majority of the Mikir population is found in the age group of 0-14 years. This is also observed in the United Mikir and North Cachar Hills District, while in the United Khasi and Jaintia Hills District majority population are found to be in the age group of 15-44 years. As the bulk of the population comes from the age-group of 0-14 years this may indicate that there is less infant mortality and when these children will attain the marriageable age there is every likelihood

TABLE

State/Districts	Total Population	Male	Female	Rural			Urbvu		
				Total Population	Male	Female	Total Population	Male	Female
Assam	121,082	62,827	58,255	120,953	62,730	58,223	129	97	32
Garo Hills	6	5	1	1	1	—	5	4	1
Khasi and Jaintia Hills	4,188	2,296	1,892	4,133	2,253	1,880	55	43	12
United Mikir and North Cachar Hills	116,887	60,525	56,362	116,818	60,475	56,343	69	50	19
Mizo Hills	1	1	—	1	1	—	—	—	—

Source : Census of India, 1961; Vol. III, Assam Part V-A, p. 187-205.

of the increase of the population. The less number in the age group 15-44 years may reflect, the premature death or though nothing definitely can be stated, unless a detailed demographic study of the Mikir population is made.

Physical Appearance

The interesting account of Lyall (1908, p. 4) throws some light about the physical characteristics of the Mikirs. "In features the men resemble Assamese of the lower classes more than most of the Tibeto-Burmese races. Their colour is light yellowish brown and the girls are often fair. The men are as tall as the majority of the hill races of Assam." Colonel L. A. Waddel's eighteen specimen 'saveraging 1633 mm. or 5.454 feet in height, the tallest being 5.583 feet and the shortest5 .108 feet. The average noticeably higher than that of their neighbours, the Khasis. The average head measurements in those specimens were, length 181 mm.; breadth 141 mm.; Cephalic index 77.9. The nose is broad at the base, and often flat, giving a nasal index of 85.1, and an orbital of 107.7. The facial hair is scanty, and only a thin moustache is worn. The front of the head is sometimes, but not generally, shown. The hair is gathered into a knot behind, which hangs over the nape of the back. The body is muscular, and the men are capable of prolonged exertion."

Measurements of Mikirs

According to Waddel (1900 cf. Gupta and Dutta, 1962, p. 9) measurements on 18 Mikirs are as follows:

	mean
Stature (mm)	1633
Cephalic Index	78.17
Nasal Index	85.84

Pakrashi Cephalic Index

The stature distribution as given by Pakrashi (1953) are as follow. The number of individuals studies by Pakrashi being large (n-100). Only few are given below:

Stature	*f*	%
Very Short	5	5.00
Short	54	54.00
Below Medium	19	19.00
Medium	14	14.00
Above Medium	7	7.00
Tall	1	1.00
Cephalic Index	*f*	%
Hyperdolichcephal/		
Dolichocephal	82	82.09
Mesocephal	17	17.00
Brachycephal	1	1.00
Nasal Index	*f*	%
Leptorrhine	20	20.00
Mesorrhine	60	60.00
Chamaerrhine	19	19.00
Hyperchamaerrhine	1	1.00
Facial Index	*f*	%
Hypereuryprosopic	20	20.00
Euryprosopic	32	32.00
Mesoprosopic	26	26.00
Leptoprosopic	16	16.00
Hypereuryprosopic	6	6.00

Thus from the above distribution on the different anthropometric measurement it is evident that the Mikirs are predominantly a short statured, long headed group with medium noses. The distribution of the facial index shows that the people are generally broad faced.

C. ECONOMY

Classification of land

Land is one of the most important economic resources of the people, their livelihood depends mainly on cultivation. The lands may be classified into five categories as land put to non-agricultural uses, barren and uncultivable land, cultivable land, cultivable waste land and land under forest.

Agriculture

The land put to non-agricultural uses include the area which is used for homestead purposes, play ground, foot paths, etc.; barren and uncultivable land signifies the land area which are unfit for cultivation; cultivable land means the land under cultivation; cultivable waste land signifies the land area which can be cultivated but is left fallow for the present time and under forest indicates the area which is covered with jungle trees and which is not included in the net area cultivated. A general pattern of land utilization in a Mikir village in the United Mikir and North Cachar Hills district is as follows:

Land Utilization

	Categories of Lands	*Areas in (Acres)*	*Percentage*
1.	Cultivable land	285	33.9
2.	Land put to non-agricultural uses	100	11.8
3.	Barren and uncultivable	100	11.8
4.	Cultivable wasteland	100	11.8
5.	Land under forest	258	30.7
	Total	843	100.0

Mikir Hill District

The distribution of land in a village governed by the Mikir Hills District (Jhuming) (Amendment) Regulation, 1966, passed by the Mikir Hills District Council. According to this regulation Jhum land is restricted to one particular area for a village which may be selected by the villagers in consultation with the 'sarthe' or 'gaonbura' of a village. If any disagreement arise about selection of jhuming site among the villagers, the 'sarthe' refers the case to the Executive Committee of the District Council and its decision in this respect is final. Individual plots within the selected area may be selected by the people themselves in consultation with their 'Sarthe'. The District Council reserves the right of disposing of the filled stuff in jhum area in any manner it considers suitable without interfering jhuming. The villagers shall be jointly or individually responsible for any damage to areas not from the Jhumed areas. Jhnm lands are generally marked by the owners with a boundary in she nature of a fence or drain or line and the 'Sarthe' of a village will see that such marking does not encroach on other's land. There is no restriction as to the size of the land alloted to different individuals, it depends upon the ability or capacity of a family to cultivate. It may be noted that a person or the family lose their right of occupation and cultivation if they leave the village or shift to other village (or another 'hawar' or jurisdiction of another 'Sarthe') for the purpose of settling there permanently. In this case they have to consult with the 'Sarthe' of that 'hawar' or village where they reside to allot them land.

Forest lands

Forest lands are of two types (1) unclassed State forest, from where the people have the right to cut trees either for construction purposes or for fuel and (2) Reserved Forest, where the people have no right to utilize the forest material. The evergreen forests are the home of various wild animals such as elephants, buffaloes, tigers, bears, deer, etc. In Mikir Hills the wild elephants are not uncommon and the wild elephants often attack villages and sometimes damage the jhum fields. Snakes of various kinds poisonous as well as non-poisonous also abounds in the jungle. Rabbits are a great pests in the jhum fields and the villagers are always for the look out of the rabbit holes and always try to scare the rabbits., Monkeys often attack the jhum fields in company. Varieties of birds break the silence of the forests with their sweet melodies.

Varieties of Trees

The forests are chiefly infested with different speices of bamboo-chek; cinnamon-Thekiching Sonaru tree Sanaru; Sal tree—Hai; Plantain tree—Phinu/Lothe; Mangoo; Tharve—Jack-fruit—Jangphong and many other trees valuable for timber. The wild plantation trees abound, in the forest and form a ready source of food for elephants, monkeys and the like.

Demand in firewood have resulted in wanton destruction of valuable forest growth. The United Mikir and North Cachar Hills District where the tribe under study is mostly found, contains within its fold the reserve forests covering appoximate-ly an area of 641,353 acres (District Census Handbook, United Mikir and North Cachar Hills, 1961, Census, Assam, p. 20). With the expection of the area under Reserved Forest, the tract bears an extensive area of unclassed State Forests. This area is forest in name only, since unrestricted jhuming has virtually eaten up almost all the forest trees rendering the whole area covered with only bamboos and grasses with a few scattered trees here and there. The forest reserves of the district, particularly for the bamboo trees. Hence with a view to improv-ing the indigenous species, a scheme for planting the bamboo trees has been undertaken in Bokajan area under the State Development Scheme in the year 1955. The species planted under such schemes are 'Wahing' (Calamus viminalls) and 'tita' (Calamus rotang).

Rearing of Livestock

The secondary occupation of the Mikir is the rearing of livestock. Poultry, goats and pigs are commonly reared either for their food and commercial purposes or for ceremonial and sacrificial importance. Milch and draught cattle are kept for milk and for ploughing the fields respectively. Fishery is not as common as the rearing of livestock because the climatic condi-tion as well as the terrain do not suit the rearing of fishes.

Cultivators

The cultivators are the predominant group in the rural area, who constitute 54.2% of the total population and 91.1% of the total workers. The change in their traditional occupation, that is cultivation, is evidenced from the table, where it observed that 6,153 persons (both sexes) or 8.54% of the total workers, 72,090 who are engaged in works other than cultivator and agricultural labourer. When the males and females are separately taken it was observed, that 886 or 2.37% males and 5267 or 15.13% females, constitute the number of workers apart from cultivator and agricultural labourer out of total of 37,289 male and 34,801 female workers respectively. Thus it is evident from the above figures that the percentages of the female workers are fairly high as compared to the male workers apart from cultivator and agricultural labourer are considered. The number of non-workers in the rural areas are 48,903 persons of 40.38% of the total population or 67.8% of the total workers. Most of them are children of school workers, other than cultivators and agricultural labourer another non-workers.

The Jhuming Cultivation

The Mikirs practise both wet cultivation and Jhuming. Those who reside in the hills generally take to Jhuming and those in the plains follow wet cultivation. Selection of the jhuming site is done by the people themselves. The village headman has generally the sole authority over the village jurisdiction called 'hawar' and he convenes a meeting for discussion regarding selection of a jhuming site. After the decision taken regarding the jhuming site, the people cut the jungle and burn the trees for jhuming. It may be noted that one person loses his right of occupation of cultivation along with his shifting to another village or another 'hawar' of a village headman. In this case the village headman can allot the land to another person who comes under his jurisdiction or to his village. Generally the people living in the hills set mark to their own plot by fencing the plot by bamboo strips. It is also observed that sometime the plots for cultivation of individual households are scattered and there is no need of fencing the plots and the clearing areas in the hills indicate the cultivable plot and the owner of the plot is also known since in average a village consist of 50 to 60 households. In selecting a particular site for jhuming the person informs the 'Sarthe' regarding the selection of his particular site. This is done only to save from any controversy which later may arise for the site. The Mikirs living in the plains have acquired the knowledge of wet cultivation from the plains people. Though it is rare it is worth mentioning that the Mikirs who have the experience of wet cultivation, do so in the hills where such cultivable land is available, particularly those who are residing in the slopes of the hills. Sometime encroachment on other land may arise, where the plot is too big for the person to cultivate though it is not very frequent then in that case, the village durbar or 'sarthe' will interfere and will allot him only such amounts which he can cultivate when the old plot is exhausted and the person want to shift to a new plot for cultivation, then they have to get the permission of the village durbar. The village durbar seldom prohibits people to shift their cultivation site as there is no scarcity of cultivable land in the hills. But it is not necessary to shift their habitation site along with the shifting of the jhuming site. Some temporary dwelling is reconstructed near the jhuming site only to stay during the operational season, if the jhuming land is fairly at a distance.

Before a plot is put to cultivation, trees are felled and jungle is cleaned. This is done in December or January. The felled trees are allowed to dry till March when they are set on fire. Tillage and spreading of ash are done usually by human labour with the help of hoe. Paddy is then sown with the first rains, in April-May. The clearing, slashing, hurning, tillage, sowing and harvesting are done by individual family and sometime with the help of daily wage labourers. No joint participation either on the basis of the village, clan or joint family is done except in harvesting where friends and relatives extend their helping hand. Paddy as is stated earlier is sown broad-cast in April or May, and is harvested in November-December. Other varieties as maize, millet, etc. are also sown along with paddy as side lines in holes so made for the purpose by hoes, in the first rains and gethered in the ensuing cold weather. The ears of paddy are out with the help of a sickle. The sheaves on getting dry, are collected and thrashed out on the spot by beating against a stone. Agricultural equipments are invariably of simple type and most of the people especially those who reside in the hills are quite ignorant of the use of artificial manures. To them dried and decomposed leaves and burnt up ashes are the only manures providing fertility to the virgin soil. The important agricultural equipments are the following ku (spade—which is brought from the market). The dao which is used in agricultural practices is of the Nopete type and the sickle is known as Nokekrangso—the blade of which is serrated, and usually 1½′ in length including the handle.

Wet Cultivation

In plains who are practising wet cultivation they keep the cultivable lands enclosed on all sides by mud walls about 8″-10″ in height. If there is any stream nearby then the canals from the stream to the river may be done otherwise the fields has to depend on the monsoon rains. In wet cultivation, the soil is made into a thick paste by means of a hoe or in some cases those who can afford bullocks for ploughing use. Weeding and transplantation are done generally by women. To protect the crops from wild animals and birds, effigies are made to stand in the middle or corner of the field. A watch house (hamtap) is also constructed in the field so that the owner or any one of his family may stay to watch the crops and to keep the animals and birds away from the fields.

Ramrongkekan

During the sowing and harvesting time some ceremonies in the form of dancing and singing are performed by boys and girls while the elderly people hoe the soil and sow the seeds. The sowing dance is known as Ramrongkekan and is done with the accompaniment of drums. They also sow the seeds in the rhythmic way accompanied by the beating of drums and dancing.

Hacha

Hacha is the dancing festival during the harvesting time, where boys and girls in their traditional dress dance.

Weaving

The most important household industry among the Mikirs is weaving. The loin loom known as 'pethrang' is a simple tension loom. The spinning wheel by which cotton is spun into thread is known as 'mithongrang'. The loom is simple consisting of the warp of manageable length and breadth, is usually fastened at one end of the wall while the other end of the warp is tied around the waist of the weaver with a cane belt (thehu). No reed is used and the shed is effected by half-wealt process which is also operated by hand. The weft yarn is inserted in the shed through a bamboo tube (nonthari langpong) and a bamboo or wooden string is used for beating up the weft. Weaving is done by women, which is a pride for them. The chief products of the loom are 'rikong' (a cloth used by men to wrap the loins), Peinki (worn by women around the waist), etc. They generally dye their threads in black, yellow and red colours. The black dyes are obtained from the juice of a certain plant called 'sibu', a yellow colour from a plant called 'Jantarlong' and that of red colour from a plant called 'Tansir'. The designs generally preferred by them are stripes in various combinations of colour. Generally the products of the loom are for their personal use. Below is given the names of some of the parts of the loin loom in Mikir terms.

Part of the Loin Loom

Mikir Terms	*Corresponding Meaning*
Thehu	A cane belt used on loin of weaver to fasten and tighten the loom.
Harpi	A piece of pointed and flat wooden or bamboo stick used as reed.
Thoning	A round bar of wood or bamboo on which threads of the loom are wrapped.
Honthari	A rod of bamboo on which thread is wound.
Honthai langhong	A bamboo tube on which 'Honthari' is kept.
Uwek	Small rods of bamboo.
Ule	Long rods of bamboo like Umek.
Takeri	A kind of bobbin.
Honlam	A bamboo or wooden stick on both sides of which small bars are fitted as 'cross' and threads are wrapped on it.

Sirki	A spool.
Thelangpong	Bamboo pipe for helping the healds.
Hi-i	Healds.
Honki chongbong	Bamboo or wooden stick used for drying Eri cocoon.
Ingthi	A reed of loom.
Ponglang	Same as 'Tholengpong' but small in size.
Therang	Round bar of bamboo wood.
Barlim	A flat and small rod of bamboo.

Bamboo and Cane Work

With the exception of weaving which is practised in every Mikir village, bamboo and cane works and blacksmithy are practised only in few villages and by those who know the art. These two household industries are done by males and the industries are taken up much for their personal use than for sale. Any male knowing the art of basketry, make bamboo or cane baskets of various kinds according to the use to which they are put. For example, baskets for carrying and storing paddy, for keeping clothes and ornaments, for storing food grains, etc. cane tables, chairs, murrah (low stool) are also made by them, particularly those who are living in the urban areas. Blacksmithy is practised only by 'Senar' and 'Milik' the sub-clans of Timung and Teron respectively. They are the only sub-clans who are practising this industry traditionally and formerly no other people or any other clan in interior villages could practise this trade, but presently there are no such restrictions on the clans possibly due to economic factors, it has been reported that few peoples belonging to Ingti clan have taken up blacksmithy, in the urban area. It could not be ascertained during the investigation why only the Senar and Milik clans practised this industry in the former times and why not other clans. It seems that they are the only sub-kurs who have specialized in this trade from time immemorial. But even when this is so there is no distinction among the clans either socially, economically or politically. The blacksmiths take the manufacturing knives and daos of various kinds, these are made out of discarded spades which are brought from the market at a cheaper price. They also collect old umbrella ribs which are utilized for the manufacture of needles and hooks for fishing. Ornaments which are fairly in good demand by the community such as girdles bracelets, rings and earrings of either gold or silver are made by the Khasi smiths. But the people who are living in the urban areas buy ornaments from the local markets which are brought from the plains area. Sometime even in the interior villages the ornaments of plains are found since the people coming and going to the urban centres collect ornaments for others as well.

The only source of income of the whole village is cultivation. The majority of the households are from the income group Rs. 301-630. The next higher income group is Rs. 601-900 which includes 12 households of the village while there are only 2 households which receive the maximums of Rs. 1201 and above. The minimum income of Rs. 300 and less is received by only 2 households in the village. The income from other sources such as weaving, bamboo and cane works are practically nil and even if there is any, the amount is insignificant. During the slack season weaving and basketry are taken up by women and men respectively and generally done for domestic purposes.

D. SOCIAL STRUCTURE

Religion

The Mikirs believe in a number of gods collectively known to them as "Arnum atum" who are invoked and propitiated so that they may grant the village prosperity and happiness. These gods are worshipped in different ways at different times. Like the Khasis, the Mikirs have no idols, temples or shrines, but they believe in the form of a fertish locally known as 'bor' which are only pieces of stones by keeping which the people believe that they can become richer and lead the easier way. There are a good number of gods who receive their names from the disease caused by them. Names of some of the gods who are known for their evil doings are as follows:

Names of Gods

Honi Arunam — Leprosy, or if killed by tiger
Peng — For general health, cause fever

Dor	—	Eczema
Hemphu	—	During Child Birth
Chinthong and Lamki	—	Evil eyes
Chomangase	—	Infest hills and valleys

Cholera or small pox are not named after any god. The people live in constant dread of these gods so they try to be in good terms with them by duly offering propitiations to them. The objects of nature such as the hills, the valleys, the trees, the streams and other rocks are manifested with evil spirits which cause disease to men and as a matter of fact these gods receive their names from the diseases caused by them. The Mikirs are in constant dread and fear of these gods and hence they try to pacify them by offering due propitiations to them. Name of some of the gods who are known for their good deeds are as follows:

Risoarnam	—	For prosperity of young boys.
Ritarnam	—	For cultivation before sowing any crop.

Barithi

However, among the gods, the one who is known as 'Barithi', the god of heaven, is the most powerful and the dispenser of good and evil. He is propitiated with a pig and the whole village takes part during the ceremony. On this occasion the priest or kurusur as he is called, selects a wide open space in the village where the animal is to be sacrificed. The blood of the animal is offered to Barithi by the kurusur and at the same time he prays to him to free the whole village from any disease and to grant them good health for the whole year. The gods who infest the hills and the valleys—Chomengase and Peng—are propitiated by the sacrifice of a goat or fowl, these are propitiated by the individual family if and when they think that these gods are not pleased with them. When an epidemic disease like cholera breaks out, it is taken to be caused by 'Ajoase' to whom propitiation must be made with a goat or pig. This god is also believed to infest the waters or streams.

Rongker

An important ceremony known as 'Rongker' is usually observed when an epidemic breaks out in the village which is believed to be caused by the god 'Ajoase'. The expense of the ceremony will be borne by the families residing in the village, in cash and kind (rice) or either of it, depending upon the economic condition. In this ceremony the 'Kurusur' kills a pig, fowl or goat, at the outskirts of the village and the condition of the intestines tells the omen whether it is good or bad. While sacrificing a goat if the head is not served from the trunk by one stroke then it is considered as a bad omen.

Bad omen

In the case of a fowl the head is served and then it is left free and it is kept for some time in the air. While dying if its body falls on the left side then it is a bad omen while if it falls on the right side then it is considered a good omen. If the Kurusur finds a bad omen then every household in the village devotes itself to prayer to the god 'Ajoase' to have mercy on them and to avert the impending calamity. If on the other hand, the omen is good then the blood of the slaughtered animal which is shed on a plantain leaf is offered to 'Ajoase' and the meat of the slaughtered animal is cooked and eaten by the village elders in the Sarthe's (Gaonbora) courtyard.

No woman can observe the sacrificial ceremony and they are forbidden to eat the meat of the sacrificial animal as it is believed that the god will not be pleased to dine together with women. But whether the omen is good or bad, the whole community is prohibited from going to work and entry into or going out from the village is strictly forbidden. The prohibition lasts for a week or until the calamity has died down. If by chance an outsider pays a visit to the village during the calamity, he will have to put up for the night in the village and may leave it only in the morning of the following day.

Thengthon

Illness or trouble of any kind is ascribed to 'Thengthon', the god of jungle and trees and a goat or pig or fowl is sacrificed depending upon the economic condition, for the propitiation of the god. Barrenness in women is believed to be caused by 'Someme' and a fowl or a goat is propitiated to ensure fertility in women. These are beside quite a number of other gods the propitiation of whom forms the main object of their worship. All the gods mentioned above are placed at the family level and each household may do so according to the nature of the disease or trouble caused by the particular god.

Arni and Chiklo

The sun and the moon known to them as 'arni' and 'chiklo' respectively are looked upon as devines, and though no propitiation is made to them they receive due honour and respect. All the sacrifices to the gods are performed by the village priest 'Kurusur'. When the propitiation is to be done on the family level then the head of the family requests the kurusur to perform the sacrifice for the ceremony. The priest occupies a high and respectable position in the society and he is to lead a good and pious life. A person can become a Kurusur provided he is, by experience, well-versed in the art and technique of sacrificial ceremonies. No particular kur or sub-kur is associated with Kurusur and when ceremony is performed no feast is given at the time of appointment of the priest. Kurusur performs duties only when need arise, and when he is requested to perform the sacrificial ceremony his services are rewarded with food and drink and in some cases with cash, the amount of which never exceeds Rs. 2.00. Sometime a small village may not be having a 'Kurusur' then in that case 'Kurusur' from the nearby village is summoned to serve and he is duly rewarded. It is the 'Kurusur' who decides what sort of illness the person has and what sacrifice should be performed to appease the gods responsible for the cause of this illness, he also performs all the sacrifices connected with the festivals.

Chomarong

As has been stated earlier, the Mikirs believe that there is a place known as 'Chomarong' or dead man's paradise where both men and women, rich or poor will go and stay after death. A person who is justified by his good deeds in his life while on earth can only go to 'Chomarong', while a man who dies leaving behind his evil deeds on this earth is bound to be reborn. The rebirth of a man is taken by them as a punishment for his evil deeds, for a reborn person has again to suffer the hardships and troubles of this hard-ridden world.

Beliefs and Practices of Non-Christian Mikirs

The beliefs and practices of the people described in the foregoing pages belong to the non-Christian section of the Mikir population, while the Christian Mikirs who are fairly in good number (12, 443 persons in 1961 Census) belong to the Baptist sect and live their life according to the tenets of Christianity.

Social Reform and Welfare

During the five year plan a number of community development blocks have been established covering almost every village in the state, there are also other organizations for social reforms and welfare, working among the Mikir community.

As early as 1949, the Mikir Welfare Centre, Sarihajan village (P.O. Bokaian, Sibsagar) started with some L.P. schools, one M.V. School, one small free hotel and simple medical aid worked under the administration of the Bharatiya Adimjati Sevak Sangh. The Assam Tribal Welfare Works organized some primary schools since 1939 in the villages of the Mikir hills area. There are also Christian Missionary activities among the Mikirs, as a result there are now a few thousand of Christian converts. The American Baptist Mission is still working among them in some parts of Nowgcng District and Golaghat Subdivision. This was the condition existing before 1950. But still Christianity, though it has had far-reaching efforts in the other hill districts of Assam, has not made much progress among the Mikirs and few only, of the total population, are Christian converts.

Mikir Seva Kendra

A few of the welfare agencies existing in the Mikir society worth mentioning are Mikir Seva Kendra, Karbi Jutang Amei, Karbi, Lammet Amei, Srimanta Sankar Mission and the Opium Prohibition Organizatian. Among these organizations, the Srimanta Sankar Mission, the Mikir Seva Kendra and the

Opium Prohibition Organization serve the people for their welfare such as modern medical treatment and abolishing the opium consuming habit which is prevalent among the community. Some trained lady workers are also engaged by these institutions to teach the village people the methods of keeping the general health in modern hygienic ways.

The Karbi Lammet Amei

The Karbi Lammet Amei or Mikir Literary Committee established in 1967 and Karbi Jutang Amei or Mikir Cultural Association established in 1966 are serving the community for the development and uplift of Karbi literature and culture.

Structure of Social Control, Prestige and Leadership

Mei

Much of the old customs of their social organization splendidly survives even in the present day administrative change. The routine administration of each village is run by the village councils known to them as 'mei'. Each council is presided over by a headman or gaonbora called 'sarthe'. All adult males of the village are members of the *mei* known as Chakri. In *mei* the number of Chakris is not limited and each one of them take active part in the organization of their village. The district council recognizes the functions and duties of the 'mei' and it does not interfere with the customary rights and previlages of the community and the right of selecting the 'Sarthe' from amongst them.

Sarthe

The Sarthe is usually selected by a consensus from amongst the village elders and as such he is generally in good standing amongst the community and also bears a good moral character. When a person is appointed as 'Sarthe', he gives a feast to his village and pigs and fowl are killed on the occasion. His tenure of office, a post which is honorary is not definitely specified, but depends upon the villagers. If the villagers find the Sarthe a good and efficient one, his service may be required for as long as he wishes to serve, sometimes until death. But if he is unfit and incapable of discharging his duties, he is deprived of his sartheship and another man is selected in his place. The District Council can only recognize the office of the Sarthe, but it cannot retain him or expel him otherwise and go against the will of the community.

Sarso

It is the duty of the Sarthe to summon the members (chakri) of the 'mei' to a sitting and it is he who puts forward proposals relating to the affairs of the village and the members to give their verdict. The Sarthe can only preside, over the *mei* but he cannot make any decision without the consents of the other members. Under the 'Sarthe' there are assistants called 'Sarso' (Assistant gaonbora) to help him in his duties and sometimes take over charge of his duties in the event of his illness or absence from the office. The 'mei' fixes the date of the festivals and appeal for voluntary contributions from the community and entrust every member with particular duty in connection with the festivals. When death occurs in the village, the '*mei*' informs the whole village of the incident so that they can go and help in the house of the death, until cremation is over. The '*mei*' also tries to settle disputes regarding land, property, adultery, assult, etc. It may impose fines on the defaulters. The fine varies with the nature of the cases. It does not, however, exceed fifty rupees in any case. Disputes that cannot be settled by the '*mei*' are referred to the District Council.

'Mei-Pi'

The '*mei*' usually plays an important role in regulating the social, economic and religious life of the community though its power has been somewhat curbed with the establishment of the District Council and all important matters like theft, murder, disputes over land or any property are now dealt with by the above body. But the '*mei*' still occupies an important place in the social organization and still retains much of its traditional powers in deciding various matters affecting the community as a whole. It should be noted in this connection that some three or four or more villages usually unite together to constitute what is known as '*mei-pi*' or a great council. This '*me-pi*' consists only of '*Sarthes*' from respective villages and it is presided over by a head '*Sarthe*' selected from among themselves and who holds office for a period of one year and may be further reselected for another term depending upon the consensus of opinion of the *Sarthes.* Serious matters such as charges of adultery, attempts at life, theft, or menace of elephant or other wild animals in the neighbourhood are referred to the '*mei-pi*' if the matters are affecting a number of villages. Matters which cannot be settled by '*mei*' or '*mei-pi*' are referred to the District Council.

Risomar Terang

The bachelors' hall or 'risomar terang' where young boys sleep at night is still found among the Mikirs in the interior villages of the high hills. Usually the 'Sarthe' or headman of the village will instruct the bachelors of the village to construct a house where they could assemble and sleep at night. Such houses are generally constructed by all the young boys of the village under the supervision of the '*Sarthe*'. Membership to the '*risomar terang*' is open to all young boys in the village irrespective of *kurs* or *sub-kurs.* Generally a boy after attaining ten years of age ceases to sleep with his parents at night and comes to sleep along with other youths in the bachelors' hall. As soon as a man gets married, he ceases to be a member of the '*risomar terang*'. Other persons whether married or unmarried, who are not members of the risomar terang are not allowed to enter the hall. The members of 'risomar terang' dance and sing with the accompaniment of the drums or flutes during the festivals or even in ordinary days if they feel like it. The elder boys help the younger ones to learn to play the drums and the flute or dancing, etc. The members of 'risomar terang' co-operate with one another in a spirit of mutual understanding and co-operation. Among the Mikirs there is no particular method of gaining leadership or prestige, it all depends upon the villagers to select their leader who is efficient and who is capable of discharging his duties and in whom the villagers have good faith. The villages which are near the urban centres, particularly where the majority of the residents of the village are Christian there the young boys of the village arrange a club where they spend their leisure time playing games. Thus in villages which are having the urban influence the 'risomar terang' is replaced by the modern club houses.

E. CEREMONIES AND BELIEFS

God's Pleasure

The Mikirs believe that the birth of a child is in God's hand. Barrenness of a women is looked upon as God's displeasure over the couple and their matrimonial life may be terminated by the couples themselves; however, there are cases where couples have no issue yet they continue to live together happily until death tears them apart. Barrenness in women is believed to be caused by '*So-meme*'. A man or woman may remarry after separation but if, again remarriage does not bear any issue, they are either again separated or content to live together, if love prevails. Regarding miscarriage or still birth, it is believed that rites and ceremonies performed during marriage have not pleased the god, so they again perform, the same rites and ceremonies as are done during the marriage, after such incidents the blood of the animal, either fowl or goat, which is sacrificed depending upon the economic condition, is poured on a plaintain leaf and offered to gods while its meat is taken by the household, friends and relatives.

Male Child Preferred

Male children are preferred by them though also the female child is received warmly and with great joy in the family but they also believe that it depends on the will of God who may bestow on the family any sex He desires. Among the Mikirs no parental practice or ceremony is performed.

The delivery of the child takes place in the mother's own house with the help of the attendant (dhai). A pregnant woman is always treated with respect and is free from doing any heavy work. She is exempted from doing work in the field and also from carrying firewood. She can only clean the house and do her normal cooking work for the period of her pregnancy.

Delivery

There is no professional 'dhai' or midwife in the village. Such work is performed by old and experienced women who are given a place of honour at the naming ceremony of the child (Osamenkeir). When the child is about to be born the expectant mother is made to lie on a mat on the floor and the attendant 'dhai' keeps watch over her. Then everything is prepared for the delivery of the child, that is, a piece of cloth, sharp split bamboo, thread, etc. When the child is born, the 'dhai' cuts off the naval cord with a sharp split bamboo and a piece of cloth is tied around it. The clothes used by the woman and the instruments are washed, either by her husband or her close relative like her sister or mother after the delivery. The placenta is buried outside the house by the husband at a corner of the courtyard. There is no ceremonial segregation for the mother remains in bed for only three or four days after birth, by that time she recovers enough to resume her normal vocation. On the day following the birth, friends and relatives come to that house to greet both the child and the mother. The naming ceremony of a child known as *Osamenkeir* is performed after a week or so according to the discretion of the parent and also depending upon their economic condition. In the case of a male child a cock is killed while in the case of a female one hen is sacrificed as an offering to the god *Hemphu.* Neighbours and relatives from far and near are invited to the ceremony in which rice, meat and rice-beer (hor) are served to the guests. There is no hard and fast rules regarding naming of a child. Names are given to a child according to the will and liking of the parents, friends and relatives suggest names for the child which if the parents like may be retained for the child.

A Mikir child is suckled by its mother for about a year or so. On approaching the end of this period or when the child is about six months old some rice which has been masticated by the mother, is given to the baby. When the child's teething period is over and all the teeth have come out, normal diet, i.e. that which adults take is given. The mother generally carries the child at her back even while she is at work. The child is allowed to crawl on the floor all by itself until it learns to stand.

No Initiation Ceremony

Among Mikir there is no initiation ceremony. Those Mikirs who are educated and those who are living in the urban areas or those who are living near the urban centres take the help of the hospital during delivery and everything goes according to the routine of the hospital authorities.

Marriage

Monogamy is the rule among the Mikirs and polygamy though permissible is rare and no such case was recorded during the survey. Marriage within one's kur is not permissible and they strictly follow the rules laid down by their traditional customs, cross-cousin marriage is generally preferred. Marriage outside the community is looked down upon by the society and the parents out of disgrace, may drive the boy or girl away from the home. Seduction is rare and if at all it occurs, the girl's parents have to give their girl away in marriage.

Adultery

Illegitimacy and adultery is very rare. The case of adultery is usually tried by the village durbar and '*mei*' and the guilty pair are tried publicly thus subjecting them to the jeers and scorn of the neighbours. They are released only after the fine imposed by the council is paid. The amount of the fine usually varies Rs. 25 to 80, depending on the case and the decision of the '*mei*'. The accused is fined and the amount is given to the injured wife or husband. The husband of the erring wife may take her back but he may also refuse to do so even when they both have children and in such cases, the children stay with the mother after separation. In such cases the husband takes a gourd of rice beer, and present it to her parents and declares himself free, after which she has to return all presents given to her by the husband. After the divorce, both parties can remarry and the ceremony is usually performed in the same way as is done during the first marriage.

Teron and Ingti

The marriage between Teron and Ingti is not possible since they consider them to be of the same family but a boy of

Mikir sub-kur of Teron can marry an Ingti girl, this is the only exception since they do not regard this union as incestuous though such marriages are very rarely observed and the reason on the account for such restriction could not be ascertained apart from the above restriction any kur can marry any other kur other than its own.

Marriage Age

The average age of marriage for the boys is between 20-25 years and for girls 14 to 20 years. The table on the next page shows the age and marital status of the Mikirs according to 1961 Census of India, 1961; Assam, Part V-A, p. 243-43.

The table shows that in the age group 0-14 years, 101 females were found to be married, thus they are in the prescribed age limit for females while in the case of males none is found married in this age group. In the 0-14 years age-group which shows 101 females it does not give any clear indication whether the females belong to the latter year or in the earlier years of this age-group so it is difficult to decipher whether the child marriage is practised among them or not.

Kur

As a rule at the time of marriage negotiations between both the parties concerned keep in view the name of the principal Kur in making the decision. This is done so as to observe the strict rules of exogamy. The descent is patrilineal and marriage is patrilocal, that is, the wife goes to stay with her husband after marriage away from her own parents.

Akejoi

If a young man fancies a girl he informs his parents who go to this girl's parents and propose the marriage of their son with the girl, though such cases were not very frequent in the former time, which is also known as 'akejoi' type and which is now-a-days preferred by the Mikirs.

Akmon

The other type of marriage is of 'akmon' type that is marriage by contract or agreement, where the husband stays in

TABLE
Age and Marital Status of the Mikirs

	Total Population			Never Married		Married		Widowed		Divorced or Separated		Unspecified Status	
Age Group	*Person*	*Male*	*Female*	*Male*	*Female*	*Male*	*Female*	*Male*	*Female*	*Male*	*Female*	*Male*	*Female*
All Ages	121,082	62,827	58,255	33,372	32,780	27,311	21,716	1,914	3,384	137	245	93	67
0—14	55,046	25,767	29,297	25,736	29,187	—	101	—	1	—	4	31	4
15—44	45,417	24,893	20,524	7,369	3,513	16,668	16,243	724	591	96	127	44	50
45 and above	20,459	12,036	8,423	138	78	10,649	5,427	1,190	2,791	41	117	18	10
Age not stated	142	131	11	129	2	2	5	—	1	—	—	—	3

his father-in-law's house and work for him for one year or more and sometimes for life according to the term of agreement Such types of marriages are usually observed where the girl is an heiress or if she is the only daughter.

Suinkeba

The boy's parents will go the girl's parents' house and propose the marriage of their son with their daughter. If the girl's parents agree to the proposal, the boy's parents give a betrothal ring or bracelet to the girl. This is known as '*Suinkeba*' or formal engagement. Sometimes in lieu of the betrothal ring or bracelet, a gourd of rice beer is offered and if this is accepted the engagement is made. If one of the parties breaks the engagements, the village council (*mei*) has the power to fine the defaulting party. In the present day the fine usually ranges from Rs. 20 to 50. In the British days the fine was equivalent to 20 to 502 anna coins, when the fine is realized it goes to the injured party and the betrothal ring is returned to the boy's party. When the formal engagement is over then the day for marriage is fixed by both the parties according to their convenience. On the appointed day the parties prepare rice beer (hor) and husk some paddy to be served to the invited friends and relatives. If the bridgroom's party happens to pass through some villages on its way to the girl's house, the party has to give a gourd of rice beer to the village headman or Gaonbora through which it passes. When the party reaches the girl's father, one of its member hands over one gourd of rice beer to the girl's father. There is no particular person who should carry the gourd of rice beer to the girl's house, but usually an old man of the boy's side carry the gourd to the girl's house. Initiated by the girl's father an argument then ensues on the point of the coming of the bridgroom and the offering of the rice beer on the occasion. The bridgroom's father would reply saying that he has brought his son to work for his (bride's father) daughter and hence this offer for marriage. The bride's father would answer back and say that his daughter is unworthy of the groom because she can neither weave nor do any household chores. The groom's party would reply, we will teach her ourselves. Next the boy's father asks his wife to enquire of the girl whether she consents to marry the boy, for without her consent, the rice beer cannot be accepted. If the girl gives her consent, the rice beer is accepted and is drunk by both the fathers. It may be noted that even in this stage the girl can still back out from the marriage bargain, in which case she has to pay a fine (varying from Rs. 25 to 50) imposed by the *'mei'* and further she has to return all the present's given to her. This argument etc. which takes place at the evening or night symbolizes the marriage ceremony for that night. Then the bride will proceed to prepare a bed for the bridegroom in the guest room (kam), but if the groom feels embarrassed he may simply send one of his garments to be placed on the bridal bed as a symbol that he sleeps there.

God Hemphu

While in the next day morning a fowl or a goat (depending upon the economic condition of the girl's parents) is sacrificed by the girl's part to the god Hemphu. This is known as Vurke-matha and the sacrifice is done by an experienced man, a male relative of the girl's father, usually his brother. This ceremony usually takes about an hour. On the plantain leaf rice is kept at one side and when the animal is sacrificed, the blood of the animal is collected and is kept on the same plantain leaf on which rice has been kept. This is then offered to the god Hemphu and is placed outside the porch with the utterence of some chants. The ceremony is followed by a feast given by the bride's father at his residence. The meat of the animal sacrificed is eaten only by the couple while the friends and relatives are entertained with food and drink according to the ability of the girl's parents. After the feast the people are pronounced as husband and wife. The parents of the girl may accompany her and they can stay at the groom's house and return after 8 days, and during their stay they are entertained with food and drink. The husband with his wife stays in his parent's house until they are able to set up a house of their own. If the marriage is of 'akemon' type that is marriage by contract or agreement, the husband stays in his father-in-law's house and works for him for one year or more and sometimes even for life according to the terms of the agreement. The ceremonies in 'akemon' and 'akejoi' types of marriage do not differ in any way.

Remarriage is allowed

Remarriage of the widow is allowed. Divorce can also be granted when the girl runs to her home after marriage and refuses to go back to her husband. In this case the husband takes and gourd of rice beer to her parents and gives it and declares himself free of the matrimonial bond, after which the girl has to return all presents given to her by the husband. After the divorce both parties can remarry and the ceremony is performed in the same way as is done in the first marriage.

Death

The Mikirs believe that if a man does good deeds in this world, he may go safely to '*chom arong*' dead man's paradise after his death, otherwise a man may again be born in this hard ridden world and he cannot have a place in paradise after death unless he lives an honest live.

The Mikirs do not normally bury the dead. Cremation is the usual method of disposing of the dead and it is done after performance of some ceremonies. The cremation ground is always outside the village. However, the body of a still-born child or a child who dies soon after birth, or a mother who dies during child birth is buried without any ceremony. Victims of small pox or cholera are buried shortly after death, but the funeral rites for the deceased are performed later when the dead body or bones are dug up and cremated according to the convenience of the deceased's relatives. In the case of a person killed by a tiger, the body or his clothes, if found, are buried at some distance from the village because the tiger is supposed to visit the burial place. Such a person even if he has done good deeds during his life time, cannot gain admittance to '*chom arong*' or dead man's paradise unless elaborate funeral ceremonies are performed.

Natural Deaths

For natural deaths, the body is generally kept inside the house for one day after death, and if an elaborate ceremony is held the body may lie for as long as three to four days according to the convenience of the family of the deceased. The body lies in the '*kut*' and members of the same kur or clan, sit around the dead body though it may be noted that there is no bar for members of other kurs to come and sit around the body. Generally only the close relatives of the deceased sit around the dead body. The members of the family cook and eat in the '*kam*' (Guest Room). Friends and relatives flock to the deceased's house to console and sympathize with the bereaved family and pay their last respect to the deceased person. The body is washed and clothed by the old men and women of the family as the case may be.

The Bier

The bier (dola) for carrying the dead body is prepared by the young men of the village of the cremation ground. No particular kur or sub-kur or any relative of the deceased family is associated with the preparation of the dola. The bier is made of wood or hamboo for carrying the dead body and during the preparation of the bier, the men are entertained with 'hor' or rice beer by the relatives of the deceased. When every thing is ready, that is, when the body is washed and new clothes are put on, then the body is kept on the bier and tied to it and the old clothes of the dead person are hung over a bamboo pole called Jambuliathon.

Jambuliathon

The Jambuliathon is a special and decorated bamboo pole which cannot be made by any unauthorized person. Only the sub-kur Langue of Teron kur is authorized to prepare the pole by the Mikir society. The pole can be carried to the cremation ground by any relative or friend of the deceased. The bier as well as the pole is then taken in a procession to the cremation ground when the body is detached from the bier and placed on the funeral pyre. The platform (Thari) is a raised portion on the ground done by means of earth and stone, over which are piled logs of wood for burning the body. The pyre is lit by a male relative of the mother's side. While the pyre is burning nobody can weep except the professional weepers. They are the old women of the village irrespective of kur or sub-kur who usually mourn over the dead person saying couplets in praise of the dead person. When the dead body is thoroughly burnt, the mourning party (chorhe atcuses) returns home to partake of the feast given by the family of the deceased. On the following day the house is washed and cleaned after which the life becomes normal.

Chomangkan

After the cremation of the deceased, a death anniversary known as 'Chomangkan' is performed by the relatives of the deceased about a year or two later or more, depending upon the economic condition of the family concerned.

Chom Arong

It is believed that by performing such ceremonies the dead man's spirit may go safely to '*chom arong*' and everything that has been observed after the death is performed again with all the rites and practices connected with it. This ceremony is generally performed by the mother's or father's brother or in the absence of mother's or father's brother by any male relative from either the father's or mother's side. This ceremony generally lasts for three days and the family go to mourning and feast is given to friends and relatives. On the first day of the ceremony, the relatives proceed to the '*theri*' to pick up the charred bones of the dead person which are specially kept for this purpose and which are then wrapped inside a piece of white cloth. The wrapper containing the charred bones is then placed inside an effigy (arang) closely resembling the dead person which is specially prepared for the purpose. The effigy is made of sungrass and bamboo.

'Arang'

This dead man's figure '*arang*' is then taken inside the 'kut' and laid on the 'palm' (bed). The mourning party (cherhe atum) again goes into mourning as if the man has just died. Then young men from the village go to the '*theri*' to prepare a funeral pyre when the '*arang*' is to be burnt. On the second day a '*doha*' or dance ceremony is held in which young boys or girls are invited. The young boys under the leadership of one of them then called '*duhuide*' play with their drums and the girls under the leadership of one of the girls called '*ochepi*' dance in the courtyard of the house of the deceased.

Risomars

The dancers (*risomars*) usually dance in pairs forming a circle, the girls' taking hold of the boy's coat while the boys catch hold of the girls from the belt (*vankok*). After this performance, the '*risomars*' are given rice beer after which follows the shield dance, where only the men take part. The dance reaches a climax on the third day when the great dance '*Kanpi*' is performed. During this dance, one of the '*risomars*' who is an expert dancer goes inside the kut and dances before the dead man's effigy. He dances there for about half an hour after which he returns to the party of the dancers. Just before sunset the 'arang' is taken out of the kut and is tied to the 'dola'. Meanwhile the maternal uncle or any other male relative from the deceased's mother's side, who is known as '*nihu*' kills a pair of fowl after going around the dancing group. If the deceased was a married person, then a male relative from the father's side who is called '*ingjir arlo*' kills a goat. The cost of fowl and the goat killed by the respective persons is borne by the deceased's family. The heads of the animals killed are thrown to the '*risomars*' who receive them as a mark of respect. The heads of the animals killed are then cooked and later eaten by them. The rest of the meat is kept to be feasted by those who remain after the burial. The '*arang*' is then taken to '*theri*' and all the people go in a procession. One of the '*risomars*' carry the bamboo post '*Jambuliathon*' stuck with the dead man's clothes and walk in front keeping step to the beating of the drums.

The follows a group of '*risomars*' and the deceased's male relatives who carry the *arang*. Next come other relatives and friends. On the arrival at the *theri* the *arang* is united and placed on the funeral *pyre*. The pyre is lit by a male relative of the mother's side and at the same time the professional weeper (charhe atum) mourn over his death, recall his past life and pray to gods (arnum atum), to guide the deceased on his way to '*chom arang*' without hindrance on the journey. Then a dance follows where the *risomars* usually dance in pairs forming a circle, the girls taking hold of the boys' coats while the boys catch hold of the girls' from the belt (Vankok). After the dance all return home. When the party reaches home, a feast is given by the members of the deceased's family in the deceased's house.

On the following day the house is washed and cleaned and the life becomes normal.

Christian Mikirs

The Christian Mikirs who are in fairly good numbers (12,443 persons in 1961 Census) belong to the Baptist Church and live their life according to the tenets of Christianity. The ceremonies followed and performed by non-Christians whether in respect of birth, marriage or death are not at all followed and performed by Christian section of the population.

Among the Christian Mikirs, in the case of a child birth though delivery may be performed by a local dhai as in cases of non-Christians, no other ceremonies are performed. Baptism or the naming ceremony of the child according to the Christian rites are performed when the child is one month old or so. The child is taken to the church and there the pastor pronounces the name of the child already selected by the parents and blesses the child. The parents may give a feast at their house with rice and meat or tea to friends and relatives, so as to honour the baptism ceremony of their child.

Marriage of Christian Mikirs

Regarding marriage, the boys and girls have free choice to select their mate and when the boys and the girls have decided to marry, they will inform their parents who settle the marriage negotiations. The boy's parents may go to the girl's parents and make an offer for marriage. If the girl's parents accept the offer, the marriage is fixed and settled. If the offer is rejected, the boy's parents will make an offer to another girl and marriage will be settled by mutual consent and agreement of both the parties. Before marriage is to be finally settled the boy accompanying his father and his relatives will go to the girl's house and there the pastor of the local church will make the formal engagement and fix the date of the marriage. The marriage ceremony is performed according to the Christian rites in the church by the pastor, who pronounces them as husband and wife, after both of them make an oath to live and to have each other 'from now and forever'. The marriage ceremony is always marked by a big feast in the girl's house in which rice and pork are generally served to the invitees. On the following day the husband will take his newly wedded wife to his own house and there they start life as husband and wife.

Deaths among The Christian Mikirs

As regards to death among the Christian Mikirs, the corpse is not cremated but is buried instead. When a person dies, the church bell rings and thus announces the death of a person. The dead body may be inside the house for 2 or 3 days according to the wishes of the deceased's relatives, during this period neighbours, friends and relatives come to the bereaved family to share their sorrow and to console and comfort them. The young men of the village prepare the Coffin and dig the grave. The burial ceremony according to Christian rites generally takes place before the coffin is lowered down in the grave after that all who accompany the deceased's coffin to the grave will sing a hymn and say a prayer for the departed soul. A wooden cross is generally erected over the grave bearing the name and the date of birth and death of the deceased. In some cases stone inscriptions are erected over the grave.

F. FAMILY AND COMMUNITY RELATIONSHIP

Nuclear Family

The Mikir family is of simple type that is a nuclear family consisting of husband, wife and unmarried children. The joint family that is, where married children live along with their parents, if found, is only for a short period, because according to their usual practice the married children usually set up a house of their own, but presently there is no such compulsion particularly among those who are living near the urban centres, where joint family is not uncommon due to the economic pressure. The size of the family (nuclear family) usually consists of 4-6 members, sometimes very large families, with more than 8-9 members, are not very infrequent.

Generally the father is the sole authority in the family. In the absence of the father the eldest son, if an adult, shoulder the responsibility and takes full charge of the family. The mother is the mistress of the house next to the father and is much respected. Both men and women enjoy equal status in the family as well as in their society save for the inheritance of property where the son is the heir.

Patrilineal

The Mikir society is patrilineal and the inheritance also follows the same line. On the death of the father, the eldest son if unmarried, takes over the responsibility of the family and also inherits the property, otherwise the responsibility of the family falls on the younger son. Generally the father divides and allots the property among his sons during his lifetime giving the eldest one the biggest share, this is because he has to take the sole responsibility after the death of his father. In case there is any dislike of the parents with the eldest son then the younger son inherits the property and also shoulders the responsibility of the family after the death of the father. Daughters have no claim at all to the father's peoperty but they share the property of their mother who distributes her property like clothes, ornaments equally among her daughters, during her lifetime. Immovable property like land is distributed equally among sons during the father's lifetime. In case any dispute may arise in this regard, the dispute is referred to the mei (village durbar) whose decision over the matter is always taken as final by the parties concerned. Such cases are, however, rare and the sons are generally well satisfied with what they get according to the provisions of the will made by the father. In case the father does not have any male issue, his property passes to his male relatives, generally to his brothers, who divide and distribute the property equally among themselves and under no circumstances shall his daughters inherit the father's property. It is the duty of the sons or the male relatives to look after the well being of the daughters of the deceased, who are looked after in this manner as they are unmarried. Similarly, the wife of the deceased is also cared for as long as she stays a widow. If she remarries she automatically looses her claim. The laws of inheritance are governed according to the age-old customs and the community never dream of seeking a change or upsetting the order of the things.

Possibly the earliest account regarding the sub-divisions of the tribe is given in the Census report of Assam 1818 (p. 81) as follows:

Divided into Tribes

"The Mikirs are divided into three tribes, namely, Chinton, Ronghang, and Amri where the first ranks higher than the third, because Amri excused itself from sending a man on the dangerous embassy to the Ahom king in Sibsagar, when a representative was required from each tribe. Hence Amri is excluded from sharing the liquor at a sacrifice, and is held in contempt by the western Mikirs especially. These latter are fourth tribe called Dumrali by the Mikirs and Tholua by the Assamese and from the fact of their acting as interpreters to the embassy, we may presume that they had been settled in the Assam valley for sometime. All four tribes, as it seems have the same divisions, a phoides, within each of which marriage is interdicted."

Allen (1905) does not subscribe to the views expressed in the report of the Census of Assam 1881. According to him they are divided into four tribes Chintong, Ronghang, Amri and Dumrali and these tribes are again sub-divided into various exogamous groups.

Sub-groups

It may be mentioned that in both the earlier account the authors have taken the sub-groups as tribes, but actually they are the sub-groups of the parent tribe, which are distinguished on the basis of geographical areas. Generally the hill Mikirs designate the plains Mikir (i.e. Mikirs staying in Nowgong, Kamrup, Darrang and Sibsagar) as Dumrali, while the plains Mikirs call the hill Mikirs as Chintong and Ronghang, but the distinction between Chintong and Ronghang could not be ascertained since the present day Mikirs (of N.C. Hills) are not very sure as to which geographical area represents Chintong and Ronghang. These division of the tribe based on the geographical areas were made centuries back and the names of the divisions are simply running down through generations

The Mikirs are divided into four endogamous groups namely, Chintong, Ronghang, Amri and Dumrali and these are again sub-divided into various exogamous groups or 'kurs'. It is to be noted that all these four groups are sub-divisions of the parent tribe based on geographical divisions and do not form separate entities.

According to Pakrashi (1953) the Kurs are the exogamous groups of the Mikirs and sub-kurs are the parts of the larger groups that is, Kurs. The sub-kurs are the parts of, in number under each principal Kur. According to him each sub-division or sub-Kur is distinguished by a special sub-name attached to the name of the original Kur and there is no precise rule in adding a sub-name. Thus it is difficult to define sub-Kurs except as special sub-names attached to the names of Kurs. The Kurs can be identified through the sub-names or sub-Kurs attached to it.

Pakrashi (1953) has given a comparative account of the Kurs and Sub-Kurs. According to Pakrashi (1953) the Mikirs have the following main exogamous groups of Kurs as E-jang, Timung, Ingti, Terang and Teron. A few names of the sub-Kurs under the different Kurs as collected by the different workers Stack, Moore, Dundas and Pakrashi are given below: (cf. Pakrashi : 1953) for reference:

	Stack	*Moore*	*Dundas*	*Pakrashi*
Kurs	Lekthe	E-jang	Inghi	E-Jang
Sub-kurs	Hanse	Hanse	Hanse	Hanse
	Tutso	Tutso	Tutso	Tutso
	Bongrung	Bongrung	Bongrung	Bongrung
	Kramsa	Kramsa	Kramsa	Kramsa
		Rongpi	Rongpi	Rongpi
		Ronghang	Ronghang	Ronghang
		Lekthe	Lekthe	Lekthe
		Rongchehon	Inghi	Inghi
		Keap		Keap

Exogamous Groups

Thus the Mikirs are divided into 5 main exogamous groups or kurs (Pakrashi 1953). It is evident from the list of the Kurs and sub-Kurs that the information regarding the sub-Kurs under the Kurs presents some difficulty. As E-jang exogamous group has been represented by Stack as Lekthe, which appears to be on the other hand as sub-Kur of E-jang. Lyall stated that the Lekthe exogamous group is said to have been the military clan (cf. Pakrashi 1953) which could not be confirmed by Pakrashi. According to Lyall (cf. Pakrashi 1953) the people belonging to Timung exogamous group represented no special status like that of the Lekthe people.

Moore and Dundas referred to the Ingti exogamous group as Ni-e and Kather respectively.

According to Pakrashi (1953) Ingti Kur is the superior exogamous group according to he origin of all Kurs of the Mikir. According to Lyall (cf. Pakrashi 1953), Ingti is said to have been in former times the priestly class. The exogamous group Terang as stated by Stack and Pakrashi has been stated by Moore and Dundas as Lo-e and Be respectively. According to Stack, the Terang people claimed the dignity of the priestly clan but the informants of Pakrashi did not support the view of Stack, but they said on the other hand, that Tarang might come next to Ingti Kur in status among the Mikirs.

The absence of Teron exogamous group from Stack's report suggests that he might have taken Teron and Tirang to be the same.

Pakrashi (1953) gave the following explanation which might explain the difficulties underlying the precise enumeration of sub-Kurs or Kurs. As Mikirs are always on the lookout for virgin sites where new rotation of jhuming can be performed, the leader of a new settlement might adopt, as a mark of distinction, a new name as a suffix to the main Kur name which he and his family members and followers might adopt. Thus this new community under a new head man might later on be distinguished from the other settlements by the new suffix adopted to the original Kur name. The name of the sub-Kur might in other words have been adopted only as a mark of distinction, though retaining the full identity and alliance of the members of the newly formed sub-Kur with the corresponding Kur.

Kur And Sub-Kur

Each principal 'Kur' is distinguished by a sub-Kur and the formation of any 'sub-Kur' in no way interferes with the intrinsic relation between the main Kur and its sub-divisions. There is no precise rule in adding a sub-Kur, and these sub-names refer in most cases to a certain local individual or objects, e.g., Dera—a place name; kiling—a river; Tesang—bechelor's house; Patok—a village headman, etc. The members of the sub-Kurs never disregard one another, for they all belong to the same Kur irrespective of the apparent difference in the names of the sub-Kurs.

Shri Lamkam Teron (1966) in his book 'Mikir Jana Jati' has given the list of kurs and sub-kurs. A few names are given below:

I. Kur Teron

Sub-Kurs

1. Kongat
2. Lange
3. Milik
4. Aai
5. Chirung aru
6. Trap

II. Kur-Inghi

Sub-Kurs

1. Inghi
2. Rongpi
3. Ronghang
4. Hansey
5. Tiso
6. Rongpi chinthoog
7. Rongi amri
8. Rongpi rongnang
9. Rongpi lindok
10. Rongpi
11. Rongchechon
12. Ronghi
13. Rong-o
14. Ronghanglindok
15. Ke-ap
16. Lekthe
17. Kebong
18. Kete
19. Durong
20. Kelum
21. Tisorongling
22. Tisorongphu
23. Tisorongche-cho
24. Tisorongchitim
25. Tisomotho

III. Kur-Timung

Sub-kurs

1. Phengcho langteroi
2. Nok bara
3. Muchophi
4. Kling rongphar
5. Rongphar phura
6. Sengnot

7. Timung rongpi
8. Tokbi dera
9. Timungkiling
10. Chalut senot
11. Kokbi chintkong
12. Tokbi ronghangaro
13. Rongpharonghang
14. Phangcho-ingnara
15. Singnar-nuchiki
16. Nongdu
17. Nonglada
18. Phangcho Voraru

Social Organization

In the social organization of the Mikirs each Patrilineal-patrilocal group is exogamous. The Mikirs always give unquestionable importance to the principal Kurs at the time of marriage negotiations. Pakrashi (1952) subscribed to other remarks made by Stack that the children are counted to their father's Kurs, and cannot marry within it. They may, however, marry their first cousins on the mother's side, and indeed this appears to have been formerly the most usual match." There is no preference for any Kur in marriage save that the Kur must marry outside its own Kur. Formerly when the Mikirs lived in the Khasi hills, intermarriage with Lalungs though permissible was not preferred and was looked down by the Mikir community.

If a Lalung boy marries a Mikir girl, then the children will get the litle of the Mikir sub-Kur name after the mother, while, if a Mikir boy marries a Lalung girl, the children will get the sub-Kur name of the Mikir father. Thus in both the cases the Mikir sub-Kur name will be retained by the children. This is because the Lalung is a matriarchal community while Mikir is a patriarchal community. Presently such marriages are very rare. There is no particular association of Kurs with particular occupation, though, the 'Senar', a sub-Kur of Timung and the 'milik' a sub-Kur of Teron generally practise blacksmithy, also there is no social or economic distinction among the Kurs. There is also no restriction as regards to the taking of food among the Kurs and sub-Kurs.

Kinship

Among the Mikirs the kinship terms express certain obligations, privileges, rights, etc. and these terms are inherently dependent upon the very superstructure of the society. A study of the Mikir kinship terms clearly reveals certain traits. Lyall (cf. Pakrashi, 1955) noted the following facts:

(i) Most of the names are the same for both sexes and that the sexes are distinguished only by words, as pointed in the index for the males and the females.

(ii) Again, the same words appear to be used in different sense, as ong is maternal uncle but ong-so is the wife's brother; Osa is both nephew (sister's son) and son-in law. Te is sister but tepi is brother's wife. Simlarly, Kor is sister (or brother), Korpi is wife's sister, Korpo sister's husband and so on.

(iii) It will be observed that brothers and sisters and brothers-in-law and sisters-in-law use different form of address when speaking of their relationship.

Pakrashi (1955) noted that among the Arlengs the kinship terms are distinguished with regards to seniority and juniority in age between the sibings.

(iv) In general usage, qualifying terms like ik, mu and so are very frequently used to express distinct sense of seniority or otherwise in age. These words mean elder, younger and little respectively in the kinship terms of the Mikirs.

(v) The female speaker always denotes her own brother chekle and sister as te in contrast to the Kor and Korte which are commonly used.

(vi) Ingjir-pi denotes elder sister but this usage is allowed on the part of the male speaker only.

(vii) Osa and osopi commonly denote a boy and a girl, yet they address the sons and daughters by the terms Sopo and Sopi respectively and, moreover, the speaker adds the generative prefix to sopo and sopi in order to emphasize his or her own sons and daughters. Among Mikirs ne means 'my' or 'our'.

Pakrashi (1955) did not attempt to examine to what extent socio-economic and psychological factors have acted upon the

Mikir Kinship system in building up the present structure and also how kinship terms are changing through contact with the Assamese speaking people.

Relation among the Different Segments of the Community

It has been stated earlier that Mikir tribe as a whole is divided into four sections namely, Chintong, Ronghang, Amri and Dumrali and these are again sub-divided into various exogamous Kurs which are further sub-divided into sub-Kurs which vary greatly in number under each principal Kur. The four sections of the Mikirs that is Chintong, Ronghang, Amri and Dumrali are the geographical divisions of the tribe. Thus Dumrali is the plains Mikirs while Chintong, Ronghang and Amri are the Hills Mikirs. The exact geographical division of Chintong, Ronghang and Amri is quite obscure.

Chintong, Ronghang, Amri and Dumrali are said to have their own traditional status or rank. It was said that Chintong and Ronghang rank higher than Amri socially, simply because of the fact that the Amris excused themselves from sending a representative on the fatal mission to the Ahom in Raha when a representative was required from each of the four divisions Dumralis acted as interpretors to the embassy and were therefore allowed to have a share of the liquor whereas Amris were excluded from sharing the liquor since they excused themselves from sending a representative.

In the ancient times there might have been some social distinction among these groups as evidenced from the earlier account given but presently there is no social distinction among the Mikirs as to high and low classes and all Kurs are socially equal. In former times, however, it was reported that each Kur occupied its traditional rank in society. Thus Ingti is said to have been the priestly clan; Terang was also the priestly clan but occupied a lower rank, Lekthe a sub-Kur is said to have been the military clan. Timung and Teron represented the rest of the people.

Jealousy and suspicion occasionally arise among the Kurs and when there is a dispute on land between persons of two different Kurs, the members on each side would appear as partisans and sometimes foment to discord. But generally such discords are temporary and are appeased by the members of the 'mei'.

Meetings are sometimes held between the members of the Kur in which the well being of the Kur is more concerned than the welfare of the community as a whole. The different Kurs come together and unite only in cases which affect the village or the whole community as such. The observance of religious rites and other ceremonies are performed in a spirit of mutual understanding and co-operation.

The Christian and non-Christian sections of the population are living in perfect amity and there are no tensions among them. They help one another in times and work hand in hand in their fields. During festivals and other religious ceremonies they invite one another to the party without any distinction. In short, the relations among the different segments of the community is healthy and cordial.

Inter-Community Relationship

The Mikirs who are living in the urban areas may engage the services of barbers and washermen, tailors, and shoemakers from other communities, but the Mikirs who are far away from the urban centres never employ the services of such persons from other communities except their own. Untouchability is absent and they do not forbid any one who belongs to another community to interdine with them or take water from the same well. Inter-marriage with communities other than their own, though not at all forbidden is not very much approved by the society. One such case has been found in Dokmoka, about 52 miles from Diphu where a Mikir boy has married a Boro Kachari girl and they are staying within the Mikir village and they have not been socially boycotted by the Mikirs.

Tribal Ways of Life

The Mikirs who are living in the hills are more attached to their tribal ways of life than those living in the plains. The Mikirs who are living in the plains are surrounded by Assamese and Bengali neighbours and their long experience and steady contact with them has resulted in certain changes in their customs and manners as compared to the Hill Mikirs. Those

Mikirs who are living in the hills have no prejudices with regard to food but the plains Mikirs would never eat the flesh of a cow or buffalo; possibly these are the effects of contact with Assamese and Bengali neighbours. As early as 1891, Mr. Baker (Assam Census Report 1891) noticed a strong leaning amongst the Mikirs to Hinduism. Their dress has also been influenced by their neighbours, so that the Mikir males of the plains have now-a-days substituted their loin cloth (rikong) for a dhoti and their waist-coat (choi) for a long shirt, while those in the hills retain much of their traditional dress. As regards to occupation, a change from jhuming to wet cultivation is seen among those who live in the plains whereas those in the hills still attach greater importance to jhuming, since even if they are away of it they are not in a position to follow the wet system due to condition of the terrain. Those Mikirs who are in the plains and near the urban centres are more in advance than their brothers in the hills, as regards to education. This may not be due to the much educational facilities given to the plains men rather it may be the effect of their contact with the neighbouring communities, that is, Assamese and Bengalees. Also another factor is the conservative outlook of the hill Mikirs. Mikirs are rather reluctant to accept the change of their social milieu, while their brothers in the plains are apt to adopt change according to the needs of the time.

G. DWELLING, DRESS AND FOOD

Dwelling

The Mikirs generally reside in clearing patches of the forests in the hills and their villages are always set up within easy reach of the plot which they are actually cultivating. Villages are always kept apart from one another in isolated blocks for the convenience of cultivation. The main factros which determine the location of a Mikir village is the nearness to the cultivating plots and to the source of water. Even in compact village the arrangement of houses are dispersed in such a manner so as to provide space for rearing of livestocks and for the Kitchen garden of each of the houses. There is no kurwise or sub-kurwise clustering of houses and they are built according to the convenience of the individual. Houses are generally large, and the shape of the house looks rectangular and the structure as a whole is raised about 3 or 4 feet from the ground supported by stout wooden posts. The whole structure of the house including side walls is made up of split bamboo finely woven and knitted together so firmly that no mud plastering of the short is necessary. But now many well-to-do families, particularly those who are living in the urban areas have their houses mud-plastered. The roof of the house has slopes on either side attached with sungrass which is generally replaced after four or five years, when it gets rotten or damaged by natural forces. The floor of the house is covered with knitted bamboo strips which are fastened at each end to the posts which support the roof of the house. The inside of the house is dark except for the scanty light that creeps in through the openings in the split bamboo wall. Generally there is no window or chimney, the main door and the tiny slits in the bamboo walls serve as a source of ventilation. Usually the house is divided lengthwise by a partition into two or three rooms with one portion on one side, these types of houses are usually observed in high hills. In the urban areas the 'L' pattern of the house is preferred. The 'L' shape pattern of the house which is observed in urban areas consists of a room meant for outsiders or guests known as 'Kam' which is usually on the right-hand side when one enters into it (left-hand side ones are also not very unfrequent) and where the only door into the house leads to it and the other which is 'kut' is meant for the family.

Kam

The 'kam' is further divided into two by a partition and the outer portion of the kam opens to the open space in between the kam and the kut. The hearth is placed in the outer part of the kam almost touching the wall. The household goods are also kept at the one corner of the kam. In the 'kut' a kind of platform called 'tobung' is raised about 2 feet high above the floor and runs along the wall. The 'tobung' serves as a sleeping place for the members of the family. There is a fire place called 'mehip' made of three upright stones laying at the back of the 'kut' and by the side of the fire place there is another kind of platform called 'damtak' which is also attached to the wall, where the heads of the family, that is the father and the mother sleep. In this room (kut) also stands a paddy receptacle (ingkro) made of bamboo. Behind the fire place (mehip) there is a place called 'dambuk' which is attached to the 'damtak' where the young and unmarried girls sleep. The front porch is known as 'hongkup' in which are kept the loin loom, firewood, baskets, mortar, pestle, and daos etc.

Household Equipments

Hak	Basket made of bamboo for carrying paddy and other goods.
Khailum	Basket with cover for keeping valuables, having two layesr—upper made of cane and lower layer made of bamboo.
Linkhoi	Wooden pot for mailling sesame.
Lamgbong	Direct gourd used for keeping water.
Lamhar	Small wooden pot.
Sohak	Wooden ladel, big size, generally used for distribution of rice.
Anthong	Wooden saucepan for keeping boiled rice.
Kindor	Bamboo basket used for keeping rice at the time of worship.
Ington	Bamboo basket for keeping food stuff.
Burupso	Small cup like thing made of bamboo for keeping dried chilli.
Sae	An equipment made of bamboo like seive, used for refining rice beer.
Harbong	Small dried gourd for offering rice beer.
Longpongsi	Bamboo pipe used for bringing water.
Long-Lengpong	Wooden paddy husking equipment along with its wooden stick.
Therang	Loin loom along with its accessories.

Equipments Connected with Economic Pursuit

1. Krue (Hoe for jhum).
2. Nepak (Dao).
3. Nahirangso (sickle).
4. Nakanti (Dao-differs from the former one in structure).

5 Song (War shield made of thinocerf's skin).
6. Nok (War sword).
7. Thai (Bow and arrow)
8. Sir (Hunting spear)
9. Paron (An implement for fishing, made of bamboo, like basket).
10. Choklet (Another implement for fishing, made of bamboo)

Musical Instruments

1. Cheng (Big drum).
2. Chengbruk (Very small size drum like Dambru).
3. Muri (Wooden flute).
4. Pangsi (Bamboo flute).

Household goods are of simple variety, meant for purpose of utility rather than for decoration. A block of wood is enough to serve as stool (inghoi) to sit on. There are baskets of various shapes and sizes and bearing different names for different uses. They are generally used as cupboards for storing paddy, clothes, ornaments and other articles of daily use. Bamboo joints each with a node on one end an opening on the other are used for carrying water and also for keeping powdered chillies, salt, fat of animals, rice beer and other things. Utensils of brass and aluminium are also used. Vessels of brass and pitchers of kerosene tins are also used for storing water. Enamel plates and mugs are also among the utensils possessed by them.

Dress

The dress of both males and females is simple. The males commonly put on a piece of cloth known as 'rikhong' which is wrapped round the loin. Sometimes on their heads they wear turbans called 'poho'. Adult males also use a waist coat called 'choi' with a long fringe which covers the buttocks and comes round in front. An endi cloth called 'peingki' is also used by them during the cold season. Generally boys do not put on 'choi' or 'poho' but will sometimes put on 'rikong' along with shirt or with shirts and pants. In some cases adults also use shirts, pants and coats, particularly those who are living near the urban centres. Those who are living in town always wear the European dress, which has become the fashion. Women put on a petticoat known as 'peni' which is fastened by a kind of belt round the waist, sometimes with an ornamental girdle of silver coins or usually adorned with fingures of flowers woven on cloth called 'wamkok' or in some cases with simply a belt made of cotton cloth. Another cloth known as 'pekok' or 'jiso' is used to cover the upper part of the body which is tied under the arms and drawn tight over the breast. Over and above, these cloths one or two pieces of cloth 'jiso' are hung on either side of the shoulders covering the breast. The use of frocks, skirts or blouses are also not very uncommon among the young girls.

Long Hair

Women generally keep long hair and it is straight and tied in a knot (chubi) behind the head. Males cut their hair short and seldom care to comb their hair, if at all they do, they comb in flat. Sometimes old men keep long hair and tie it in a knot at the back of the head just as in the case of women (chubi). Nails are trimmed with a knife and teeth are cleaned with a piece of jungle tree usually of Neem or Mangoes in the interior villages, but those who are living in the urban centres or not far away from the urban centres use the modern paste or tooth powder for cleaning the teeth. Footwear is seldom used both among the males and the females particularly in the villages away from the urban centres. The Mikirs who are living in the urban centres particularly those who are office goers use modern footwear.

On ceremonial occasions both males and females will generally put on their traditional dress except in a few cases, especially among the youths who are much influenced by the urban ways of life. The priest (gursur) put on the common dress i.e. 'rikong' and 'choi' in normal occasions, but on ceremonial occasions he will put on a dress called 'rikong sales' meaning 'holy dress' which is wrapped around the loin. He also puts on 'choi' on such occasions.

Ornaments

The Mikirs are very fond of ornaments. Women of post pubertal age and particularly those who are married put on a characteristic silver ornament known as 'nothangpi'. The ornament is made of silver and consists of three parts, the central shaft, the front part and the rear part. The front and the rear part of the ornament lies in front and behind the perforated ear lobe respectively. The ornament is a short of cylindrical ringed structure with spiral ridges around it outside. The young girls wear 'Norik' which is much like 'nothangpi' but only it is small in size. It is made of silver and is inserted into the lobe of the ear. Grown up men particularly those who are living in the villages wear 'norik' or earrings of gold and silver suspended from the lobes of the ear. Women also wear necklaces of beads known as 'lek' and threads of the necklaces are made of silver. The 'lek' are of two types. Lek pengkhra where the thread of the silver is round and Lek ruve where flat plate of silver thread is used. Finger ring or 'urnam' and bracelets or 'rol' both of either gold or silver are worn by women irrespective of age. Another form of urnam, is worn by males in general. All these ornaments used by them are either obtained from the Khasi smiths, or they are purchased from the local markets. The use of either gold or silver ornaments depend mostly on the economic status of the household.

Tatoo

Tatoo or 'duk' is practised by grown up women only. After attaining puberty they usually draw a perpendicular line of indigo colour most generally along the middle of the forehead, down the nose to the upper lip and chin. This is done only to ward away the evil eyes. No other part of the body is tatooed except the face.

Staple Food

Their staple food is rice and they eat all kinds of meat with the exception of beef and buffalo. Meat is taken either roasted or cooked after it is throughly dried over the fire. Sometimes meat is also dried in the sun. Dry fish is most preferable which they store in small baskets. The following are the common vegetables and fruits and spices which they usually take:

Pumpkin	Benghom

Brinjal	Hepi
Potato	Phurui
Carrot	Mula
Tomato	Bokbok
Watermelon	Thoithe
Yam	Hon
Oil Seeds	Nempo
Chilli	Birik
Mustard	Hanjang
Sugarcane	Nok
Jackfruit	Jangphong
Mango	Tharve
Ginger	Hanso
Onion	Harsum keer

All the members of the family eat together in the same house. Meal is generally taken three times a day, in the morning, at the afternoon and in the evening. At every meal a small quantity of good is usually set aside as an offering (Kathok) to the gods.

Hor

Rice beer or 'hor' is their favourite drink. There are three kinds of rice beer, namely 'arak' which is the strongest variety, 'thap' medium in strength and 'hor' which is mild and ideal for a common family drink. The latter one is their favourite drink and figures prominently in the observance of their ceremonies and festivals. Outsiders and strangers are also offered with it for the sake of courtesy. Generally the adult males smoke a small tobacco pipe (thenghpong). Tobacco in their tonge is known as Duma. Betelnut (kore) and pan leaf (bikon) are consumed by both sexes.

Musical Instrument

The name of some of the Mikir musical instruments are also given below. These musical instruments are indigenous. The most important instrument is the drum which shows variety of size and shape.

Cheng	Big drum

Cheng bruk	Very small sized drum like Dambru
Chengso-so	A musical instrument made of brass metal
Muri	Wooden flute
Pangsi	Bamboo flute
Chang chickli	Big drum
Thekeleachang	Small drum
Achang	A kind of Bina

Recording of Time

The Mikirs generally record the end of the night with the cock's crow which they call 'wokuthoni' or 'wokuththom' meaning the time between one and two or three times of cock's crow. When going on a journey the time is generally recorded by the eating of a piece of betelnut which generally takes fifteen minutes for each piece. This is only in villages where watches are an uncommon sight among the villagers. Those who are living in the urban areas, particularly office goers are found to be having clocks. In interior villages, 'space' or 'adak' is referred to as between the earth and the sky called sining pen longle adak. Generally short distances are expressed in terms of Tharlon (a bamboo pole about 12′ length) expressed as so many Tharlons. Long distances are indicated by the distance of a hill in sight, 'inglong' (hill), 'isi-inglong' (one hill), 'hini khelo' (two hill distance), meaning one hill or two hill distance. Generally they measure the weight through the medium of 'holon', a kind of basket, 'hag' a big size basket and 'mantung'—a cloth bag which is prepared from Mikir bed-sheet.

H. VILLAGE LIFE AND RECREATION

Sanitation

Houses in Mikir villages are not compact, this is because each house requires a large open space for the sheds for the domestic animals and for homestead gardens. Generally pigs, goats, poultry and even buffaloes are kept either below the plinth of their 'Chang' houses which are very common in the Mikir villages, while in the urban areas the domestic animals are kept in space just adjacent to their houses. Owing to the keeping of their domestic animals very close to their houses, the areas surrounding the houses always remain very dirty and stinky and rubbish is thrown all around the house as there is no particular space outside the house for throwing the rubbish. Pigs and dogs act as scavengers although their own excreta make the whole atmosphere foul smelling but the people are used to such things and they seem to be not worried about it. Sanitation in the real sense of the term is totally absent in the Mikir villages. There is no drainage system and foul water finds its way to the village streets and then it serves as a water pool for domesticated animals.

Lavatory

There is no lavatory or latrine. Only nearby jungle offers a good place for the evacuation of bowels where dogs and pigs would swarm for their food and serve as scavengers. The Mikirs who are living in the rural areas are having lavatory or latrine at one corner of their house away from the main rooms. The village people do not care to clean their clothes and generally they will do so only on occasions like festivals or other ceremonies. Usually they put on the same clothes every day until it is in such a condition that it cannot be worn by the person any more due to its torn condition. They will only wet their feet and face to soothe away their fatigue and weariness after coming from their hard days' work in the fields. Cooking utensils and dishes are washed after every meal. Their houses are dark and one cannot see what is inside unless he is accustomed to the darkness. Doorways and in some cases windows or the opening in the walls serve as sources of ventilation and as there is no chimney the smoke is like a cloud in the ceiling of the house until it is forced by the wind to come from outside through some opening.

Diseases and Medicine

The common diseases are dysentry, exzema, constipation, malaria, boils and other skin diseases. Some of the Mikir names for the common diseases are as follows:

Dysentry	Pokpari
Small Pox	Piamir or Arnum
Cholera	Mavur or Toman
General Fever	Phukeso

In the villages for away from the urban centres they do not much rely on the modern medical facilities but rely on their indigenous medical herbs with which they treat all kinds of diseases. There is no particular medicinemen but the old and experienced persons, generally the priests, give medicine to the diseased person. The villages near the urban centres are using the modern medicines, while in the interior villages where the facilities of the modern medicines are not available, they use the indigenous medicine and worship the god, thinking that the disease is because the god is annoyed with them. After observing the symptom (deuri) of the disease, the priest suggests the relatives of the diseased, whom to propitiate for the particular disease. Then the illness of a person is taken to be the cause of evil spirits and the priest or gurusur is consulted. It is the gurusur who decides what kind of illness the person falls victim to and decides what sort of sacrifice would be performed to appease the spirits and also the number of animals or birds to be sacrificed. It is only when they fail to cure the disease by sacrifices to the spirits which caused them that, they resort to the modern medicine. Even if the town is far away from the village, they have to go to the town to collect the medicine for the diseased person.

Recreation

Mikir men and women work together in their fields from morning until the sun sets and then relax themselves only after coming from the fields, they remove the fatigue of the day's work by sitting around the hearth snapping stories and gossiping about his fields and crops, and the prospects of the coming harvest. When they meet with friends and relatives the inevitable subject of crops always comes up for discussion amongst them apart from some family matters or other matters. Though they have to undergo the rigours of nature which make their life hard yet their hearts are full with hope and joy and they are satisfied with what they have. Sometime they sing in chorus while working in the fields or sing simple melodies while thrashing the crops. It seems to dispel fatigue and weariness from both body and mind. They are the children of the nature and find music in the winds, streams and woods which fill their mind with much delight.

Hide and seek

Generally boys and girls play not many games, what they play are some of the modern games borrowed from the outside, generally learned through their school mates. Hide and Seek is played by both boys and girls. In this game a seeker will search the party of the boys and girls who are hiding in some secret place and the one who is caught while hiding by the seeker, will play the part of the seeker, thus in this way it goes on as long as the participants of this game wants it to.

Foot Ball

Foot ball is a favourite game among the boys and sometimes teams are formed among themselves for friendly matches, sometimes they take part in tournaments for a cup competition. Indoor games as carrom, iudo and cards are also played by both young and old. Those who have received some education read newspapers, story books etc. or sometimes listen to the radio or the transistor set if available in a neighbour's house or if possessed by them. The household chores such as fetching water, cooking, cleaning and washing, etc. and whatever little time they could spare spent in gossiping with visiting friends and relatives. The young men frequently go during their leisure time for shooting some wild games or fishing in the nearby ponds. The villages young men particularly those who are staying in the interior villages generally spend their leisure time in a bachelor's house called 'risomar terang' where they play their drums, dance and sing, discuss some problems which they come across in their day-to-day life and exchange their experiences.

Risomar Terang

Dancing takes place not only during their recreation period but also during their festivals and ceremonies. Men and women of all ages who are able to dance join together in the dance with the accompaniment of drums and flutes.

I. LANGUAGE AND FESTIVAL

Festival

Of the festivals observed by the non-Christian the most important is known as 'Chojun' or harvest festivals. It is usually performed once a year in late December or January after the harvest or once at least after 2 or 3 years according to the convenience. The festival is observed by each and every household and generally last for one day. This festival may be done also by the village as a whole, where every household of the village contributes in cash and kind. Whether done individually or by the village as a whole the ceremonies held are not different in any way On the appointed day the 'Kurusur' or the village priest takes a pig which is called 'pirthat-aphak' which has been specially kept for the purpose of sacrificing it to 'Thankarnam' or god of the locality, who is suposed to be the giver of good or bad harvest. The pig is usually killed outside the village. The spot where the pig is to be killed, there is an alter called 'duran' which is built by the Kurusur. The blood of the sacrificed pig is collected on a plantain leaf and is placed on the 'duran' along with some cooked rice as an offering to 'Thankarnam'. The meat of the slaughtered animal is cooked and eaten by all those who accompany the 'Kurusur'.

Horbong-Arnam-Kepu

Another harvest festival observed by them is known as 'horbong-arman-kepu'. This community festival is generally observed by two or more villages and only the village elders take part in it, that is those who constitute the 'mei' or village durbars of the participant village. The festival is observed sometime in the month of January but that does not necessarily mean that all villages perform it at the same time. The place as well as the date of the festival is fixed by the members of the 'mei' of the participating village. This festival may even be performed after one or two years according to the convenience of the 'mei' or village durbars of the participant village. The festival lasts only for one day. In this festival 'Barithe' or the god of heaven is invoked and propitiated. Fowl and pigs are killed by the 'Kurusur' or by an elderly person of the 'mei' in the courtyard of 'the kup' of the 'Sarthe' (Gaonbora). The blood of the slaughtered animals is collected in a wooden vessel called 'anthong' and is offered to 'Barithe' as a token of respect. Two days before the commencement of the festival, all the participating members gather at the house of the 'Sarthe' at night to prepare rice beer and to husk paddy. On the appointed day the 'Kurusur' performs the sacrifices of the animals after which the meat of the slaughtered animals are cooked and eaten by the participating members. Thus eating and drinking continues at the house of the 'Sarthe'. Sometime drinking reaches an excessive stage leading to petty drunken bouts but these are soon forgotten when the eating and drinking is over.

Hachakkakan

There is another festival known as Hachakkakan which is performed after the harvest in the month of January or February and is celebrated by the whole village as well as individually, depending upon the economic condition of the individuals. The festival is more common among the hills and is performed at night. In this festival the young boys of the village dance and sing in a circular form. The leader of the boys who are participating in the dance stand in the centre and sing, he is known as Lunse. The boys make a circle around Lunse and dance along with the rhyithmic song of Lunse and move with a circular fashion performing different styles and movements of the hands and body. The songs are not accompanied by musical instruments. The singing and dancing continues throughout the night until dawn comes, when the dancers get exhausted and retire. When the dancing is over the villagers who collect to see the dancing return home and take rest and eat, drink and make merry.

Among the Christian Mikirs Sunday is a sacred day and every body is exempted from work on this day to attend Church services. On this day the pastor or any elder of the Church will preach from the Bible and utter prayers and hymns. Services are also held in the house and with the same rules of preaching. Christmas and New Year are the two festivals observed by the Christians. Christmas is associated with the birth of

Christ which is observed at the midnight of the 24th of December; the moment is announced by the beginning of the church bells at that time and the people come to attend the church service in which songs, prayers and hymns are performed. This is followed by merriment and feast. The New Year Day is also celebrated with much merry-making. On the night of the 31st December just at 12 o'clock the church bell rings and thus announces the beginning of the New Year, which is welcomed with much merriment, and songs and prayers are held in the church and the pastor or a church elder delivers a sermon. The day is marked with joy and merriment and the church members, young and old only have a dinner party of rice and pork, on a valuntary contribution either in cash or kind.

Language

According to Lyall (1908) the language spoken by the Mikirs belong to the great family of Indo-Chinese speech called 'Tibeto-Burman'. In the Linguistic Survey of India by Grierson (1904-1928) it is considered as a member of the Naga-Bodo sub-group in which it is classed together with Empco, a Kaccha Naga and Kabul and Khoisao. He has also given a grammatical sketch of the Mikir language, which was the first published attempt to explain the fact and mechanism on the language.

Script

Mikir has no script of its own. The first publication printed in it, a short catechism issued by a missionary press at Sibsagar in 1985, used the Assamese script, since then, so far as is known the Roman alphabet has always been employed to express the sound of the language. The Gospel History written in Roman alphabet entitled 'Birla Kema' (Glad Tidings) was published in 1904 by the American.Baptist Mission Press. Their folk tales are lively and the themes have been appropriated and assimilated to the social conditions of the Mikirs. It approved that during their sojourn in the Khasi hills, the Mikirs had assimilated much of their customs and manners. Not only dress and ornaments but the methods of divination and funeral ceremonies and memorial stones and also personal names are all borrowed from the Khasis. The Khasis have also contributed many words to their common speech, for example, the prefix 'Ka' in women's names is manifestly taken from the Khasi usage. According to Lyall (cf. Report on the Census of Assam, 1881, p. 78) there are sufficient indications to declare Mikir to be the Kinsman of Bodo rather than Khasi.

Literacy

So far as literacy is concerned, the majority of Mikirs are illiterate. The 1961 Census (Census of India, 1961, Assam; p. 282-302 reveals that out of the total population of 121, 282 persons 106, 394 or 87.8 percent are illiterate out of which 51, 612 are males and 54,782 are females. The literates without any education level accounts for 7,345 males and 2,747 females 3,849 males and 721 females have primary or junior basic education and 21 males and 6 females have matriculation or higher secondary standard when compared with the general education of the State as a whole, the percentage of literacy of the Mikirs is 27.4% and with the general education of the scheduled tribes as a whole the percentage of literacy of the Mikirs is 23.6%. A good percentage of educated and literate persons are met within the urban population, which speaks of better educational facilities in the urban area.

Books

Below is given a list of the books published in Mikir language:

1. Achambb Akitap
2. Kalakha Akitap
3. Haa-li
4. Brukachen
5. Cheb Langtham
6. Admmchas
7. Karbi Kapuchan
8. Chekarbinour Akitap
9. Karbi lamburu
10. Kacharha akitap
11. Char lamthe
12. Rong Keche

13. Karbi Bhasar Chamu Parichaya
14. Mikir Jaha Jati
15. Tam hidi
16. Kitap Kuni

CHAPTER XIV

KACHARI PEOPLE

Assam State of India, has multiracial and linguistic groups of people with different cultures of whom the Boro Kacharis or the Bodos form a very important section of these groups and are believed to be among the earliest settler of Assam. At one time they built a powerful kingdom with their capital at Dimapur and then at Maibong and Khaspur. The spread over the Brahmaputra Valley, North Bengal and Bangladesh and constitute a very important group of Indo-Mogoloid people of the East. Those who live in scattered hamlets along the foothills of the Himalayas in the North-East as well as in scattered areas of the Brahmaputra Valley, have now been mixed up with the neighbouring peoples. But they still call themselves 'Boro or Bodo' although they are otherwise known as 'Kacharis' in the Assam Valley. A section of this tribe who have gradually become Hindus, speaking Assamese and considering their status to be higher than that of the Kacharis who are known as the Koches. In the Brahmaputra Valley, the greatest concentration of this tribe is in the districts of Goalpara, Kamrup, Darrange and Nowgong. They also skirted the southern bend of the Brahmaputra and occupied the Garo Hills where the Garos still show close affinity with them. South of the Garo Hills, they spread in northern Mymensingh where the semi-Bengalized Hajong tribe shows that it is of Bado origin. In the borders of North Kachar Hills and Dimapur, there are two distinct groups known as Dimasas and Meches who also call themselves Bodos or Kacharis. In the range of the hills, south of the Surma Valley there are the Tipperahs whose language is a branch of the ancient Bodo.

Attempts were made to find out the local belief about their

origin, but most of the villagers practically knew nothing about it although some of them were of the opinion that they are the direct descendants of Hirimba, a wife of Bhama. Such mythological origins are however common in Hindu India.

Sri M.M. Brahma, research scholar of the Tribal Culture and Folklore Research Department of the Gauhati University, in his collection of the 'Folk-songs of the Bodos' remarked that "In so far as the Bodo language is concerned, there is little doubt that the language is very rich in vocabulary and is specially noted for its phonological peculiarity." Though the language is widely current not only in Assam but also in some parts of West Bengal, there is no Bodo alphabet as such. In an article 'Boro Lipi' (Boro alphabet) by Shri Gahin Basumatari published in the issue of Asom Bani dated November 22, 1963, it is stated that in the Brahmaputra Valley the Boro Kacharis use both the Assamese as well as the Roman alphabets in Bodo literature. Since times immemorial, the Bodos living in the districts of Goalpara, Darrange and Kamrup have composed Bodo songs, poems and dramas in the Assamese alphabet and the first Bodo journal, the 'Bibar', was also published in the Assamese alphabet in 1923. Due to the interaction of cultures, it is found that words of both Assamese and Boro languages are found in either language. The Kachari Rajas, during their reign, took immense interest in the growth and development of Assamese literature. Dr. S.K. Bhuyan, in his 'Kachari Buranji', thoroughly discussed this point and according to him, one king of Cachar was the patron of Madhab Kandali who translated the Ramayana into Assamese.

The majority of the people of this community are bilingual in the sense that they use their own Bodo dialect in speaking among themselves while Assamese is used as the medium of expression with the neighbouring Assamese people.

Race and Physical Appearance

Considering the linguistic affinities of the Kacharis with the Garos as well as the tribes known under different names as Dhimal, Chutiya, Koch, Rabha, Mech, etc. many authors infer the possibility of existence of some ethnological relationship between these tribes, but without thorough anthropometric data, it is difficult to say to what extent such racial affinities exist among them. Some scholars like Prof. S. K. Chatterjee include the Bodos under the Indo-Mongoloid stock, while Haddon finds the Dolichocephalic Platyrrhine (Pre-dravidian) racial elements in the tribe. In physique, the men and women are as a rule medium-statured and well built, strong and healthy.

Religion, Caste and Community

The villagers generally call themselves Hindus, although one section is under the influence of the Brahma Samaj—a reformist cult. The Brahma Samajis have adopted a new mode of worshipping the deities and all the religious parts connected with their social occasions are performed according to the Hindu rites. The main annual festival amongst this Brahma group is the 'Mahalaya'. They perform the religious ceremonies through the observance of the 'homa ceremony' and frequent offerings are made to fire through the enchanting of 'slokas' from the religious scripts. The other non-Brahmas who also call themselves Hindus still owe allegiance to their traditional tribal deities and still annually perform the 'Kherai and Garja' community worships. They believe in the existence and active interference in the affairs of men of certain invisible spiritual beings, considered as evil spirits which cause one's sickness and other natural calamities and are for the most part influenced by malevolent motives, the ill effects of which towards mankind is overcome by frequent offerings of rice, plantain, pigs, goats, poultry, etc. to the household deity, Bathau Bodo or Mainao, and also by performance of the Kherai puja or the Garja puja. There is of course a tendency among them to identify the tribal deities with the Hindu gods and goddesses through a process of syncretism and hence Bathau is being frequently identified with Siva and Mainao with Lakshmi—a typical symptom of the influence of Brahminism.

Language

The language of the people is Kachari and the speakers of this language consist of Boros, Bodos, Garos, Hajongs, Koches, Lalungs, Meches, Rabhas, Chutiyas, and Tipperahs. In the Census Report of 1961, this language is grouped under the Tibeto-Burman family which is a branch of the Sino-Tibetan or

Tibeto-Chinese family according to the Linguistic Survey of India.

As the plains tribals live along with the Assamese people and nowhere are they in big concentrations, it has become necessity for them to learn Assamese and they do speak Assamese while conversing with their neighbours. But among themselves they speak their own language. With independence and a new realization of their selfhood, the Kachari people are now definitely trying to rediscover their personality as well as their old traditional customs, manners and beliefs. The 1961 Census has revealed that the number of speakers of Boro is 280,343 apart from the Dimasa, Kachari, Lalung and Rabha speakers who number 32,077, 64,421, 10,576 and 38,308 respectively. Compared with the figures of the 1951 Census and earlier Censuses, these figures do not fail to show that the plains tribals are now all out to rediscover themselves. The Kacharis are now having primary schools in their own mother tongue and they are also clamouring for higher secondary schools and high schools with Kachari as the medium of instruction in areas where they are in concentrations.

In the sphere of their community life, the villagers form what looks like one large joint family where people commonly share their pleasures and pains, joys and sorrows. Mutual co-operation and help, both in individual and common cases, are exchanged whenever occasions demand, either in social or economic life. They are deeply attached to their social and religious customs and usages. When the young folk sing and dance, in which respect they are very rich, they forget all the worries of life. The followers of the Brahma religion also still maintain the tie of relationship with those who are yet to come under the same canopy of their religious principle and interchange of marriages is still prevalent between the two groups.

The people are peace-loving and easy going. Any dispute among themselves is still settled by the 'Gaonbora' and they need hardly refer any case to the Kachari Samaj—a bigger organisation which controls the entire judiciary of the tribal population with its own jurisprudence. But the wind of change has started blowing, and sooner or later the naive people of this beautiful hill, will be cast into the mainstream of social, political and economic upheaval. May its people withstand the stress and strain of the change-over and may they preserve for ever what is good and distinctive in their tradition.

A. ORIGIN AND HISTORY

The Mongoloid people of India, speaking various languages and dialects of the Sino-Tibetan language family appears to have started to come to India through the Eastern and Northern gate of the country from over 3,000 years ago. The Basic Mongoloid element which gives the tone to the population of Assam is very largely a contribution of the Bodo tribe (Chatterjee 1959). According to Chatterjee (1959) the Bodos at one time had formed a solid block of a Mongoloid people throughout the whole North Bihar, North Bengal, East Bengal and the Brahmaputra Valley, with extensions in the Kachar Hills, the Garo Hills and the Tripura Hills. Local Austric and Dravidian elements were in possibility absorbed by the Bodos.

In the Mahabharata (which dates back to the middle of the 10th century B.C.) mention has been made of Bhagadatta—a powerful king—who came with his host of Kirata and China troops and took part in the battle of Mahabharata as an alley of Kauravas. Kirata appears to be the name by which the Aryan speakers knew the Indo-Mongoloid. The Bodo (Bara) tribes are linguistically connected with the Nagas, whereas the Nagas have always remained isolated, but the Bodos spread over the whole of the Brahmaputra valley and North Bengal as well as East Bengal, forming a solid block of Indo-Mongoloid (Kirata) people in Eastern India (Chatterjee, 1951).

In the Puranas, mention has been made of the ancient dynasty of Assam consisting of Hinduised Bodos, as belonging to the family of Narakasura of which Bhagadatta was a branch, and appear to have ruled over Assam, right down to the middle of the 1st millennium A.D. (Chatterjee, 1959). We do not have any direct evidence of happenings in Assam from the time of the Mahabharata right down to the time of Bhaskara Varman (7th century A.D.). According to Chatterjee (1959) the Bodos have kept up their tribal identity by maintaining their language which has dispersed in several detached pockets in Kachar (both hills and plains) and in Chutiya area to the North of Brahmaputra, and in Central and Western districts of Assam as well as in the North and East Bengal, where they are found as Rabhas, Mechs, Rajbansis and Garos (within the Garo Hills), as well as Hajongs and as Tipras in Tripura. Thus it would appear from the foregoing account that the inhabitance of Kachar (of hills and plains) are of Bodo origin as evidenced linguistically.

According to Endle (1911, p. 4), the people known to us as Kacharis and to themselves as Bada (Bara) were in earlier days the dominant race in Assam. By Bada or Bara he implies the Bodo race as evidenced from his monumental work on the Kacharis (1911). Endle divided the Kachari group into two broad groups:

1. Northern group;
2. Southern group as follows, where the Brahmaputra was taken roughly as the dividing line.

Name	*Area of Habitation*
I. Northern Group	
1. Bara (Kachari)	Western Darrang, Kachari Duars and in North Kamrup.
2. Rabha (Tolata)	Goalpara.
3. Mech (Mes)	Do
4. Dhimal	North-East Bengal.
5. Koch	On Northern Frontier from Jalpaiguri to North-West Darrang.
6. Solanimiyas	Only in Mangaldai Sub-division.
7. Mahaliyas Phulgariyas Saraniyas	Western Darrang. All slightly Hinduised Kacharis.
II. Southern Group	
1. Di-ma-sa "Big-water folk"	North Cachar Hills.
2. Hojais	Do and Nowgong.
3. Lalungs	South-West Nowgong and adjoining districts.
4. Garos	On Garo Hills and at foot of same.
5. Haijongs	On plains adjoining southern slope of the Garo Hills.
6. Hill Tippera (Tripura) People	

According to Allen (1905, p. 23) the Kacharis or Bara (mis-pronounced Bodo) as they call themselves, belong to the great Bodo tribe, whose original habitat was somewhere between the upper waters of the Yang tse-kiang and Haang-ho, and they gradually spread in successive waves of immigration over the greater part of Assam. Kacharis who had ruled in different parts of Assam from time immemorial to the middle of the Nineteenth century A.D. are traditionally known as Karatas (Nath, 1959). Kacharis of North Kachar Hills are known as Dimasa Kacharis (Allen 1905).

Dimasa Kachari is a scheduled tribe of Assam as given in the President's Scheduled Castes and Scheduled Tribes List Modification Order, 1956.

Allen (1905) has given the following account for the separation of the Bodo and Dimasa, but according to him no trace of the story has been found amongst the Kacharis of Darrang. "Long ago the Dimasa fought against a powerful tribe and were beaten in pitched battle. They were compelled to give ground, but after a time further retreat was debarred by a wide and deep river. In despair the king resolved to fight again on the following day, out in the night a god appeared to him and told him that the next morning the army could cross the river if they entered it at a spot where they saw a heron standing on the bank. No one, however, was to look back while the movement was in progress. The dream proved true......A heron was seen standing on the bank, and the king and a great portion of his people crossed in safety. A man then turned to see whether his son was following, when the waters suddenly rose and swept away those who were in the river bed and prevented the others from crossing. The Dimasa were those who succeeded in reaching the further bank of safety."

Allen (1903) stated that this legend accounts for the separation of the Bodo and the Dimasa find no place among the Kacharis of Goalpara (Kacharis of Goalpara are known as Mech). Thus one tribe style themselves as Bara and the other Dimasa, though both use languages of Bodo origin. According to Allen (1903, p. 45) the Mech tribe is believed to be absolutely identical with the Kacharis. But the Dimasa Kacharis of the N.C. Hills do not support the views expressed by Allen (1903) in total, but they have not denied that the Mechs are also a branch of Kacharis which got separated in distant past, but how and when is not known, probably lost in the mist of the history.

Allen (1905, p. 90) stated that the Totlas are a superior section of the Kacharis, and occupy an intermediate position between the Kacharis and the Koch. Kacharis when they are converted to Hinduism, were generally incorporated into the ranks of the Koch caste, in lower Assam (Assam District Gazetteers, Vol. VII, 1905, p. 86-87). According to Allen (1905, p. 76) the Kacharis at Nowgong are divided into two sections, those who live in the Barbhangha, Dhing and Khatoalgaon near the Brahmaputra are said to be Bodos akin to the Kacharis of Darrang, while those in the valley of Kapiti are Dimasa. The former are known as Jharuas or Chaidvaria Kacharis, the latter as Hojais.... There are no subdivisions amongst the Jharuas, but the Hojais are said to be divided into endogamous clans as Rabha, Ramsa, Kheremia Thengal, Sonwal and Jaladha."

The Kacharis may perhaps be described as the earliest known aboriginal inhabitants of the Brahmaputra Valley. They are identical with the people called Mech in Goalpara and North Bengal. These are the names given to them by outsiders. In the Brahmaputra Valley the Kacharis call themselves Bodo or Bodo fisa (sons of Bodo). According to Endle (1911) the Kacharis became widely separated as the Western (Bara) and Southern Dimasa, a corruption of Dima fisa or "sons of the great river". They were known to the Ahoms as Dimisa, clearly a corruption of Dimasa, so that this name must have been in use when they were still in the Dhansiri Valley (Gait, 1963). According to Endle (1911, p. 4) "It is indeed not all unlikely that the people known to us as Kacharias and to themselves as Bada (Bara) were in earlier days the dominant race in Assam; ...have left traces of this domination in the nomenclature of some of the physical features of the country, e.g., the Kachari word for water (di; doi) apparently forms the first syllable of the names of many of the chief rivers of the province, such as, Diputa, Dihong, Dibong, Dibru, Dihing, Dimy, Desang, Diku, etc. and to these may be added Dikrang, Dipu, Digaru, etc., all near Sadiya, the earliest known centre of Chutiya (Kachari) power and civilization."

"The origin of the word Kachari (the first is short in Assamese and long in Bengali) is difficult to trace, but it may be mentioned that, according to the Limbu legend of creation given by Risley in the Tribes and Castes of Bengal, one of the two progenitors of the human race settled in the Kachar country, which is the name given by the Nepalese to the tract at the foot of the Hills between the Brahmaputra and Kosi rivers; and there became the father of the Koch, Mech and Dhimal tribes, or the head-quarters of a powerful Mech dynasty, the member of the tribe in Assam may well have been called Khacharis or Kacharis. The Kacharis are believed to very closely allied to the Koches, and also, so far at least as language is concerned, to the Chutiyas, Lalungs and Morans of the Brahmaputra valley, and to the Garos and Tipperas of the Southern hills. Having regard to their wide distribution, and to the extent of the country over which Bodo languages of a very uniform type are still and current, it seems not improbable that at one time the major part of Assam and North East Bengal formed a great Bodo Kingdom" (Gait, p. 1963).

Ahom, a branch of the Shan race, crossed the Patkoi (Patkai) range to the South-East of Assam in the early years of the 13th century A.D. (1228 A.D.) under the leadership of Sukapha who was compelled to leave his ancestral kingdom of Nara as he had no prospect of sovereignty there. The Ahoms ruled in Assam from A.D. 1228 to 1826 A.D. till it passed into the hands of the British by the Treaty of Yanadaboo (Bhuyan, p. XVIII, 1933). According to Hem Barua (1926) the Ahoms are a great Mongoloid race of Hukwang (Hukawang) valley, who migrated into Assam in the 13th century, through the Patkoi range.

According to Anderson (cf. Endle, p. XVI) the Dimasa, Great-River-Folk (di—means "rivers" or "water"), were driven out of the valley of the great river Brahmaputra in historical times, and finally became rulers of what is now known as the Cachar District.

There are no written records of Kachari rule, and the traditions current amongst the people, consist of little more than long lists of kings, on the accuracy of which it is impossible to rely. According to Fisher, the Kacharis of North Cachar believe that they once ruled in Kamarupa, and their royal family traced its descent from Rajas of that Country, of the line of Hatsungtsa. How long this kingdom existed, it is now impossible to say; but what is known with some degree of certainty is, that they were engaged in a prolonged struggle with the Ahoms, a section of the great Shan (Tai) race, who crossd the Patkai Hills from the South and East about A.D. 1228 and subdued the Morans, Borahis and other Kachari tribes living near the Northern slopes of these hills (Endle, 1911, p. 6).

According to Barman (unpublished manuscript, 1968), originally, this eastern region of Bharata was termed as Kachchha Desha, indicating land of Runn or narrow sea gulf, and the people of this region used to be termed as Kachchari, meaning the inhabitants of the land, called Kachcha.

The Ahoms gradually subdued the Kacharis, who drove their opponents to take refuge in or about Dimapur on the Dhansiri at the foot of the Naga Hills. In Dimapur the Kacharis were in comparative security and they appeared to have attained a high degree of material civilization evidenced from the architecture and archaeological remains though not fully excavated of the Kachari kingdom.

This section of the Kacharis are known as the Dimasas. According to Barman (1966), "Hidimba-pur (pronounced as Hirhimbapur) was the real name of this capital and kingdom. Reference is there in the Mahabharata, that Bhima, the second of the Pandava brothers, married the demon princess, Hidimba (Hihimba), sister of the local potentate of terrible ways, then called Rakshasa...The ruling family of the Kachchharis, since the days of antiquity, therefore, assumed the distinction of Hidimbba-chha, meaning the progeny of Hidimba, their generic mother. This term, Hidimbas-chha, got distorted into Dimabaachha, and then into Dimachha or Dimasa in the later phase."

The Dimasa Kacharis could not live in peace and prosperity for a long time because their ancient foes, Ahoms, followed them up to their new capital Dimapur, and about the middle of the sixteenth century the Ahoms succeeded in capturing and sacking Dimapur itself. The Kachari Raja thereupon removed his capital to Maibong which is at a considerable distance from Dimapur (Maibong literary means "much paddy"). At Maibong the Kachari dynasty would seem to have maintained itself for some two centuries (Endle 1911). According to Endle (1911), under pressure of an attack by the Jaintia Raja the Kachari sovereign withdrew from Maibong to Khaspur in Cachar (circa 1750 A.D.). There they seem to have come more and more under Hindu influence, until about 1790 the Raja of that period, Krishna Chandra, and his brother Govinda Chandra made a public professian of Brahminism. They were both placed for a time inside the body of a large copper image of cow, and on emerging thence were declared by the Brahmins to be Hindus of the Kshatriya caste, Bhima of the Mahabharata fame being assigned to them as a mythological ancestor. Hence to this day the Darrange Kacharis sometimes speak of themselves as "Bhim-ni-sa" i.e., children of Bhim, though as a rule they seem to attach little or no value to this imaginative ancestry.

According to Endle (1911, p. 7), the region of the last Kachari King, Goivnd Chandra, was little better than one continuous flight from place to place through the constant attacks of the Burmese, who finally compelled the unhappy monarch to take refuge in the adjoining British district of Sylhet. He was, indeed, reinstated in power by the aid of the East India Company's troops in 1826, but was murdered some four years later, when his kingdom became a part of the British dominions. His commander-in-chief, one Tula Ram, was allowed to remain in possession of a portion of the sub-division now known as North Cachar, a region shown in old maps of Assam as "Tula Ram Senapati's country". But on the death of this chieftain in 1854, this remaining portion of the old Kachari Raj was formally annexed to the District of Nowgong.

As regards this last mentioned migration, i.e., from Maibong to Khaspur about A.D. 1750, and the conversion to Hinduism which soon followed it, "it would seem that the movement was only a very limited and restricted one, confined indeed very largely to the Raja and the members of his court. The great majority of his people remained in the hill country, where to this day they retain their language, religion, customs, etc. to a great extent" (Endle, 1911).

Even to this day they are sticking fairly rigidly to their old customs and practices unlike the Ahoms.

Population

The Dimasa section of the Kachari people are mainly concentrated in the United Mikir and North Kachar Hills. The district covers an area of 5891.7 square miles and has a population (1951) of 165444 in which the Dimasas number 14,714. It is larger than any autonomous hill district of Assam and it shows the lowest density barring the NEFA region, being only 28 per square mile.

The earlier census figures of the Dimasa Kachari Population is as follows:

1931	—	14,680
1941	—	15,971
1951	—	14,714
1961	—	68,718
1981	—	73,927

The total number of the Dimasas in Assam, according to the Census of 1981 is 73,927.

Population trend of Dimasa Kachari/Kacharis from 1911:

Year	*Male*	*Female*	*Total*
1911			228,528
1921*	105,364	101,902	207,266
1931	7,439	7,241	14,680
1941			15,971
1951			14,714
1961	36,575	32,143	68,718

*In 1921 Census (p. 99) figures on Dimasa Kachari are not given as such but as Kacharis as a whole, further, Kacharis were divided into Hindu and Animist and the poled value has been presented here.

Population of Dimasa Kachari:

State/District		*Persons*	*Males*	*Females*
Assam (Hills)	R	68,405	36,359	32,046
	U	313	216	97
Garo Hills	R	1,309	615	694
	U	11	7	4
U.K. and J. Hills	R	17	14	3
	U	83	69	14
U.M. and N.C. Hills	R	67,069	35,725	31,344
	U	213	140	75
Mizo Hills	R	10	5	5
	U	4	—	4

R—Rural ; U—Urban.

The table above shows the distribution of the Dimasa Kacharis in the State of Assam, Meghalaya, Mizoram and in the different hill districts of Assam.

Physical Appearance

Endle (1911, p. i) has given a brief outline of the physical characteristics of the Kacharis as such in general, the same is given as follows. "They are certainly not a tall or handsome race and in general appearance bear some resemblance to the Nepali, being as a rule shorter and stouter than the people of the North-West India, though well fitted to bear up against physical fatigue and hardships. In face and figure they show a distinct approximation to what is known as the Mongolian type i.e., they have square set faces, projecting cheek bones, with almond shaped eyes, and scanty beard and moustache, the last-mentioned being often wanting altogether." The mean stature of Dimasa Kacharis is 163.9 cms.

The Dimasa Kacharis are short to medium statured people. The mean stature of the Dimasa Kacharis is 163.9 and which is close to the mean value of 1630.5=5.9 observed among the Kacharis (cf. Gupta and Dutta 1966).

Majority of the Dimasa Kacharis are of medium brown colour with low waves in hair form. They have a shallow to medium nasal root with normal wings in most of the cases. As far as the Mongoloid characteristic like eipcanthic folds and eye slits are considered, they suggest more of the non-Mongoloid features as evidenced from the frequency distribution of those characters.

The appearance of the non-Mongoloid features in the Dimasa Kacharis may be due to their mixing in the biological sense with the plains people of Assam through centuries and this might have brought the caneasoid features more to the surface.

They have round to broad faces with prominent chins. Majority of them do not show prognathism and they have medium lips with prominent cheeks.

B. ECONOMY

Agriculture

Land is one of the most important economic resources of the people, their livelihood mainly depend on cultivation. The lands may be classified into the following categories, (1) uncultivable land, (2) cultivable land and (3) land under forest.

The lands which are used for homestead purposes, playground, footpaths, etc. are included in the non-agricultural lands, uncultivable land signifies the barren land areas which are unfit for cultivation and the land under forest indicates the area which is covered with jungle trees and which is not included in the net areas cultivated. In addition to this there is another type of land known as cultivable but it is left fallow for the present time.

The jhum land in a village is restricted to a particular area for a village in consultation with the Sarthe or the 'gaonbora' of a village. If any disagreement arises about the selection of the Jhuming site among the villagers, the gaonbora refers the case to the District Council, whose decision in consultation with gaonbora is taken as final. Individual plots within the selected area for jhuming may be demarcated by the individuals in consultation with the gaonbora. There is no restriction as to the size of the land alloted to different individuals, it depends upon the ability or capacity of a family to cultivate. A family or a person loses the right of occupation or cultivation if they leave the village or shift to another village for the purpose of permanently settling there, which is under the jurisdiction of another 'gaonbora'. When the old plot is exhausted and the person wants to shift to a new plot for cultivation then they have to get the permission of the gaonbora. Sometime a temporary dwelling is constructed near the jhuming site only to stay during the operational session if the jhum land is at a fair distance from the house.

The village people obtain the fuel from the felled trees while clearing the forest for jhuming, which they may also store for future utilization. If needs arise the people have the right to cut trees either for construction purposes or for fuel from the unclassed state forest i.e. the forest areas near the village which are not reserved. This area is forest in name only, since unrestricted jhuming has virtually eaten up almost all the forest trees rendering the whole area covered with only bamboos and grasses with a few scattered trees here and there. Reserved forests are those where the people have no right to utilize the forest material. The forests reserved of the district are potentially very rich which give a very good revenue to the district, particularly for the bamboo trees. The evergreen forests are the home of various kinds of wild animals such as elephants, wild buffaloes, tigers, bears, deers, etc. The menace of the wild animals in the villages is not an uncommon sight. Rabbits are a great pest in the jhum fields and the villagers are always on the look out for the rabbits holes and always try to scare the rabbits. Various kinds of poisonous as well as non-poisonous snakes abound in the jungle, and the villagers have to tread with an open eye while moving through the jungles. Monkeys often assail the jhum fields in company. Varieties of birds break the silence of the forest with their sweet melodies.

The forest is chiefly infested with the different species of bamboo, cinnamon, sal, devdar and many other trees for valuable timber. The wild plantain trees abound in the forest and form a ready source of food for elephants, monkeys and the like.

Livestock Rearing

The secondary occupation of the Dimasa Kacharis is the rearing of livestock. Poultry, goats and pigs are commonly reared either for their food and commercial purposes or for ceremonial and sacrificial importance. Milch and draught cattle are kept for milk and for ploughing the fields respectively. Deer and wild pigs are frequently caught, sometimes by the use of large nets, enclosing a considerable extent of grass land in which some keen eye has detected the presence of the much prized game. The net gradually encloses the prey which comes within the reach of the man or the party, hunting, and then the dao speedily brings an end of the animal.

Fishing and Implements

Fishing by the Dimasa Kacharis is a very favourite pastime as well as an occupation. On certain prearranged dates men as well as women of the village, some, if not all, in a group go to fishing in the nearby streams. The day for fishing is fixed by mutual consultation. The fishing implements used are of a very simple nature and are commonly prepared from materials which are indigenous. The river water being shallow the nets are rarely employed for fishing. Zakhi and Palha are the two implements commonly used for fishing, the former being employed chiefly, but not exclusively, by women. Both implements are made of split bamboo fastened together with cane. The Zakhi is a triangular basket, open at one end, the three triangular sides closing to a point at the other end. This is attached to a bamboo handle some three or four feet in length. By holding the bamboo handle one enters the stream which is usually very shallow, and lowers the basket to the bottom, keeping the open end in front of the person and then quickly lifts the basket and examines the content, and if any fish is found trapped, it is rapidly transferred to the fish basket. Palha is the other fishing implement. It is made of split bamboo fastened together by cane strips and is about 4½ feet in height and about 3 feet in diameter at the base. The upper portion is drawn somewhat closely together, leaving an open space at the top sufficient to allow the admission of a man's hand, the whole structure being quite light and easily manipulated by one hand. With this in hand the fisherman quietly enters the shallow water at any likely spot and places the basket closely clutching the ground, and the fish so enclosed are then withdrawn by the hand through the opening in the upper part of the instrument.

Another instrument used by the Kacharis in catching fish is a small, pointed spearhead attached to a light bamboo. With this fishes like eels are caught by spearing. This instrument have become obsolete even in interior villages, instead rod and line has become popular particularly in urban folks more so those who are having white collar jobs.

Cottage Industry

One of the important household industries among the Dimasas is the culture of the eri silk-worm and the manufacturer of the eri cloth. They also manufacture muga cloth.

The loom employed for weaving the eri silk is simple tension loom and is made from the material available in the village. The loom is unlike the loin loom. The loom is usually kept under a thatched cover which protects the weaver from the scorching sun. The weaving is always done by the lady of the house or by one of her daughters. The cloth which they weave are mainly for their personal use and if there is any surplus they sell it in the market. But this does not happen very often as almost all the house holds are having their own looms. Among Dimasa women weaving is a must; a woman who does not know the art of weaving is looked down upon in the society. With the exception of weaving which is done by the females, the bamboo and cane works are done by the males only. The black smithy are done by their Bengalee or Assamese neighbours. Bamboo and cane works are taken up by the males mostly for their personal use than for sale. The person knowing the art of basketry makes bamboo or cane baskets of various kinds according to the use of which they are put. For example, baskets for carrying and storing paddy or food grains or for keeping clothes and ornaments, etc.; cane tables, chairs, murrah (low-stool) are also made by them, particularly those who are living in the urban areas.

Jhuming Cultivation

After the allotment of plot of the jhum land to the individuals of the village it is put to cultivations, trees are felled and jungle is cleared. The felling of the trees are allowed to dry until March when they are set on fire. Tillage and spreading of the ash, obtained from burning the trees, is then done with the help of the hoe.

Agricultural Implements

In the interior villages, the agricultural implements are invariably of very simple type and the manure they use is the dried and decomposed leaves and burnt up ashes. The important agricultural equipment is the following: the axe (rowa), the spade and sickle another dao. All these are obtained from the market or are prepared when ordered by blacksmiths, particularly in the interior villages who usually do not get ready made things for use.

Paddy Cultivation

Paddy is then sown with the first rains in April-May. Everything regarding cultivation like, clearing, slashing, burning, tillage, sowing and harvesting are done by individual families and some time with the help of daily wage labourers. Joint participation at the family or the clan level is not found, except in harvesting where friends and relatives extend their helping hands. Paddy is sown in April or May and is harvested in November-December. In addition to paddy other crops like maize, millet, mustard, etc. are also sown along with paddy as side lines in the holes so made for the purpose by hoes. Thus the sowing is over, before the first rains and the harvesting is done in the ensuing cold weather. The ears of paddy are cut with the help of a sickle. The sheaves, on getting dry are collected and thrashed on the spot by beating against some stone.

Wet Cultivation

Those Dimasa Kacharis who are much influenced by their Bengali or Assamese neighbours who are having plain lands for cultivation and adequate water supply for their fields from near-by streams take to wet cultivation if they can afford it. In wet cultivation the soil is made into a thick paste by means of a hoe or in some cases those who can afford to use bullocks for ploughing. Weeding and transplantation is done generally by women. Some times no transplantation is done, where the water is not adequate, and some time plants which are blown off by the wind is carefully re-planted. Sometimes a watch house is also constructed in the field so that the owner or any one of his family may stay to watch the crops and keep the animals and birds away from the field, particularly before harvesting.

Source of Income

The only source of the income of the whole village under discussion is cultivation. The majority of the households in the village, fall within the annual income group of Rs. 301-600, comes to be 28 households. The second largest number of households, i.e., 16 households are in the income group of Rs. 691-900, while 7 households are in the income group of Rs. 901-1200 and only 6 households are in the income group of Rs. 1201 and above. The villager takes to other jobs other than cultivation, like some unskilled jobs in the Public Works Dept. or Govt. hospitals or some other offices, but such services are only taken up when the agricultural operations are over.

The expenditure incurred by each household in the village for paying revenue is Rs. 3/-, paid to the District Council. Among the higher income groups the expenditures are comparatively higher than that in the lowers income groups. Household which fall in the higher income groups like the above Rs. 1200 usually spend a large amount on food and other necessities like furniture, etc. The economic conditions of the households are fairly good since the village is free from poverty and there is none living in acute want and poverty or much economic distress.

C. SOCIAL STRUCTURE

Religion

Though the Dimasa Kacharis claim themselves to be the followers of Hinduism their religion can hardly be regarded as covered within the fold of Hinduism. It appears as if their religion is an outcome of the reactionary forces of their traditional types of religion, commonly known as animistic and Hinduism. The general conversion of the Kachari people into Hinduism took place in the later part of the eighteenth century. The Ahoms succeeded in capturing and sacking Dimapur about the middle of the sixteenth century, thereupon the Kachari Raja removed his capital to Maibong, where the dynasty seemed to have maintained itself to some two centuries, and finally when attacked by the Jaintia Raja, the Kachari Kingdom was shifted from Maibong to Khaspur in Kachar in Circa 1750 A.D. It is during this period that the Kacharis were more and more under the Hindu influence until about 1790 the Raja of that period, Krishna Chandra and his brother Govinda Chandra made a public profession of Brahminism. It is said that they were both placed for a time inside the body of a large copper model of a cow and on emerging from there were declared by the Brahmins to be Hindus of the Kshatriya caste, and Bhima of the Mahabharata fame was assigned to them as a mythological ancester (Endle 1911, p. 6).

The conversion to Hinduism was formerly limited only to the members of the Royal family and the great majority of the Dimasa people retained their language, religion, custom, etc. to a great extent intact. But as the time passed more and more people were influenced by Hinduism, particularly the Barman Kacharis who are residing in the plains of Cachar. But Hinduism in its strict sense is not found among the Dimasas.

The Dimasas have many gods and godesses, of which there is one supreme called Madai. Under him there are many other Madais, some are family deities and some are evil spirits. The progenitor of these family deities or Madais is known as 'Airekhidima', who is supposed to have the form of a big female bird. According to traditional beliefs, the bird (Airekhidima) after looking for a suitable place for her nest at last came to the banyan tree and built her nest on it. In the course of time the bird laid seven eggs. The first one to come out of these eggs was 'Braisibrai'. It was then followed in succession by 'Aloomaja' (also known is 'Dooraja'), 'Naiphuraja', 'Waraja', 'Morangraja' and 'Hamaido', when the last egg was not yet matured and Hamaido being impatient kicked at it. The egg broke and the liquid content fell hither and thither on the land, water and thus turned to evil spirits or Madais. These Madais or evil spirits trouble the people and hence they were deprived of being treated as deities. 'Braisibrai' being the eldest one is worshipped as a common god by all the Dimasa Kacharis and the last one 'Itamaido', because of his Misdeed was not worshipped as an ancestral god. The remaining Madais became the family deity or Nokhoni-Madais and are worshipped as such by the Dimasa Kacharis annually but there is no fixed time, for it depends upon the wish of the family members.

Community worship is done periodically at an interval of three or more years when 'maisingba' or sacrifice of animal is offered to a presiding deity at a 'Madaikho' gods' house or temple. These are located in certain fixed places, some of the clans combine to form a big circle and each such circle has one Madaikho. As the clans are spread over vast areas so they have to get together whenever such ceremony takes place. Before the community deity, goats which are completely black are sacrificed in addition to pigs, fowls, pigeons, eggs, etc.

There is no authorised priestly clan among the Dimasa Kacharis. In common Hojai represents the priest. In one village there may be 2 or 3 priests but in other villages there may not be any priest. In such cases, a priest is borrowed from the nearby village. The following are the office bearers who deal with the religious practices:

I.	Dainya	Performs the sacrificial ceremony
II.	Janthai	Assistant
III.	Gisia	Highest Priest
IV.	Phatri	Through him god speaks or through him comes the divine utterances.

In early days all these offices were hereditary but now except the Gisia others are not hereditary. They can lead a married life but all have strictly to follow a good and devout life. They should not partake food from other's hands. These office bearers may be classified on the basis of the food they take:

(a) Misham—i.e. those who take all the food or takes food without restriction.

(b) Gathar— i.e. those who do not take pork, crab, snail and vegetables like Bairethai and Yaulaisa.

All these officials perform religious ceremonies during the community worship.

For worshipping in the family level only two categories of the priest perform the religious functions, they are :

(a) Hojai — Priest
(b) Barowa — Assistant

These officials are not hereditary and any one who knows the art of worshipping becomes Hojai, and to them there is no restriction for eating. The deities are not represented by any figures or object but by small mounds of earth and these are known as Habim.

Among the family deities, the 'Mykhone Madai' is the most important. The performance of the ceremony is different from that performed in the community level. Here the priest sacrifices the animals besides performing the duties of prayer and rites. This ceremony is usually performed just before the sowing season for bringing about the prosperity of the whole family. Another performance known as 'Madaima daimba' is performed for the well being of an individual in the family.

Community worship is generally held at the times of famine which brings successive failure of crops due to draught etc. A meeting of the village priests and eldermen takes place and the date and place is fixed where such ceremonies are to be performed and the representatives of the respective village bring their animals and birds to be sacrificed.

Society

A number of community development blocks have been

established covering almost every village in the state, there are also other organisations for social reform and welfare, working among the Dimasa Kachari. The 'Dimaraju' organization look after the welfare of the Dimasa. There are branches of this organisation throughout the North Cachar Districts in all important places like:

Barakhola	Jaipur	Tungpreng	Haflong
Maibong	Sheoratal	Diphu	Dhanashri
Hojai	Haoraghat	Dimapur	Lamding
Lanka	Bikrampur	Dhalai	Thaligram

There is a good number of members in all these centres ranging from 12 to 107 persons. The Assam Tribal Welfare works have also organised some primary schools in the villages where the tribal children get free education.

Since the Dimasa Kacharis are not much influenced by Christianity so there is no missionary welfare organization working in the Dimasa Kachari Villages.

Social Structure

The Dimasa Kacharis have been influenced by their Assamese and Bengalee neighbours particularly those who are living in the plains. Much of their old customs of their social organization has survived even in the present day administrative change. The routine administration of each village is run by the Village Council, particularly by the village head man, the 'Gaonbora'.

The jhum land in the village is distributed by the 'Gaonbora' whose voice in this matter is final. If any disagreement comes then only the case goes to the District Council. The 'Gaonbora' is elected by the village people, who are usually elderly persons and commands respect of the villagers. The District Council is simply an approving authority and has no say in the election of the 'gaonbora'. The District Council recognizes the functions and duties of the 'gaonbora' and does not interfere with the customary rights and privileges of the community.

There is no authorised priestly clan among the Dimasa Kacharis. In common Hojai represents the priest. Gisia is considered to be the highest priest and only 4 or 5 village combined may have one Gisia and all the religious ceremonies are performed under his supervision. In early days the religious offices were hereditary but now except the Gisia, the highest priest, others are not hereditary. Gisia commands respect from all the village people as well as from distant villages which does not have any Gisia of their own, but they take the services of the Gisia from other villages. The other offices of the priestly clans are not hereditary and any one who knows the art of worshipping becomes Hojai.

It is the duty of the 'gaonbora' to summon the members of the Village Council to a sitting and it is he who puts forward proposals relating to the affairs of the village and the members discuss the matters and give their verdict. The 'gaonbora' can only preside over the village council but cannot take any decision of his own without the consent of the members of the Village Council. The Village Council plays an important role in regulating the social, economic and religious life of the community, though its power have been somewhat curbed with the establishment of the District Council and all important matters like theft, murder, disputes over land, which cannot be setteled by the Village Council are settled by the District Council. The Village Council still occupies an important place in the social organisation and still retains much of its traditional powers in deciding various matters affecting the community as a whole.

D. CEREMONY AND BELIEFS

Birth of a Child

The Dimasa Kacharis believe that the birth of a child is at God's hand. A pregnant woman is always looked upon with care and is not allowed to do any heavy work. She is exempted from doing work in the field and is also exempted from carrying firewood and other such things, but is allowed to do light household chores. Delivery of a child generally and preferably done by an experienced elderly woman among the relatives. In return the dhai is paid in cash or kind. When the child is about to be born the expectant mother is made to lie on a mat on the floor and the attendant dhai keeps watch over her. Then all the things like piece of cloth, sharp bamboo split, thread, etc. are kept ready for the delivery of a child. When the child is born the dhai cuts off the naval cord with sharp split bamboo and a piece of cloth is tied around it. After she has given birth to a child she is kept in isolation. This confineness lasts till the performance of the 'dausthaiba' ceremony which is usually dried up and comes out by itself. This ceremony is done so as to be free from the bondage of debt incurred during the delivery from the relatives and friends.

In this ceremony a pair of chickens are sacrificed and the killed animals are given to the 'dhai' by he parents. Before the delivery the women are given normal diets as is taken by the other members of the households, while after the delivery she is given Mudru i.e. boiled vegetables. In addition as a substitute of milk she is given the juice of Mishage, a plant leaf, which is a good substitue for milk.

Name Giving Ceremony

The naming ceremony of the child is also performed by the 'hajaijig'. The child's name is usually selected by its parents or grand parents according to their likings. This ceremony is known as Nanabasinjiriba and in this the horoscope of the child is prepared and then one chicken is sacrificed and the boy is presented with Thali, Bati, clothes and jewellery, etc. Not all are able to perform this ceremony, particularly the poorer sections and as it is not obligatory. So, only those who can afford it perform this ceremony. A feast is held on this occasion in which friends and their relatives are invited and zu and pork or other meat with the exception of beef are supplied to the invited guests.

Until about a month the mother is held unclean and is subjected to certain restrictions in social and religious matters. That is, she is not allowed to approach the domestic altar in which her relatives offer rituals and offerings to the gods. This period of ceremonial uncleanliness is usually terminated by the use of the holy water (dithar) by the priest (jonthai), which is sprinkled on the mother as well as at the different places and corners of the house. Then only the mother is considered from the social and religious limitations and is at full liberty to resume all her social and religious duties.

The child is fed with he mother's milk until the end of the

suckling period which usually lasts about seven to eight months when the child is old enough to be fed with rice. On approaching the end of the suckling period the child is generally given rice masticated by the mother. When the child's teething period is over and the teeth have come out, normal diet, that is, which adults take is given. The mother generally carries the child at her back, while at work, when the child attains an age of 3 or 4 months. The child is allowed to crawl on the floor all by itself until it learns to stand.

The Dimasa Kacharis who are living in the urban areas or those who are living near the urban centres take the help of the hospital during delivery and every thing goes according to the routine of the hospital authorities.

Marriage

Marriage among the Dimasa Kacharis is strictly monogamous. Marriage within one's sengfong or jaddi is not permissible and they strictly follow the rules laid down by their traditional customs. Marriage outside the community is looked down by the society and the parents out of disgrace, may drive the boy or girl away from their home. Seduction is rare and if at all it occurs the girl's parents have to give their girl away in marriage. Illegitimacy and adultery is very rare and if at all any such case is detected it is usually tried by the Village Council and the guilty pair is tried publicly thus subjecting them to the jeers and scorn of the neighbours. They are released only when the fine imposed by them is paid. The amount of the fine varies from Rs. 50 to Rs. 100 depending on the case and the decision of the Council and the amount is given to the injured husband or wife.

A younger brother may marry his elder brother's widow, but an elder brother cannot marry the widow of his younger brother. Marriage with one's wife's younger sister (after the death of the former) is permitted but not the elder. Child marriage is not found and the above rules are strictly enforced and any breach of them renders liable to be outcast from the society.

Generally the boy's father will go to the girl's parents for formal negotiations though only after ascertaining the wishes of the boy. In absence of the father a close relative like an uncle will represent for the marriage negotiations. The marriage negotiations are done in a short of set pattern of phrases. When the proposal is accepted the girl's father receives a basket (made of cane and leaf) full of salt weighing about a seer (½ L). This is known as 'Saudidang Singpha'. If the girl's father does not accept the proposal even at the later stage, then the salt has to be returned to the boy's father and the engagement is broken. After the formal engagement the girl's father seeks approval from the clan members and conveys the same to the boy's father who comes after for finalization of the marriage. At this time the boy's father goes to the girl's father with two or three gourds of rice beer accompanied by some of the close relatives for finalizing the marriage day. This is known as Laotai langba, i.e., taking of gourd. Then after sometime again a meeting is held between both parties and on this occasion the price of the bride known as 'Kalti' is fixed. The amount of the Kalti varies from Rs. 50 to 200, according to the economic position of the bridegroom's father as well as his position in the society. The number of animals to be sacrificed during the marriage as well as the quantity of rice beer, is finally decided and settled along with the Kalti. The proposal being thus finalized, the date of the marriage is set according to the conveniences of both parties. The Kalti is paid on the date set for the marriage. Thus the actual marriage ceremony takes place usually after five or six months from the first day of negotiations. According to the Dimasa Kacharis the following days of the week are not auspicious, as Saturday, Tuesday, Sunday and the birth day of the daughter or son. The marriage ceremony is held at the bride's house. If the groom is of a distant village then the groom's party reaches a day earlier than the actual marriage day, as it is on this day that the bride's price is given. The arrangement for the staying accommodation of the groom's party is done by the friends and relatives of both parties. The marriage ceremony is completed before the end of the afternoon. Both the parties assemble together in some open space in the village or if the house of the bride is fairly large enough with a big courtyard, then the ceremony is held at the bride's house.

In this ceremony the members of both the parties varying from about 200 to 300 members sit in the open space on either side facing each other. The sitting arrangement is so made that the 'Khunang' or Village Headman sits at the centre, the groom's party sit on the right hand side, the bride's party on the left and the invitees in the front. When this is done, the bridegroom is summoned to bow and touch the feet of elders of both parties and each of them touches him on his head and blesses him. The groom moves towards each of the relatives and members of the other side under a cover, usually, a big umbrella or a big canopy, held by his six or seven friends, when the blessing by the elder members is over then the 'Sampradana' ceremony takes place. In this the elder members of both the parties have verbal fights, which is followed in a traditional way, over the eligibility of the boy or the girl in the marriage, in which the groom's party will invariably win and the girl's father will offer his daughter in marriage.

In the earlier days the bride did not come to the courtyard before the public, but now in families who are influenced by the urban way of life, particularly their neighbour, the Bengalees and the Assamese, come out in the court along with the relatives and friends during the 'Sampradan' ceremony. Thereafter the bridegroom accompanied by the girl's relatives goes to the house of his father-in-law leaving the guests behind to feast merrily. The bridegroom spends that night in the outer chamber (nok-hung) apart from the bride. He is admitted the following day into the inner chamber (noshing), to live with his newly wedded wife. On the third day after marriage, the bridegroom with his bride and relatives and friends return to the parent's house. This is known as 'phira phoiba' or the visit of the daughter-in-law. After staying for some time he along with his wife again returns to his father-in-law's house to stay with him as long as he desires which usually lasts for about a year. This period of staying with his father-in-law is known as 'min-ha-bha'. During this period the newly wedded couple help the bride's parents in jhuming and other domestic work. The groom stays in his in-law's house until he is able to build his own house and start a life at their own accord.

Divorce

A man may divorce his wife on any reasonable ground but

he will not get back the Kalti paid by him on the day of marriage. If the wife commits adultery and she is divorced she should return the 'Kalti' to thc injured husband. She has also to pay to the husband Rs.40 to Rs.50 as a fine and all presents given to her must also be given back. Should the husband commit adultery the wife may divorce him and he will not be entitled to get back the 'Kalti' as well as the presents which he has given to the wife either on the day of marriage or during their stay as husband and wife. If the husband and wife agree for separation the 'Kalti' is not returnable but may be kept with the wife or her parents. The children invariably belong to the wife if the husband does not come to claim them. In all cases of divorce both the parties are free to remarry and all the ceremonies are performed as in the case of the first marriage. The decision of divorce always comes through the 'Khumang' whose decision is final and when he announces it publicly then only the legality is valid. The only act performed by the husband or the wife for divorce is the tearing of a betal leaf into two pieces, indicating thereby that their married life is severed for ever.

Death

The Dimasa Kacharis always cremate the dead body except in cases where a person has died of unnatural death as well as in the case of a child's death. The body of a child less than two months old or where no errupation of tooth has taken place, their burial is the usual practice; but where in a child is having at least one tooth the body is qualified for cremation. A woman dying in child-birth is buried and no feast is held and friends and relatives generally do not assemble except the close elderly relatives who attend the burial and all the personal belongings of the woman are thrown out in thc jungle or burnt. The belief behind this practice is that if any one takes it the same fate will befall the person. Dimasa Kacharis believe that all deceased persons go after death to the place called, Habscn, i.e., the place above the earth. And people who have done good deeds during their life are able to go to Dambra or the heaven.

When a person dies the relatives of the deceased inform close friends and relatives who flock to the house of the deceased.

The ceremony starts with the killing of a fowl. The dead body is then washed and dressed in clean cloths by any elderly man or women of the family depending on the sex of the deceased and then the body is put on a mat on the floor. The dead body is placed to lie flat with the head towards the west. Then the friends and relatives who have flocked to the deceased's house console and sympathize the bereaved family and pay their last respect to the deceased person by placing a gift like a place of cloth or money by the side of the dead body, depending on the ability of the person. When all the guests have seen the dead body it is taken on a bier (doli) to the cremation ground (mankulungling) which is generally situated on the bank of a river or stream. Seven layers of dried wood are raised to form the funeral pyre (thairik) and over this pyre the corpse is placed and fire is lighted by a male relative of the father's side. In case the body does not burn well it is stated that the cause is due to the absence of some relative or friend. In such cases any of the male relatives standing there throws some grass and states the reason of the relative's absence. This practice is known as 'dohongsuba' throwing sungrass which is usually done when two thirds of the body is burnt. When the body has been thorougly burnt the bones and ashes are collected and thrown into the nearby stream except the frontal bone (tain) which is retained and placed in the memorial house (Mangkilong) which is errected on the cremation ground preferably on the spot of cremation. The structure is made of bamboo and looks like a small temple. The bone so placed in Mangkilong is allowed to remain there until the shraddha ceremony takes place. The date of the shraddha ceremony is set by the relatives, which must be over before the harvest or the Bihu Festival. Until the shraddha ceremony (maimutharba) is over the family is considered to be in mourning and throughout the period meal has to be offered after the name of the deceased person at Mangkilong or if the structure has not been erected then the meal to the deceased person may be given in the house on a plaintain leaf. On maimutharba ceremony the memorial house a Mangkilong is burnt, friends and relatives who took part in the cremation of the dead body are given a feast. On this occasion only rice beer is served. Burning of the Mangkilong is performed on the day set for 'shraddha'. While returning from the cremation ground every individual has to dip their big toe in a half open bamboo pipe where water is kept. 'Shraddha' is usually held with great pomp and the ceremony lasts for two days. Animals like pigs and fowl are killed and rice beer is prepared and all these are served to the invitees. Thus with the end of the shraddha the death ceremony or the purification ceremony is over.

On the death of the husband, a wife takes off all her ornaments and remains in mourning, until the next harvest festival. For the first three days after death she is not allowed to take rice. Similarly, on the death of one's wife, a widower remains in mourning until the harvest festival. On the death of parents, children are not allowed to eat until the following night. During the period of mourning neither widow nor widower can remarry.

E. FAMILY AND COMMUNITY RELATIONSHIP

Family

The Dimasa Kachari family is ordinarily of simple type, that is a nuclear family consisting of husband, wife and unmarried children. The system of residence can hardly be called patrilocal (Ghosh, 1964) as the husband often settles in his wife's village after marriage. This tradition has been operative from olden times, as it is found that out of ten inter-village marriages (Ghosh : 1964) which took place from the age-group of 40-60 years, five bridegrooms whose parents have already died, frequently prefers to live in his wife's place. When an inter-village marriage takes place and if the man decides to shift to his wife's village, he first lives with his mother until he can build a new house of his own. When marriage within the village takes place, the newly wed man prefers to build his hut by the side of his wife's father's hut.

The family type among the Dimasa Kacharis is usually composed of the parents and their unmarried children. Thus the households are normally small, this is because of their system of residence, where the family can never be extended either vertically or laterally as the sons become separate from the parents after marriage. Thus the Dimasa family splits up when the sons and daughters get married. Generally, within a year a man should be able to set up a new house of his own. Though the splitting of the family takes place, nevertheless, due to the characteristic residence pattern among the Dimasa Kacharis, the process of proliferation thus always goes as most of the families in one village are related to each other by some ties of kinship.

In order to understand the nature of the residential arrangements, it is necessary to examine their rules of discent as both are intimately related.

Clan and Kinship

The Dimasas follow a characteristic lineage system, which is quite different from that of other neighbouring tribes like the Mikirs and the Nagas. The male children reckon their descent along the father's line or Sengfong. This is their primary affiliation; but they also feel related to the mother's clan or Jaddi which is the secondary affiliation and is avoided in marriage. Similarly, the female children reckon descent along their mother's line or Jaddi, but they feel secondarily related to the father's clan Sengfong until marriage. After marriage a woman is adopted formally into the husband's clan and secondarily attached to her husband's Sengfong. The secondary clan affiliation entails certain duties for both men and women towards both respective clan members. Thus among the Dimasa Kacharis the choice of mates are regulated specifically by means of clans instead of otherwise as is observed among the Hindus where marriage is avoided in one's gotra as well as with the members of one's kin-group. Thus Sengfong and Jaddis play a very important part in the regulation of the Dimasa Kachari marriage system. The son and son's son all belong to the Father's Sengfong while the daughter and son's daughter's daughter belong to their respective mother's Jaddi. Thus all the sons of all the brother's follow the same Sengfong while the daughters differ in Jaddi. Thus patrilineal and matrilineal forms of descent are present among the Dimasa Kacharis. The patri-clan is functionally more important than the matri-clan and the old rules of primary and secondary relationship to the clans is more or less strictly maintained with regard to marriage. Ghosh (P965) reported cases in the village of Hajadisa (Mikir Hills) where the rule of avoiding the patriclan had been broken in 16 out of total of 44 marriages, while there was not a single case of breach of the rule regarding avoidance of the matri-clan for the some purpose. In all the 16 cases of the breach of the custom of exogamy the guilty persons were found and then allowed to remain as husband and wife. But the usual rule as laid by the ageold tradition regarding the breach of the custom of exogamy is punishable by excommunication.

In case of the other 4 villages in North Cachar Hills District, no case of breach was observed at all in regard to either the Sengfong or the Jaddi.

Due to their system of residence, the family among the Dimasas can never be extended, either vertically or laterally as the sons become separate from the parents after marriage, thus the family tends to split up. When marriage within the village takes place, it has been found (Ghosh, 1964) that the newly-wed man prefers to build his hut by the side of his wife's hut. After marriage a man may live about a year in the wife's house this being known as *minhabba.* But it is found that many people have settled in their wives' villages though they were at liberty to construct houses in their fathers' villages.

The patri-clans and matri-clans among the Dimasa people are widely dispersed. Each clan has its distinctive names; though totem like names are used to designate clans, but totemism in its true sense is not found among the Dimasa Kacharis. Thus, the objects which have given names to the clan are not regarded as totems, as they are merely names.

There are 42 patri-clans and 42 matri-clans in all. It is said that there were only 7 Sengfongs (Ghosh, 1965) when Dimapur was the capital of the Kachari Kingdom. It became 12 in number when the capital was shifted to Maibung, and lastly became 42 at Khaspur. Upto Dimapur period (middle of 16th century), there is no evidence of jaddis. According to Dimasa Kacharis the creation of the jaddis by the Kachari King, in all probability of Maibung, was done to prevent the Kachari men from marrying the women of other communities like Kuki Naga etc., who were found around the Kachari Kingdom.

The clans have no hierarchial demarcation, all of them (42 Sengfongs and 42 Jaddis) enjoy equal status. Out of these, following 4 Sengfongs and 4 Jaddis are called Danga, that is those who lived near the king and took a leading part in all royal activities.

Sengfongs : Riae, Khemprai, Phonglosa, and Seingyung.

Jaddis : Mairungma, Saidima, Miungma, and Bangalaima.

A short list of Sengfongs and Jaddis among the Dimasa Kacharis are given below :

	Sengfongs	*Meaning*	*Jaddis*
1.	Naidingsa	Son of Scout	Gachauna
2.	Nabingsa	Son of Angler	Rajama
3.	Seingyunsa	Son of Big sword	Saidima
4.	Khemoraisa	—	Miungma
5.	Adosa	—	Madarma
6.	Daudungsa	Son of a kind of Bird	Buguma
7.	Maibangsa	Plenty of paddy	Longmaisajilu
8.	Keras	—	Anumajilu
9.	Parbasa/Girisa	Bill of mountain	
10.	Laobangdisa	—	
11.	Diphusa	Name of a river	
12.	Jrambusa	—	
13.	Mitherfansa	—	
14.	Baderbagia	—	
15.	Monisa	—	
16.	Swurungfansa	—	

Inter-Community Relationship

The Dimasa Kacharis who are staying in the urban areas may engage in services of barbers, washermen, tailors and shoe makers from other communities, but the Dimasas who are far away from the urban centres in the interior villages never allow persons other than their community members. Untouchability is absent and they do not forbid any one who belongs to another community to interdine with them or take water from the same wells though this is observed only in urban areas or among those who are educated. Inter-marriage with other communities like Burman Kacharis, Mech Kacharis are permissible since they are having the Sengfong and the Jaddis like Dimasa Kacharis.

The tribal ways of the Dimasa Kacharis are still persistent

among the people living in the hills than those living in the plains. The Dimasa Kacharis who are surrounded by the Assamese and the Bengalee neighbours in the plains and their long experience and steady contact with the plains people has resulted in certain changes in their customs and manners as compared to the Hill Dimasa Kacharies.

Dipali Ghosh (1965) observed that "the Dimasa have recently developed a tendency to conceal the presence of their matri-clans and matrilineal descent of their women from outsiders. Nowadays girls are being sent to school and they are being given the surname of their father (which is that of his Sengfong) as in the case of their Assamese or Bengali class-mates."

Marriage is not prohibited between the Burmans of Cachar District and the Hill Dimasa of the North Cachar Hills as both of them observe the rules relating to Sengfong and Jaddi. In contrast to the Dimasa Kachari, the Boro Kachari have no concept of matri-clan or Jaddi. So no marriage takes place between the Dimasa and Boro.

The dress has also been influenced by their neighbours in so far as the Dimasa Kachari males of the plains or the educated Dimasa Kacharis are concerned. Most of the males who have come in contact with the plains people have substituted their traditional cloth for dhoti, pants and shirts. While those in the interior hills still retain much of their traditional dress. Most of the people have changed from jhuming to wet cultivation, possibly due to the influence of their Assamese or Bengalee neighbours. Even if they are aware of it they are not in a position to follow the wet system due to the condition of the terrain. The Dimasa Kacharis who are living in the urban areas or in the plains are more educated than the hill people, possibly this may not be due to the fact that there is lack of proper facilities in the urban areas rather this may be due to an urge to get educated which may be the effect of their Bengalee and Assamese neighbours, a competitive attitude, which is a healthy sign of a community. Another fact is that the Dimasa Kacharis of the hills are reluctant to accept the change of their social customs, while their brethren in the plains are apt to adopt change according to the needs of the time.

Different Segments of the Community

The people generally known to us as Kacharis, as they call themselves Boro or Bodo (Endle, 1911, p. xv). There were once a very powerful and widespread race in the whole of Assam. Through the passage of the centuries this large and powerful groups of Bodos gradually broke up into a number of segments, in different geographical regions of Assam, and they can only be linked with the common language. According to Endle (1911, p. XVII), no one who has heard members of the five branches of the Bodo race speak their respective languages can fail to recognize that they belong to the same linguistic group.

The Kachari or Bodo group comprises the following groups within its folds, as based on the account given by Endle (1911) and Gait (1961):

Bara (Kachari)
Rabha (Totala)
Mech (Mes)
Koch
Sonwal Kachari
Garo
Hajong
Dimasa
Hojais
Lalungs

All these tribes are the branches of the great Bodo race. Most of these tribes have been influenced in varying degrees by the veneer of Hinduism. Each group is strictly endogamous though there are instances where marriage has taken place among Dimasa Kachari and Burman Kachari or Mech Kachari. Such alliances are as a rule not looked upon with favour and they are generally outcastes from the society but peace may set in by providing feast to the follow-villagers or by paying the fine imposed by the village elders, but even in that case the couple has to stay in the outskirts of the village.

F. DWELLING, DRESS AND FOOD

The Dimasa Kacharis generally reside in the clearing patches of the forest, in the hills and the factors which determine the location of the Dimasa village is the nearness of the cultivating plot and the source of water In the hills the villages are demarcated not by fencing around but by the natural objects like ditch, small streams, or hillocks, which marks the limit of a village. Villages are kept apart from one another in isolated blocks on the foot of the hills nearby a stream or a river for the convenience of cultivation. This is also evidenced from the name of some of the Dimasa villages as Majadisa, Northdisa, Nablaidisa, Didambra. The word *disa* or *di* in the Dimasa language means river. A Kachari village in the hills is much more compact as the houses are being built more closely together than their brethren in the plains or the Assamese. Even in a compact village the arrangement of houses are dispersed in such a manner so as to provide space for rearing of livestocks and for the kitchen garden for each of the houses. The houses in the Kachari village are not clustered clanwise (Sengfong-Jaddis) but according to the convenience of the individuals.

In former times the Goanbora belonging to a particular Sengfong was generally surrounded by the people on his Sengfong in the majority thus forming a clustering of a particular Sengfong. Each house, with its granary and other out buildings, is surrounded by a ditch and fence. The fencing is usually done by ekra reeds, jungle grass or split bamboo, etc. The ditch, some three or four feet in depth, surrounds the whole homestead and the earth (mud) taken from it is used in erecting a mud wall some 2 or 3 feet in height very close to the dwelling house. But those villages which are having some urban influence have fencing around the house with open spaces in between the fence and the dwelling unit, which is utilized for rearing poultry or for kitchen gardens. Houses are generally large and the shape of the house looks rectangular and the structure as a whole is raised about 2 feet from the ground, supported by stout wooden posts. The whole structure of the house including the side walls is made up of split bamboo finely woven and knitted together so firmly that no plastering of the sort is necessary. But those who are rich or those villagers in the vicinity of the urban areas who can affored this, prepare mud plastered houses.

The roof of the house slopes on either side thatched with sun-grass (Shan, Bengali; Thiri Dimasa term) which is generally replaced after three or four years, when it gets rotten or damaged by natural process. The floor of the house is dark except for the scanty light that creeps in through the openings in the split bamboo wall. Generally, there is no window or chimney, the main door and the tiny slits in the bamboo walls serve as source of ventilation. The house are of rectangular type varying in length from 35′—45′ and with breadth of about 20′ and is usully divided into two rooms by a partition. The outer room is called Nokhung and inner room is called Noshing, The outer Nokhung is used by the males of the household and is also meant for the outsiders or guests. There are only two doors, one connecting Nokhung to the outside which serves as the entrance to the houses and the other door connects Nokhung with Noshing which is meant for the family. The hearth is placed at one corner of Noshing almost touching the side wall. The household equipment is generally kept in the inner room.

Given below is a list of household equimpment of a Dimasa Kachari house:

Bengali	*Dimasa Kachari*
Kalshi	Damsura Dik
Kalshi (earthen)	Ara
Thala	Kopra
Hatha	Khuku
Bati (of Bell metal)	Bela
Bamboo pipe for storing water	Diphong
Axe	Rowa
Small stool	
Bamboo baskets	Khamplai
Clothes	Zapsi
Cereals	Maikho

It may be noted that the people from other Sengfong are

not allowed to touch the Maikho. Almost all the households equipment are of brass or bell metal and are made by the Bengali smiths, which may be obtained from the nearby market.

Household goods are of simple variety meant for the purpose of utility rather than for decoration. There are baskets of various shapes and sizes and bearing different uses. They are generally used for storing cereals, clothes and other articles of daily use. Bamboo pipes each with a node on one end and an opening on the other are used for carrying water and for storing spices.

Dress

The dress of both males and females is simple. The males commonly put on short Dhoti (Gamcha) and shirts, particularly those who are residing nearby the urban areas. In the interior villages the upper part of the body is covered by a rectangular sheet of cloth like Gamcha called Rimchau and is worn like a cross belt, the border of which is embroidered in various colours.

The Dhoti (Gainthou) is short and is wrapped round the loin unlike the Bangalees-Assamese. The males sometime wear a turban (Sidaupha) more so in festive occasions which generally has a length of about 20 arm-lengths or about 7 yards and in width about a yard. Boys generally put on shirts and pants instead of Dhoti particularly those who are living near the urban centres. Those who are living in town almost always wear the European dress which has become the fashion of the day. Women put on a short petticoat called Righ fastened around the waist by means of a belt made of cotton cloth. Another cloth known as Rizamphain is used to cover the upper part of the body which is tied under the arms and is drawn tight over the breast. Over and above these clothes is placed Rikhausa a sort of veil which covers the head and the face and is hung on either side of the shoulder covering the breast. But this is not generally in use except in marriage and other religious ceremonies. Their ceremonial dress is similar to the types described earlier except that they are multicoloured and looks gorgeous.

Women generally keep long hair, and tie it in a knob behind the head. Males cut their hair short and seldom care to comb.

They comb hair with their fingers which usually perform the functions of the comb. Though the Dimasas staying in the urban areas or those who have experience of the urban life or influenced by the plains people like Assamese or Bengalees cut their hair in the fashion of the plains people. Nails are trimmed with a knife and the teeth are cleaned with a piece of jungle tree or sometimes only with the fingers along with some tooth powder if available; while those who are staying in the urban areas and are enlightened, use tooth paste for cleaning the teeth.

Footwear is seldom used both by the males and females particularly in the villages away from the urban centres. The Dimasas who are living in the urban centres, particularly those who are office goers use modern footwear.

On ceremonial occasions both by males and females will generally put on their traditional dress except in a few cases, especially among the youths who are much influenced by the urban ways of life. The priest or Hojai, put on the common dress i.e., Gainthou or Rimchau and the turban Sidaupha, these are the common dress put on by the priest but they are always worn clean that is which are not used eirlier on ordinary occasions and are set apart for only ceremonial purposes. Those who can afford to put on a new dress, do so.

The Dimasa Kacharis are very fond of ornaments. Women of prepubertal age put on a nose ring (Khamauthai) and necklace of beads shells (Lick). Rangbarsa is another necklace made of silver beads which are matched with Pearl beads. The thread is also made of silver.

Women of post-pubertal age wear Khadu in hand which is made of pure silver and is fairly heavy and weighs upto 15-20 totals. Khadu is also worn in anklets but it slightly varies from that worn in hand in that it remains open at one side instead of forming a complete ring.

Ornaments are rarely worn by men even in the interior villages. In earlier times men used to wear an earring of copper called Khirik. As no ear ornaments are worn by the males so there is no ear-piercing ceremony. No tatooing is done among the Dimasa Kacharis.

Food

Their staple food is rice and they eat all kinds of meat with the exception of beef. The following type of rice is generally taken by the Dimasas as—Maisa—common rice (Maima and Maisa—larger and smaller grains); maizu—used for the preparation of Zu; Bairing—a special variety known as '*Biron chaul*' in Bengali.

Meat is taken either roasted or cooked or after it is thoroughly dried in the sun. Dry fish is mostly preferable which they store in small baskets. The following are the common vegetables and fruits which they usually take—sweet pumpkin, corn, gourd, snake gourd and different types of vegetable leaves. Curry is prepared using Khar (Soda) and oil. Only mustard oil is used. Naphalam is an indigenous product and is prepared from a fish (Punti in Bengali) and mixed with Khar, salt and chilly, and is kept for 2 or 3 months. According to them it is very nourishing and is almost always taken along with rice. There is, however, one common article of food, which no orthodox old fashioned Kachari will ever touch, i.e., milk. Usually no cows are found in the village as they consider them to be an unclean animal. But presently this prejudice against the use of milk seems to be passing away.

All the members of the family eat together in the same house. Meal is generally taken three times a day, in the morning, in the afternoon and in the evening. Rice beer or '*Zou*' is their favourite drink and figures prominently in the observance of their ceremonies and festivals. Outsiders and strangers are also offered with this for the sake of courtesy.

An essential ingredient in the preparation of this most popular form of refreshment is the condiment known as *emao* which is usually composed of at least three or four distinct elements. To a definite proportion of (1) husked rice is added (2) the jack-tree leaf and Dhetai (a jungle plant) (3) another jungle plant-poison fern. All these ingredients are vigorously pounded together into a powder which is then sieved for at least two times. The powder so prepared is then mixed with water and is made into a paste, these are then left for drying for some weeks and are made into small discs after that they are kept covered for some time by the rice straw. They are then exposed in the hot sun for another four or five days, so as to become thoroughly dry. Finally they are kept suspended over a fire place in an earthenware water-vessel and from there they are taken out when required for. The adult people smoke and consume betel with areca-nut, the latter is more common and is consumed by both the sexes.

Recording of Time

The Dimasas generally record the end of the night with the cock's crow. In the interior villages the time or the period after day is known by the position of the sun or when going on a journey the time is generally recorded by the time taken for the eating a piece of betel nut which generally takes fifteen minutes for each place. The periods of the day and night are as follows:

Dawn	
Morning	Phoron
Ascending Sun	Saindaphuba
(9 to 10 a.m.) Midday	Sainjev
Descending Sun (1 to 4 p.m.)	Sainjerkheraba
Evening (5-6 p.m.)	Sainblee
Dusk (6-8 p.m.)	Sarifon
Night	Flar
Midnight to Dawn	Hakjer

Measure of Weight

The recording of space and weight by the Kachari is done according to their Bengali or Assamese neighbours. The use of Seers, Feet, etc. are common even in the interior villages. The type of weights and measures used before the pre-British days could not be ascertained but all are of the opinion that they used some different types of measures other than what they are presently using, as for example, in some of the interior villages even now they are using the unit—'mai'.

1 Mai=4 Seers (approximately)

Measured by means of a bamboo basket 12 Mai=1 Bain (48 Seers).

G. VILLAGE LIFE AND RECREATION

Sanitation

Dimasa Kachari Villages are not compact, because they build their homes on the foot of the hills, on a large open space. Almost every Dimasa Kachari house is having space for the sizes of the domestic animals and for homestead gardens. Generally pigs, goats, poultry are kept in a separate enclosure adjacent to the main house. Those who are rich and can afford, build the sheds for the domestic animals a little away but within the boundary of the individual house. Owing to the keeping of their domestic animals very close to their houses, and as rubish is thrown all around the areas surrounding the home, always remains very dirty and smelly. As there is no common place for throwing the rubbish so it gets accumulated all around and the pigs and dogs act as scavengers. Although this makes the whole atmosphere foul smelling, the people are used to such things and they seem not to be bothered by this, thus sanitation in the real sense of the term is totally absent in the villages. There is no drainage system and foul smell finds its way to the village streets. Sometimes such drain water accumulates in the ditch and serves the bathing purpose for the domesticated animals.

There is no lavatory or laterine and the nearby jungle offers a good place for this. and where dogs and pigs would swarn for their food and serve as scavengers. The Dimasa Kacharis who are living in the urban areas are having lavatory or latrine at one corner of their house away from the main rooms. The village people generally do not care to clean their clothes, but only do this on festive occasions while those who are rich usually take to new clothing. The common people who are having urban influence wash their clothes with soaps. But the poorer sections put on the same clothes every day until it is in such a condition that it cannot be worn by the person any more due to its torn nature. In any case, even the poorer section of Dimasa Kacharis apparently looks much cleaner than their neighbours the Semis and the Mikirs. They clean their face and feet and soothe away their fatigue and weariness at the nearby stream or well while coming from their hard day work in the fields.

Cooking utencils and dishes are washed after every meal. Their houses are dark and one cannot see what is inside unless he is accustomed to the darkness. Doorways and in some cases windows or the opening in walls serve as source of ventilation and as there is no chimney the smoke hovers like cloud in the ceiling of the house until it is forced out by wind through some opening.

The common diseases are dysentry, boils, malaria, and other skin diseases. Some of the Dimasa Kachari names for the common diseases are as follows:

Small pox	—	Linthai
Cholera	—	Murkhi
Ordinary Fever	—	Limba
Dysentry	—	Kamri

In the villages far away from the urban centres, they do not rely much on the modern medicine, but rely on their indigenous medical herbs with which they treat all kinds of diseases, which they can diagnose. There is no particular medicine man but the old and experienced person gives medicine some times voluntarily to the deceased person. The villages near the urban centres are using the modern medicines and are getting all the modern medical facilities in the Municipal hospitals, while in the interior villages, where facilities of the modern medicine are not available, they use the indigenous medicine and worship and propitiate the God Madaikho. The propitiation is done by Hojai and the family has simply to bring the materials for the desired propitiations.

Recreation

The Dimasa Kacharis who are staying in the villages and are agriculturists, work in their fields from morning until evening and relax themselves only after coming from the fields. The men and women sit around the hearth snapping stories and gossiping about the fields and crops and the prospects of the coming harvest, thus removing the fatigue due to the day's work.

When they meet with friends and relatives the inevitable subject of crops always comes up for discussion amongst them apart from some family matters or other matters. Sometime they sing in chorus while working in the fields or sing simple melodies while thrashing the crops, which seems to dispel the fatigue due to the hard labour and weariness from the body and mind. Though they have to undergo through the rigours of nature which makes their life hard, yet their hearts are full with hope and joy and they are satisfied with what they have. They are the children of the nature and find music in the winds, streams and woods which fill their mind with much delight.

Games

The little boys and girls in the village do not play any specific game. To them, games are like climbing trees, or throwing stones, or other similar activities with which they remain engaged and thus spend the day until they feel tired and go to their homes. The grown up boys and girls play some of the modern games borrowed from outside, generally learned through the school mates or from the plains people. Hide and seek is played generally by girls. Football is a favourite game among the boys especially those who are staying in the urban areas. Sometimes teams are formed among themselves for friendly matches for a tournament in a competition. Indoor games like carrom, ludo and cards, etc. are also played by both young and old. Those who have received some education read newspapers, and story books, etc. or sometimes listen to the radio or transistor if available, in a neighbour's home or if possessed by them.

The housewives and elderly women are hard pressed with their household chores such as fetching water, cooking, cleaning and washing, etc. and whatever little time they get to spare as leisure time they spend in gossiping or visiting friends and relatives. The youngmen frequently go during their leisure time for shooting some wild game or fishing in the nearby ponds. The village young men particularly those who are staying in the interior villages generally spend their leisure time in dancing or singing or playing on the drums or discuss problems which they come across in their day-to-day life and exchange their experiences.

H. LANGUAGE

The Dimasa Kacharis speak the Kachari language, which is followed by the other sections of the Kacharis like Burman Kachari, Mech Kachari, Sanwal Kachari, etc. Sir George Grierson (Linguistic Survey of India, Vol. III, Part II) classed the Kachari language in the Naga-Bodo group. In 1921 census there were 259,587 Bodos, Mech and Plains Kachari speakers, (p. 58) while Dimasa speakers (p. 59) were 11,040 persons of which 5,519 were males and 5,521 were females. In 1931 census (p. 228-229) Bara, Bodo or Plains Kacharis were 282,582 of which 143,544 were males and 139,038 were females. While the Dimasa or Hill Kacharis numbered 14,680 of which 7,439 persons were males and 7,241 were females.

The total number of Dimasa Kacharis who have stated their mother-tongue as Dimasa Kachari in given below (Census of India : Assam : Vol. III, Part V.A., pp. 370-381):

Total Speakers

Tribe	*Males*	*Females*	*Mother Tongue*
Dimasa	2,323	1,920	Assamese
Kachari	6,641	5,460	Bengali
	31	61	Bodo/Boro
	10,874	9,490	Dimasa
	—	45	Garo
	6	—	Haijong
	8,604	7,482	Kachari
	8,087	7,683	Mikir
	1	1	Naga-Unspecified.
	8	—	Rabha

The table above shows that the Dimasa Kacharis who had reported Dimasa to be their mother-tongue are maximum in number, the next in descending order comes Kacharis and Mikirs respectively. Thus it is evident that the Dimasa Kachari have reported different languages as their mother-tongues. Majority of the Dimasa Kacharis belong to the Dimasa, Kachari, Mikir Bengali and Assamese language groups.

There are a few publications like magazines and books in the

Dimasa language with the Bengali script. Some of them are translations of famous Bengali Books like *Naukabilas*.

A list of the few books are given as follows:

1. Jamyani Rajthai
2. Malsokhruni Malsothsothai Ranghha Dihahaihe
3. Dimasa

The literacy percentage of Dimasa Kachari is 8.89 per cent while the literacy percentage is 29.57 per cent among the Scheduled Tribes of Assam and 0.65 per cent when the total population of the state is taken.

CHAPTER XV

ETHNIC GROUPS IN MANIPUR

From time immemorial Manipur had been the home of a number of ethnic groups broadly categorised in modern times under the appellations of Meitei, Naga, Kuki, etc. The Meiteis who became a major community as a result of confederacy of a number of cognate groups like Angom, Khumal, Luwang, Moirang, etc. which became its exogamous units might have been one of the earliest settlers. The fact that the Meiteis were able to establish against many odds, a well settled and close society and also a kingdom with a written chronicle dating from the first century A.D. speaking not only of the antiquity of thair settlement but also the endeavour leading towards the growth of a distinct culture in this small kingdom.

Scholars are of a view that Manipur had been in the past one of the trade routes between the east and the west and naturally a meeting place of immigrants from the east as well as from the west. The eastern stream consisting of mostly the Burmese which got assimilated into the Meitei society was known as the "*nongpok-ha-ram*". Since the wake of Hinduism in the Meitei society the flow of western stream became more regular than before and the assimilation of the western stream or the "*nong-pok-ha-ram*" underwent into three directions: first, the assimilation of the Brahmin immigrants within the Meitei Hindu society to form the Brahmin caste; second, the assimilation of other non-Brahmin Hindu immigrants; and third, the assimilation of the Muslims by retaining their Islamic faith. The adoption of Meitei language, family names and dress, among others, were the major features of assimilation of the Muslims. The native Meiteis along with the assimilated non-Brahmin Hindus became the Kshatriya caste and within the Meitei Hindu society they have a close-knit dual caste organisation of the Brahmins and the Kshatriyas.

Though Hinduism had its roots in Manipur prior to 18th century, it was only during the time the of Garib Niwaz, an 18th century Meitei King, that mass proselytism of the natives took place into the fold of Rama cult. Ramaism while in its teething stage was overshadowed by Krishnaism under the Chaitanya school whose *Bhakti* cult, absence of caste rigidity and devotion through singing of *Sankirtan* found a firm foundation to become the state religion in the Meitei Hindu Society. The reason for the popularity of Chaitanya Vaishnavism may be attributed to *Sankirtan* itself which, infused by the artistic genius of the Meiteis created an atmosphere where dance and music become the dominant element of their religion and life, providing an emotional outlest of the people.

As a result of a strong force of cultural identification of Manipur with the Hindu India coupled with the political situation prevailing during the past one or two hundred years, the flow of immigrants from the west went on increasing ultimately in the growth of separate ethnic groups represented mostly by those coming from Assam, Bengal and Bihar. The late settlers from the west who retained their communal identities from the minor ethnic groups, mostly engaged in trade and commerce, their actual involvement in the social milleu or the mainstream of social life with the other major ethnic groups is found to have been very much ingrained.

One of the most interesting features regarding the growth of ethnic groups in Manipur is the spread of medley of tribes in its hills. The settlement of the major Naga groups like the *Kabui*, *Mao* and *Tangkhul* in Manipur may undoubtedly be said to be one of the oldest enjoying in the past autonomy within their territorial boundaries. The eastern hills of Manipur are the ancestral home of the Tangkhul while the northern and western hills remain the abode of the Mao and the Kabui respectively.

It will not be possible to have an exhaustive account of all the tribal communities and their distribution pattern in Manipur. It may, however, be mentioned here that the large number of separate ethnic groups is due to the influx of mostly the tribal groups liberally grouped under Kuki from the Burmese territory during early times. Naturally the south and south-eastern hilly areas of Manipur have been settled mostly by these tribal groups. The settlement of the Kuki in the areas between the plains of the Meiteis and Burma and also in the hill slopes close to the fringe of the plains suggests the policy of the early Meitei Kings towards having buffer communities for saving the plains from the onslaught of external forces.

A large number of tribes received constitutional recognition as the scheduled tribes of Manipur as a result of the modification of the list of the scheduled tribes of Manipur in 1956. Accordingly the Naga and Kuki appleations have been dropped and individual tribal names, numbering 29, have been recognised as the scheduled tribes of Manipur. These 29 tribes are as follows: Aimol, Anal, Angami, Chiru, Chothe, Gangte, Kabui, Kacha Naga, Koirao, Koireng, Kom, Lamgang, Mao, Maram Maring, Mizo, Monsang, Moyon, Paite, Purum, Ralte, Sahte, Sema, Simte, Tangkhul, Vaiphei and Zou.

If we go back to a few decades it will be found that tribal population in Manipur in 1941 showed a declining rate of 1.3 per cent over that of 1931. However, in 1951 the growth rate hit 26.8 per cent. The only possible reason for this alarming growth of tribal population in Manipur from 1941 to 1951 may be attributed to the influx of tribal population from Burma for shelter in the hills of Manipur as a result of the last World War II. It will be pertinent to have a glimpse of the tribal population of Manipur in the last two censuses of 1961 and 1971 and the decadal growth rate.

Tribe	*1961*	*1971*	*Growth Rate*
Aimol	108	836	674.0
Anal	4868	6670	37.0
Angami	632	70	—802.8
Chiru	1809	2785	53.9
Chothe	1035	1905	84.1
Gangte	4856	6307	29.9
Hmar	15365	23312	51.7
Kabui	29218	40257	37.8
Kacha Naga	9734	13026	33.8
Koirao	406	1620	299.0

Tribe	1961	1971	Growth Rate
Koireng	531	458	—15.9
Kom	5477	6550	19.5
Lamgang	1866	2622	40.5
Mao	28810	33379	15.8
Maram	4928	4539	—8.6
Maring	7745	9825	26.8
Mizo	2746	7483	172.5
Monsang	1342	930	—44.3
Moyon	647	1360	110.2
Paite	17029	24758	45.4
Purum	82	—	—
Ralte	80	154	92.5
Sema	4	3	—33.3
Simte	2818	4177	42.8
Sahte	—	3	—
Tangkhul	43943	57851	31.6
Thadou	47994	59955	24.9
Vaiphei	8215	12347	50.3
Zou	6761	10060	48.8

It will be seen that between 1961 and 1971 there has been a very irregular trend of growth of the tribal population of Manipur. Higher decadal increase or fall of population is often found among the less populous tribal communities than among the more populous ones. This phenomenon is indicative of the irratic changes in ethnic identification of the less populous tribes on the one hand and the affiliation of a few unscheduled tribes to this or that scheduled tribe on the other. A probe into the factors or the circumstances leading to the steep rise or fall in population among some tribal groups from 1961 to 1971 will be a very significant socio-demographic study.

The inter-ethnic relationship between the different groups of people particularly between the people of the plains and the tribes of the hills was largely determined in the past by two factors (a) geographic distance and (b) religion. The physical distance between the plains and the hills of Manipur was aggravated by unsatisfactory communication facilities or the absence of roads, and situation, though very much improved, today leaves much to be desired when it comes to wider coverage of interior tribal villages. A strong force of social distance began to operate between the plains people and the hill people as a result of the conversion of the plains people particularly the Meiteis into the fold of Hinduism some three hundred years ago. Hinduism with its concept of "Purity" and "Impurity" created a social distance between the Hindus and the non-Hindus in the past though it has been considerably minimized today as a result of expanding growth of urban population increasing rate of literacy and introduction of democratic institution. Besides, the increasing growth of trade and commerce having a contageous effect upon the interior rural areas including the remote hilly areas helped narrow down social distance of the past to a considerable extent thereby creating a climate for the growth of healthy relationship between the various ethnic groups.

While the Meiteis have accepted Hinduism as their religion, the tribes of Manipur began to accept Christianity under different denominations to such an extent that the followers of traditional religions among them have become the minority group. The acceptance of a major world religion like Christianity was a major factor of social change in the tribal belt of Manipur. Apart from enthusing the fervour of a new religion, it is responsible for the adoption of the Roman script by the tribes and for an uninhibited pull of tribal culture towards westernisation.

The third major group which is more cultural than ethinc is that of the Muslims whose contributions, like that of the tribes, towards the development of the state is considerable. The early Muslim settlers, most of them being contemporaneous with the Brahmin immigrants, got themselves assimilated within the larger Manipuri society by adopting local family names, Meitei language and other facets of culture. Among the local family names of the Muslims, mention may be made of Aribam, Khullakpam, Yumkhaibam, Ipham, Phisabam, Wangmayum, Meraimayum, Khulaibam, Baseimayum, Phundreimayum, Pukhrimayim, etc. It may be of interest to note that some of the family names like Aribam, Khullakpam and Yumkhaibam are common for both the Muslims and the Hindu Meiteis. Besides, the Muslims are found to settle as close neighbours to the Hindu Meiteis. These are indicative of the receptive attitude of the early Meitei kings in their relation with the Muslims.

Since the early days there had been inter-dependence between the Meiteis, the Muslims and the tribals in one aspect or the other whether econo-political or socio-cultural. In spite of ethnic diversities, there had been a bond of unity among these three groups and they undoubtedly form the triad in the cultural history of Manipur.

A. THE GANGTE

Culture had been used and defined to convey various meanings. The famous critic and poet, Mathew Arnold, defined culture as "sweetness and light". Philosophers like Cassirer and sociologists like Sorokin and MacIver defined culture as "moral, spiritual and intellectual attainments of man." Tylor is the first anthropologist, to use the term saying that "culture or civilization is that complex whole which includes knowledge, belief, art, morals, law, customs and any other capabilities and habits acquired by man as a member of society." In short, by culture he means "social heritage".

Functionalists like Malinawski and Radcliffe-Brown take the holistic view of culture and define heritage as to "consist of a material part and a non-material, intangible, imponderable part." Lowie defines culture as "the whole of social tradition", while a more recent view of Linton is that culture is "social heredity" or inheritance. The latest view on culture is that of Kroeber who says, "Culture is what we learn from other man, from our elders or the past, plus what we add to it." This is the same with what Tylor means by "capabilities and habits acquired by man" and Lowie by "the whole of social tradition", which in fact "conveys much the same meaning as Linton's "social heredity" or inhertance.

It is, therefore, clear that by culture it means, what is socially transmitted, what is received from tradition and what is acquired by man as a member of society.

In much the same way, the terms Tribe and Clan have been indiscriminately used without any clear definition.

In the Notes and Queries on Anthropology (1929) edited by a Committee of Section H of the British Association for the

Advancement of Science, "*clan*" has been defined as "An exogamous, unilateral group of persons all the members of which (clansmen) are held to be related to one another and bound together by a common tie of clanship. This tie may be a belief in common descent from some ancestor, real or mythical, it may be the common possession of a totem (sic), p.76, or the common habitation of a village or district. *Sib*, *sept*, *gens*, *totemkin* have been used synonymously with Clan." The Notes and Queries on Anthropology (1929), basing on Prof. Wissler's definition of Tribe in his "An Introduction of Social Anthropology", selected the following as the outstanding characteristic of a tribe:

(1) Designation by a specific name
(2) Possessing unity in speech or a dialect peculiar to a group
(3) Claiming possession of a definite range or habitat
(4) Constituting an inbreeding or intermarrying group

Based on the above definitions, Tarakchandra Das in his *The Purums* (an old Kuki tribe of Manipur) does not agree with persons such as Col. J. Shakespeare, earlier writer on the Kukis, who called the Aimol, Anal, Chothe, Kom, Lamdang, Chiru, Purum, Tikhup, Gangte, Paite, Khotlhang, Vaiphei, Lusei, etc. as clans and claims that they are definitely tribes and not clans. His main contentions are that exogamous and unilineal principles being the two most important characteristics of the clan, the Purums and other groups cannot be called clans. They are by and large endogamous groups with "lapses on rare occasions" and as such should be treated as tribes In support of his arguments he made references to Prof. T.C. Hodson, who, in his writing on the "Naga Tribes of Manipur, 1911"* called the Chirus as a tribe and not a clan and to Prof. Lowie, who in his "Primitive Society", gave emphasis on the exogamous nature of the clan when he said, "We find as one the most common traits of the sib, the law of exogamy" and "that exogamy is one of the most common characteristics of the *sib*." He further quoted Prof. J. H. Hutton, who in his introduction to the Lahkers by Mr. N.E. Parry and the Notes of the Thadon

Kuki Clan by Mr. W. Shaw treated them as tribes in spite of the fact that the people are being given clan treatments by the writers.

It is no doubt true that the Purums, so also the Gangtes and others, are not exogamous groups. But basing on one rigid definition of the clan to come to the conclusion that because the Purums or the Gangtes are not exogamous groups, they cannot be called clans presupposes subjective approach. There are a number of clan systems and as such a definition applicable to a particular clan system may not be applicable to other systems. Keeping this in view, therefore, Radcliffe-Brown said that in a society where a clan was divided into sub-clans, lineages and sub-lineages the rule of exogamy was in application only to a smaller group of persons on limited degree and commended to the excellent description made by Prof. Evens-Pritchard on such segmentary clan system of the Nuer and by Prof. Fortes on the Tallensi. This is true in the case of the Gangtes, the Thadous, the Vaipheis, etc. etc. They are segmented into sub-clans, lineages and sub-lineages and the rule of exogamy is applied only within three generations, details of which will be dealt with a later stage. Radcliffe-Brown further said that "a clan system, however, also provides a division of the tribe into a number of distinct separate groups, each having its own identity", and added that "the unilineal principle of reckoning relationship in one line (male or female) is utilised in a great variety of ways in different kinship systems" and that "one important way in which the unilineal principle may be used is in the formation of recognised lineage groups as part of the social structure." The unilineal principle is prevalent among the Gangtes and so also the various ways of utilisation of the principle which will also be described in detail. Added to this, the characteristic of clanship in regard to belief in common descent from an ancestor, real or mythical, is also found among the Gangtes and will be discussed in detail.

Gangte is a generic name originally used to denote the children of Tukgek, who had three sons, namely, Thanglun, the eldest, Hilkheng, the second, popularly known as Teklah and Thangjom, the youngest. They all once lived in a valley called Gang which was believed to have been located somewhere in

Burma. Gang stands for the valley of Gang and *te* stands for the people. Therefore, literally, Gangte means the people of Gang.

The children of Thanglun are not numerically large. Almost all of them live today in Pangen village, while the children of Hilkheng, alias Teklah, are slightly bigger in number than the children of Thanglun and are concentrated in two villages called Sempat and Luongpi. The children of Thaegjom numerically preponderant over the children of the two brothers. The children of these three brothers form separate sub-clans in order of seniority. The children of Thanglun are the senior most sub-clan of the Gangte (Tukgek) clan, then comes the children of Hilkheng (Teklah) while the children of Thangjom are the junior most in relation to the elder two sub-clans. The children of these three brothers still claim to belong to one and the same ancestor called Tukgek (alias Gangte). These sub-clans are further segmented into sub-lineages. In the case of the Thanglun and Hilkheng sub-clans their number are not large and as such I will not be dealing with them in detail. I will mainly be dealing with the Thangjom sub-clan.

The Gangtes are a patrilineal society and their descent being based on the unilineal principle is reckoned from father to the eldest son. Thangjom sub-clan can be divided broadly into eleven lineages, which are shown below in a heirarchical order of seniority:

1. Suktung
2. Saknung
3. Helthang
4. Chôntou
5. Jathuom
6. Phalchung
7. Sitsuong (alias selpho)
8. Kaihmang
9. Tuipite
10. Munthang (alias Saichangte)
11. Tuokim (alias Bailong)

These lineages are further segmented into sub-lineages and

so on. In fact the segmentation of the Gangtes into a number of sub-clans, lineages, sub-lineages, etc., etc. is determined by the number of male members born in a society and that the names of these sub-clans, lineages, sub-lineages, etc. are personal (male) names. The sub-clan which bears the name of the eldest person is the seniormost sub-clan. Seniority and juniority of the persons in the family, in other words, seniority of the sub-clan is based on the direct lines of the genealogical trees. The same procedure is followed when the sub-clan is divided into lineages and sub-lineages.

The senior sub-clan or lineage or sub-lineage is known as Upa in relation to the junior sub-clan or lineage or sub-lineage which is known as Naopa. Consistent with the unilineal principle followed by the Gangtes the right of inheritance is vested in the eldest son of a man who is known as Upa who is associated with a number of prerogatives. These prerogatives are institutionalised in the village organisation called Haosa (chieftainship) and its council of Ministers, collectively known as Sehmangupa. Thus the institution of Haosa is the centrifugal force where the Gangte culture and tradition, law and custom, etc., stem from.

The question of Upa and Naopa is entirely the outcome or the product of marriage and as such the institution of marriage should have consistency with the right of inheritance based on the unilineal principle. As has been rightly described by Prof. Radcliffe-Brown in his introduction on African Systems of Kinship and Marriage, "Marriage is a social arrangement by which a child is given a legitimate position in the society, determined by parenthood in the social sense." Marriage among the Gangtes is purely governed by social values accorded to it.

Normally, a Gangte family is of monogamy, but there is no restriction to the practice of polygamous form of marriage as well. Polygamous marriage is mainly practiced by the chiefs and outstanding persons and is considered as an expression of their social status. However, there arises complication in regard to giving what Radcliffe-Brown has termed as "a legitimate position in society" in the case of polygamous form of marriage. But in so far as the Gangtes are concerned this does not give much complication. In a Gangte family of polygamous marrige, the eldest son of the first wife known as Khunpi Cha has the legitimate position irrespective of his age compared to the sons of other wives. For instance, A marries B but unfortuately no heir was born out of this wedlock. Several years after the marriage, A with the full consent of his wife B and also his parents and his Council of Ministers, marries C the second wife, who has been blessed with a son. It so happened that after the birth of the son out of the second marriage with C, B the first wife, has also been blessed with a son. Now the son of C the second wife, is elder by age than the son of B, the first wife. But the rule of inheritance is that it goes from father to the eldest son. Therefore, the question arises as to who should be the heir. Since it is said that the right of inheritance goes from father to eldest son, it is quite natural that the son of C, the second wife, should be the heir. But it is not so among the Gangtes. Marriage being a social arrangement by which a child is given legitimate position in society determined by parenthood in social sense, although younger by age, the son of B, the first wife, is the rightful heir of A. This is true in the case Phalchung and Sitsuong lineages of the Thangjom sub-clan. Phalchung was the son of the first wife and Sitsuong was the son of the second wife. But although senior to Phalchung by age, Sitsuong being the son of the second wife, was not given the right of inheritance.

The Gangtes prefer Mother's Brother's daughter, known as Neihnu marriage. If a man has no Neihnu or does not marry the Neihnu it is still preferred that he should marry a girl from his mother's side who can still be regarded as representing the Neihnu. Father's sister's daughter, known as Tunu, marriage is strictly prohibited. Any girl from father's side is taboo for a man and cohabitation with such a girl is incestuous. They belong to a man's exogamous group. But in exceptional cases a man can marry a girl from his father's side if the distance of their relationship is three generations above. Any marriage lower than this is not allowed for they still form an exogamous group. When father's father's father's brother's son's son's daughter marriage take place the children of such marriage will call their mother's brother as Hepu who would have otherwise been called paternal uncle, Hepa Ngak. But such marriage is not encouraged because it disturbs the social structure as evidenced from the relationship between a man and his mother's brother.

Marriage price among the Gangtes varies from lineage to lineage ranging from three to seven Mithuns. Bride price is taken on the consideration that the parents of the bride suffer economic disadvantage as a result of their daughter being taken away from them. This is coupled with sentiment and prestige of the bride's family.

In a man's social life among the Gangtes there are three sets of indispensable relatives without whom a Gangte appears unable to exist. Life is a vaccum to him without such relatives; and such relatives are the outcome of marriage. Kinship terminologies of such relatives are, namely, Tucha, sister's son or father's sister's son, or in other words, receiving relatives and Song-gao, mother's brother, or mother's brother's son, or, in other words, giving relatives. These two sets of relatives are reciprocal relatives. If a man is a Tucha relative to another man, the latter is Song-gao relative to the former, and vice-versa. The third set of relative is called Behcha. Two persons who stand in a Behcha relationship call each other Behcha. They are in self-reciprocal relationship.

In case a Gangte lives among the people with whom he has no close relation, he will in some way establish these three sets of relatives by extension of classificatory terminologies of Tucha, Behcha and Song-gao. He will find out someone as his Tucha relative whose relatives have married from his own lineage or sub-clan. In the same way he will establish the Song-gao relative with some body to whose lineage or sub-clan he or his father or distant relatives have married. Song-gao relative is, in fact, inactive and therefore is not very essential as is a Tucha. But this relative in turn gives him a chance to be a Tucha relative to his Song-gao relative. But in the case of Behcha relative, one need not go to the extent of establishing such relationship. If such Behcha relatives are not available, any person with whom a man has a very good friendship can be a Behcha relative.

Although there are instance of love marriage, arranged marriage is the practice of the Gangtes, and that the parents of the boy and the girl take the initiative in such case. When the parents of the boy think that time has come for their son's marriage they will first of all approach the parents of the girl, called the Neihun of their son, accompanied by their Tucha and Behcha relatives, who will officiate everything on their behalf.

The parents of the boy together with their Tucha and Behcha relatives will take one Jar of Ju (rice bear) called Jubel with them, and over the Jubel negotiation will commence. If the parents of the girl resent to the proposal, they will give them one Jubel in return signifying their disapproval to the proposed marriage. In case the proposal is acceptable to the girl's parents, the boy's parents will go again for the second time to finalise the negotiation. At this stage, certain categories of persons, such as, a widow or widower, or a person having any defect on the part of the body or a person who has more than one wife cannot take part in the negotiation. On this day, the marriage price, the date of marriage and any other matter relating to marriage are discussed and finalised.

On the approaching day of the date fixed fcr the marriage, the boy's party will leave for the girl's home. In that party the boy will not be included. Either of the parents or both the parents of the boy together with their Tucha and Behcha and the young boys and girls of the village will go to fetch the bride. Full payment of the bride price may not necessarily be made on this day, but certain token bride price in the form of clothes called *Phawipi* and *Puondum* should be paid.

On their arrival to the girl's village they will be intercepted by the young boys of the bride's village and there ensues wrestling between the boy's party and the bride's party. This wrestling is called *Buontuolkhaw.* Strong and expert wrestlers from both sides will be selected and their will be competition among them. But conventionally the boy's side allow the girl's side to take the upper hand in spite of their stronger strength and dexterity in the art of wrestling. It is considered that the boy's side had already won the competition by winning the hands of the girl and therefore, they should be equalised in wrestling as a consolation.

The parents of the bride will give a feast to mark the departure of their daughter. One half of the animal killed for the purpose is given to the boy's party to be taken along with them. The neck portion together with some portions of the spleen and the heart will be specially prepared and will be eaten by the boy's father or whoever represents him together with his Tucha and Behcha on the one hand and the bride's parent's Tucha and Behcha on the other hand, as witness meat for the payment of the bride price or for the witness of the balance due to be paid.

The next morning, when all the necessary formalities are over, the girl will be sent off and must compulsorily be taken away from the village before sun rise.

The marriage rite takes place at the boy's residence being officiated by the village priest.

Within one year after the marriage, the boy's party together with the bride will go back to the bride's parents and is called *Mousulleh.* On their arrival at her natal home, the village priest will perform a cleansing rite for the bride so that she can thereafter take the liberty of taking food in her parents house.

When a child is born in a Gangte family, a boy or a girl will be sent to the residence of the maternal uncle of the child to herald the birth of the child, who will give one Cock and one Pot of rice bear Ju (Juum Khat). This is called *Nro Akla.* This Naoakla takes place within five days after the birth of a female child.

A name is given as soon as a child is born and is called Nao Min Chu (fighting for the name of the child). This is done because of the superstition that if a child's name is not immediately given after the birth, the Thitha (evil spirits) give their own name to the child, resulting thereby to the ill-health and short-life of the child. However, after some days the name of the child is given formally. If the child is a boy and is the first issue of the parents he is named after the last syllable of the name of his paternal grand-father which in turn become the first syllable of his name. If the child is a girl and is the first issue of the parents she is named after the last syllable of her paternal grand-mother which in turn becomes the first syllable of her name. The second boy and the second girl will be named after the choice of the parents, but preferably they go to the parents of the mother of the children, i.e. maternal grand-parents.

When a male child is about five years old formal christening of the child called *Naominsak* is done. One pig will be killed on this day. Ju will be taken (sipped) by turn in the manner described below. The father of the child will sip first. He will then request the chief of the village to sip next. After the chief, will come the senior most Sehmang of the village, and then the Thiempu, then the other Sehmangs in order of seniority. Lastly, the Khawsam of the village council's turn comes. This turn of sipping the Ju is called *Julep Chep*. This will be preceded by *Juphi* performed by the priest. He fixes the sipping pipe from which all will have to sip the Ju. He then sips the Ju himself and then spit it out in scattered drops which is called *Juphi*. The significance of this Juphi is an act of propitation for the good health of the family who performs the Naominsak.

Sipping of the Ju for the second phase continues. But here the Jule pchep is not done. This phase of sipping Ju is began by the Behcha of the family and then followed by the villagers present on the occasion.

The Tucha of the family will arrange for the sipping of the Ju which is called Lengsik. This is the standard with which the turn will rotate. Behcha of the family will commence this turn of sipping and then the Tucha will come. Every Behcha and Tucha will call each of the family members after their turn. This is called Kitok. In between the Kitok young boys and girls will be called for sipping.

In the evening a feast will be served. Here also the social structure as expressed in the sipping of Ju is indicated. The head of the animal called Sapang will be taken only by the chief and his councillors. Before eating the feast the Thiempu (village priest) will perform Sakao Paih (offering of a token piece of meat). The manner of performance of this rite is that the priest will throw a piece of meat together with a piece of bamboo. This rite is performed with an act of prayer for the good health of the participants of the feast.

In the daily life of the Gangtes the social actions and behaviours are an expression of the social structure. In much the same way in their drinking, in food also an expression of their social relationship could be observed. As has been described by Professor Fortes among the Kachin of Burma in respect of distribution of meat, so also among the Gangtes social structure is observed in their distribution of meat on the occasion of Naominsak.

Tuchas and Behchas have their own portions or snare to the animal killed on the occassion. For Tuchas fore-legs, for Behcha the hind-legs. The senior most Tucha is given the right fore-leg. In the same way for the senior most Behcha, the right hind-leg is given while for the second Behcha, the left hind-leg is given. Usually there are four Behchas who share hind-legs. So the two hind-legs are cut into four parts and distributed amongst the four Behchas. The senior most Behcha will be given the uppermost part of the hind-leg of the right side. The second Behcha will be given the same portion as given to the senior most Behcha of the left hind-leg. The lower portions of the right and left hind-legs will be given to the third and the forth Behchas respectively. The same is true with the Tuchas. These shares of meat are called Tucha and Behcha sa.

Before killing of the animal for the purpose the Thiempu will perform a rite for the appeasement of the soul of the animal to be killed which is known as *Gantha Tain.* Then the animal will be pinched with a sharpened or pointed bamboo or wooden bar just at its front right leg pit.

When it is killed the Tuchas will clear its belly and be busy with the intesting work. It is called *Sagil Sak.* The Behchas will burn the animal and then they will cut into pieces preparing for cooking. When it is cooked the Behchas will prepare for serving the meal. While male Behchas are engaged in distribution of the meat, the female-behchas are engaged in distribution of the rice.

Female-Behchas (behcha nupi) will cook rice while female-Tuchas (tucha nupi) will draw water. When the feast is over, all the cleaning of the utensils and pots are done by the Tucha Nupis.

The following day is *Sa-Aw-Jelni.* Behcha-nupis will twist thread and make Sa-Aw for the baby and the mother. The Thiempu will put the twisted thread (saw) on their necks. A portion of the animal killed the day before (on the Naominsah day) the Sa-aw-jelni was set aside. This is known as Sa-aw-jel-sa. This portion will be cooked on the day of Sa-aw-jelni, performed on the following day of Naominsak ni. This portion is taken from the part of the top of animal killed. This is called Ahuoi. Angong-vel (the skin of the neck) is also included in the Saw-aw-jel-sa. On this day Sa-aw-ju is taken.

When Naominsak is done a portion of the animal killed is kept aside for the Upa. This portion contains the head, intestine, spleen, heart, flesh and skin portion of the stomach. These portions are taken only in parts excepting that of the head from which the jaw and the lower portion of the head are taken out. The portions mentioned above will be sent to the Upa along with Ju. This is called Salu Thak. The meat will be carried by a small girl, chosen from amongst the villagers whom the performer of the ceremony likes best. Along with the girl will go the performer's family, their Tucha and Behcha. This must be in the evening, most preferably at dusk.

From what has been discussed it is clear that the characteristics of a clan, such as a unilineal principle, the belief in a common ancestor, segmentation of clan into sub-clans, lineages and sub-lineages, etc., providing a number of distinct separate groups, each having its own identity are prevalent amongst the Gangtes and as such I am tempted to call the Gangtes as clan rather than a tribe. Moreover, it is clear that Gangte is not a clan name in as much the same way as the Paites, the Hmars, the Simtes, the Zos, the Vaipheis, etc. are not clan names.

Das has taken one definition applicable to a simple society and comes to the conclusion without going deep into the social structure of that particular society. The society and the nature of social structure should not be studied in isolation of one another. A society should be studied in the context of its social structure and function.

B. THE TARAO

Tarao is a small tribe. They are found in three villages like Laimanai and Leishokehing of Tengoupal District and Sanakeithel village in the midst of Tangkhuls in East Districts. The total population of the tribe is 472 according to a census I made in 1981. This population of 472 is distributed in 75 households. The largest number of households of the tribe is found in

Sanakeithel. It consists of 27 households in this village. There are three families living outside the three villages mentioned above. Tarao is not a recognised tribe by the Government of India. However it is a very important and distinctive tribe of Manipur from cultural point of view.

Origin

In common with the Chin-Kuki-Mizo tribes, the Tarao believed that they emerged out of a hole or cave called "Tukleikhur" in the earth. The cave was supposed to be situated at the foot of Enthlouna Hill or Haobi Hill on the bank of the Burmese Chindwine River. They lived in a subterranean world before they sprang out of a cave. They did not like to live in the underground world. They liked to leave the place. A man named Katrimsha explored how to come out of the cave into the surface of the earth. He found an outlet leading to the upper world. But a fierce tiger was guarding the mouth of the cave. The tiger killed Katrimsha and ate him up. There was none to inform his whereabouts and the people did not know what to do. The second man, Chana made his attempt to lead the people out of the cave. But he was also killed and eaten by the tiger. The third man named Khurpuin made his attempt to come out of the cave and lead out the people on to the world. He was the master of the cave of Takleikhur. He dressed himself in war costume. He also met a tiger at the mouth of the cave. He took a branched tree resembling horns of an animal. He challenged the tiger. He said that he would fight the tiger with a branched tree and the tiger would attack with its sharp teeth and that they would see who could get the upper hand over the other. Then Khurpuin charged the tiger with the horn-shaped branch of tree. The tiger was frightened and ran away. He asked people to come out. He led the people out of the cave and settled on the surface of the earth.

Affinities

The Tarao people have more affinities with the Chin-Kuki-Mizo tribes than any other ethenic groups. Linguistically they are very akin to the tribes of Chin-Kuki-Mizo group at least in respect of sharing a common belief in the cave theory and linguistic affinity. Sarabjit of Calcutta University made a study on the Tarao Tribes in 1932. By that time he could meet informants who could assert a tradition that the Tarao were from the Pawis of Falam in the present Chin State of Burma. The Pawis of Falam are the central Chins belonging to different tribes locally known as Laizo (Zahau), Matu, etc. The same author stated that the Marings formed one of their colteoral branches originating from one of their ancestral brothers. Assuming that the Tarao and the Maring were of Chin origin, the tribes in Falam area in Chin state are the R-group of tribes in their speech as in the case of the Tarao and the Maring. The Chin-Kuki-Mizo tribes can broadly be divided into two divisions as the R-group and the non-R-group basing on linguistic factors within the Chin-Kuki sub-group of the Tibeto-Burman linguistic family. The Laiza (Zahau) and Matu of Burma and Lushai and Hmar of India belong to the R-group of languages and they have other distinctive dipthong sounds formed by TL, HM, HL etc. which the non-R group of people do not have in their speech. The non-R-group include the Paite, Tedim, Chin, Thadon, Vaiphei, etc. So the Tarao and Maring of Tengnoupal District of Manipur belong to the R-group besides having dipthong sounds of TL, HM, HL as other R-group of people have in their speech. Interestingly the tribes of Falam and Hake of Chin State have a style of keeping the hair in a knot over the occiput of the head in a way a man among Maring does. There are other points which suggest the affinity of the Tarao and Maring tribes with the Chin-Kuki-Mizo tribes particularly the central Chin tribes.

Populalion

The population of the Tarao was at the verge of extinction at different points of time in the past. Lieutenant Col. Dun recorded that there were 25 persons in 1891 having only six persons that could fight. After 29 years in 1910 the total number of the Tarao came to only one hundred. After 22 years in 1932 there was a marked decrease of the population to only 18 adults with 4 to 6 old men distributing in 20 households. As stated earlier the population of Tarao now rose to 472 distributing in 75 households in three villages after 49 years in 1981.

There has been a high rate of mortality among the Tarao. There were 63 cases of death during 1950-70 and 50 cases of death during 1970-81 among the Tarao. The percentage of mortality is worked out at 35% for a period between 1930-70.

The Tarao believed that they were the chosen people of God called Rapu or Sangku. The name of the present oldest village is Laimanai meaning servant of God in Meitei language. The Meitei king in the days passed believed that the Tarao were the chosen people of God and that they were the servants of God to do the works of God. On that ground the king exempted the Tarao from forced labour for the State.

The relationship of the Tarao with the Meitei king and God seemed not always favourable. Their spiritual relationship to the God and the political relationship to the Meitei king fluctuated. The Tarao people used to water betel vines of the king. They felt tired of the work assigned to them. So they poured hot water to the vines and they withered. The king got angry and cursed the Tarao people. He cursed them that the Tarao would never exceed 20 households in any single village. They believed that they would not exceed 20 households till recently when their household exceeded this limit in the Tarao villages mentioned above.

In 1967 one hundred and ten persons migrated from Laimanai to Sanakeithel out of some discord in the parental village. Out of the 110 persons, 25 persons died of dysentary within a year.

Tarao is a patrilineal society. The traditional way of marriage is by service for three years by a boy. The boy was to serve for three years for his father-in-law and stayed there till the completion of the term. The tribe is divided into three exogamous clans. The exogamous clans are (i) Khulpuin, (ii) Chana and (iii) Katrimsha. Each of these clans is further sub-divided into a number of lineages.

(*i*) *Khulpuin*

This clan is the most important from the time of their mythological emergence out of the cave to the present day for their spiritual well being. The original form of Khurpuin changed into Khulpuin when the descendants of the original person adopted it as their group identity. However, the meanings of the two forms are same. (Khur cave in the R-group of the Chin-Kuki tribes and Khul also means cave or hole in the non-R-group.) Hence Khulpuin or Khurpuin means master of the cave. Khurpuin became the leader of the people after he led them out of the cave. The legend states that he became the first chief in Houbiding village. He had a daughter named Thapcha who had given a virgin birth to Sangku, the goddess. She eventually saved the world of the Tarao from a deluge at the sacrifice of her own life.

(*ii*) *Katrimsha*

This clan is divided into four segments. They are Toleksanai, Tuilamthangna, Salaisanai and Longlan. The Longlan social unit has been extinct. There is no living member representing this unit now.

(*iii*) *Chana*

Chana is also divided into two social units. They are Tlaitlap and Thanonin. So there is only Tlaitlap social unit now under Chana as Thanonin became extinct.

Economic aspect of the Tarao

The Economic life of the Tarao is very deplorable. They partly depend on shifting cultivation for their livelihood. They cannot make both ends meet by shifting cultivation. Life in the three villages, though equally immersed in poverty, illiteracy and illhealth has different dimentions. The villagers of Laimanai have sufficient forest land for jhuming cultivation. So also the Tarao in Sanakeithel are permitted by the village authority of Sanakeithel to practise jhuming cultivation. But the product of jhuming cultivation is not sufficient for them. Out of 180 persons in Laimanai village, 94 persons are jhumers and 71 persons take up basketry work as their secondary occupation. Male, female and children do basketry work in order to supplement their jhum products. Annual scarcity of food is the usual phenomenon for a Tarao village. 20.55% of the total population practise basketry work. Non-tribal middle men collect the baskets at a low rate and sell them at a good profit to the nearby markets. In Leishokching village there is no land either for wet cultivation for forest area or jhuming cultivation. Most of them live on odd jobs and basketry works etc. There are three L.P. School teachers, two J.B. school teachers, two drivers and two in military services among the whole tribe of Tarao. None of a Tarao holds a degree. The students form 38% of the population. After J.B. School level they find it difficult to continue their studies. Out of 16 matriculates there are 11 college students. There are as many as 282 individuals who can neither read nor write among the total population of 472.

The Moyon-Monsang

The Moyon-Monsang people live in Tengnoupal District of Manipur. They are living side by side with their fellow tribes like the Anal, Chiru and Chothe. The Moyon and the Monsang are grouped separately according to 1971 census report of Manipur. Their names were also recognised as two separate and distinct tribes of Manipur. However, the two groups are very much alike in maximum respects. Numerically the two tribes are very small. According to the census report of Manipur (1971), the Moyon numbered only 1360 while the population of Monsang was only 930.

In common with the Chin-Kuki-Mizo tribes of Manipur, Mizoram and the Chin State of Burma, the Moyon-Monsang people claimed to have emerged out of a cave or hole called Khur according to their oral tradition. Linguistically they are akin to the Chin-Kuki-Mizo tribes. As such they are a group of people classed as old Kuki in anthropological literature just to allude to the earlier arrival of the Chin-Kuki tribes in Manipur. At one time in about 1948 the Moyon-Monsang people joined a political organisation of the tribes of Manipur called Khul Union. The Secretary of the Khul Union was a man from Monsang.

Both Monsang and Moyon are divided into two moieties as in the case of the Anal. Monsang is divided into (1) Simputi and (2) Rinhe moieties. Similarly Moyon is also divided into two moieties known as (1) Simputi and Jangveni. The name of the first moieties in both the cases of Moyon and Monsang is similar and it is known as Simputi. So the Simputi moieti in Monsang is further sub-divided into (1) Ngarati, (2) Karati and (3) Thumli unilineal social segments. The Rinhe moieti of Monsang is also divided into (1) Rohin (2) Wanglar (3) The-song (4) Hiengam (5) Songsir and (6) Khartu lineages.

The Simputi moieti of the Moyon is divided into (1) Nguru (2) Langlom (3) Serbum (4) Chara. Similarly the second moieti called Jangveni is further subdivided into (1) Roel (2) Wanglar (3) Chinir and (4) Nungchim.

The Moyon-Monsang and Anal tribes have peculiarity in having moieti system in which the tribe is divided into two halves. Because of the moieti system the tribes have distinctive-ness from the rest of the tribes of Manipur. The wife-taking or wife-giving system is very much distinctive resembling the marriage circle of the Kachin of Upper Burma.

The Origin of the Moyon-Monsang

The word Moyon-Monsang is a term given by the Meitei to refer to the Moyon-Monsang people. Moyon-Monsang call themselves sirtibujur (meaning-man of the cave). But this term is not used to identify themselves in reference to other groups now. The term sirtibujur came from sirti and bujur which were originally derived from siir (meaning cave) and Jur (meaning man) respectively.

According to a legendary story the Moyon-Monsang people emerged out of a cave in the dim vista of the past. The cave was believed to be located somewhere in Central China.

Men lived for many generations in the under ground world. People sprang out of the cave. But at the gate of the cave or hole there was a tiger watching the gate. The tiger used to kill and eat people who came out of the cave. He made them his prey easily. People liked to come out of the cave and live a better life on the overground world. An intrepid man named Mirang made arrows and a bow for killing the tiger. He dele-gated a cock to see whether the tiger was at the gate of the cave or not. He further advised the cock to crow whenever the tiger was not at the gate of the cave but not to crow when the tiger was watching the gate. Mirang said that he would kill the man eater. The cock came back without crowing on seeing the tiger at the gate at first. The cock went again to the gate of the cave. The tiger was not there in the gate and the cock crowed. Mirang came with his bow and arrows to kill the tiger. He asked for help from all the birds with a promise that the birds would be entitled to eat the crops of men in their fields. The birds surrounded the tiger and overpowered it. In the meantime Mirang shot his arrow from his big bow and killed the tiger at once. Mirang sang his song of victory thus:

Hia ye, khurna kahang suhpeh
Men bo, samang pa ning o
Kiman chung ning achii
Samangpa ning-o, kiman chung
Ning o atsa ae,
Mirang Sapao Kim an chang
Sing nge,

Free translation: On coming out of the cave. A giant tiger
said, 'He is tall and strong'
But, I, Mirang killed the tiger,
So I am strong and tall.

The head of the slain tiger was cut off. Mirang sprayed the blood of the tiger to the birds to mark the agreement between man and birds that the birds will freely eat the grains in the jhum fields of human beings. It is said that the wild sparrow (bariih) is bearing the blood stain of the tiger till today. The birds are feeding freely on the grains cultivated by human beings until now as result of the agrrement made between Mirang as representative of human beings on the one hand and the birds on the other hand. As part of the said agreement the horn bill is allowed to live peacefully and happily in the woods. The horn bill agreed that his quill and tail feathers should be used on ritual and festive occasions by human beings for decoration as headgear. The cave door was closed forever. The detached head of the tiger was hanged over the cave-door.

The hanging of the head of a sacrifical animal at the gate of a house in tribal villages in Manipur indicates that the house and the inmates are under ritual taboo. No stranger coming from other village is allowed to enter the house under ritual restriction. Similarly chopped head of an animal hanging at the village gate signified that the whole village in under taboo. No outsider can enter the village. No villager also can go out during the period of ritual taboo. Any one violating the rules of restrtction is fined as the magical efficacy is supposed to be neutralised. A fresh rite is to be performed and the whole process repeated.[1]

The tiger killed many persons. But no one knew how many of them were killed. A man named Thompungpa devised a means to count the number of persons killed by the tiger at the time the people were coming out of the cave. He instructed the people that every household should bring as many stone slabs as the members of their family killed by the tiger. Each household brought stone slabs corresponding to the member of the dead in their family. Thompungpa counted the number of stone slabs brought by the people and he could determine the number of the dead. So many people were found lost and eaten by the tiger. The tradition of erecting stone at the village gate is said to be originated from the practice in this story.

The people left the cave and followed along the Phertsa river. At last reached a place called Tengpherjur quite suitable for settlement. Hence they sang song like this:

Tsajur no bongnge aii
Phertsa Kahienote ye;
Tungpherjur to kahein phaya,
Buno tiska pa ye.

Free translation:

On coming out of the cave
we followed the phertsa river,
We arrived at Tungpherjur,
And found the place suitable
For throwing feast of merit.

1. It is said that the practice of hanging head of sacrificial animal over or at the gate of a village or a house owed its origin from the hanging of a head of the slain tiger by Mirang.

C. GAMES OF MANIPUR

The people of Manipur have essentially been warriors and their incessant struggle in the past against Burma and other neighbouring kingdoms gave them their martial tradition. This tradition is reflected in their sports even today.

Sagol Kangiei (Polo) : This is a sport which is considered to have originated in Manipur. The Manipuri Puranas trace it to the mythological age when it was played by the gods. The game is said to have flourished during the reign of King Kyamba (1467-1508) and King Khagemba (1597-1652). It was introduced to India in 1863 when two teams consisting of Manipuri players visited Calcutta and played an exhibition match there. The stick is made of a cane with a narrow wooden head fixed on it at a slight angle The ball is about 14 inches in circumference and is made of bamboo root which is very light. The Manipuris play polo on ponies which are just four and a half feet in height but are sturdy and very fast. It is exhilarating to see people in their sixties and seventies riding their ponies at full gallop and playing the game with gusto.

The game of Polo was considered "the best play in the world" by Sir James Johnstone, once a political Officer of Manipur. The game with certain adaptations has now become an international game. About it the Encyclopedia Britannica writes : "The English game of Polo was introduced from Manipur where it forms a great national pastime."

T.C. Hudson, once an Assistant Political Officer in Manipur described the game thus:

"To describe the game is beyond the powers of any but an imaginative and practised pen for in respect of brilliance of play, constant excitement, dashing courage, skill and popular enthusiasm, there is no game equal to it".

Khong Kangjei (Manipuri Hockey): This is locally called "Hockey-on-foot" as opposed to Polo which is called "Hockey-on-ponies".

Manipuri hockey is played with seven players on each side and every player has a stick about four feet long shaped like a hockey stick. A player is allowed to carry the ball, which is made of bamboo root, in any manner he likes. He can even kick the ball but he has to score the goal only by hitting it with his stick. During a game a player carrying the ball can be physically challenged by a rival player and then they have to wrestle with each other before the ball can be taken up again. This trial of strength is known as Mukna (Manipuri style of wrestling) which has its own laws and is also a separate, original game in its own right.

Khong Kangjei is a game which requires much physical stamina, speed and agility.

Yubee-Lakpee (Manipuri Rugby): Yubee is Manipuri for coconut and Lakpee means snatching. This game is played between two sides each consisting of seven players. The game starts with the throwing of a coconut at one end of the field. At the other end of the field there is a rectangular space with the central portion of the goal line as one of its sides. This is called the box area. The players have to carry the coconut into the box and pass the goal line against the opponents. This game which has some similarity to the modern game of rugby, is still very popular among Manipuris.

Mukna (Manipuri Wrestling): This is one of the oldest Manipuri sports and is a trial of strength like wrestling anywhere. What makes it special is that it is generally played on the last day of Lai-Haraoba (worship of the sylvan deity) right in front of the deity as a part of the ceremonial function and the function is not considered complete without this game.

Kang (An Indoor game): This is played on a mud floor and consists of hitting targets fixed on the floor with a hard, smooth, oblong shaped flat object called tne 'Kang'. The tradition of this game goes back to ancient times and there is mention of it in the Manipuri epic legend of Khamba and Thoibi: Kang is played strictly during the period between the Manipuri New Year's day and the Ratha Jatra Festival. Common belief has it that this game has untoward effects on the minds of people if played at any other time. The ruling deity of the game is said to be 'Panthoibi', the Manipuri counterpart of the Goddess Durga who is the destroyer of enemies.

Boat Race: This sport still arouses tremendous enthuisiasm among the people. The royal boats, two in number carry symbols of Chinese dragons, known as "Chingalai", at the helm.

Seventeen rowers in each boat pull hard at the oars and the object of the race is for one boat to foul the other and trap it near a bank as it moves forward. The boats are thus close together and the race is generally won only by a boat or two.

D. WOMEN OF MANIPUR

To the world outside, Manipur is a land made famous by its women through dancing and weaving. Manipuri women are seen as tendriis in the breeze given to swaying rhythmically or as retiring housewives leisurely ticking at the loom. But they are much more.

They are like the legendary and contemporary heroines, firm rulers and disloyal subject when necessary. When the political struggle in the land assumed a popular character, it was inevitable that Manipuri women should ferment the dough with the yeast of their militancy. Since 1891 there were two events in the valley, known in Manipuri as "Women's War" I and II. These upheavals which took place in 1904 and 1939-40 are now considered an integral part of Manipur's fight for independence and democracy.

In 1904, when the house of the Assistant Political Agent was burnt down by some unknown persons, the British Resident, Maxwell, suspected political incendiarism. As an example and a warning to those responsible, Maxwell ordered the rebuilding of the house by forced labour, the public to supply all the material locally available.

The women went into action protesting and demonstrating collectively against Maxwell's order. This incident is referred to as "Nupi Lan" in the history of Manipur. It means "Women's War".

A few years later, the women were again on the warpath. Some time in 1930, the government decided to introduce a new tax. The women resented it. The President of the Durbar, an Englishman, was in earnest about the new impost. When he came to check up on reported resistance, the women bundled him into a pond. Later his successor, a certain Stewart, came within an ace of plummeting into more dangerous waters. There was a dispute about fishing in the Loktak lake and he came to inquire into it. Stewart put out in a boat with some leaders of the area while a crowd of angry women screaming abuse stood on the shore. The decision Stewart took was bang in tune with the women's demand.

In 1939, extensive damage was caused to standing crops by floods. Although this did not affect Manipur's self-sufficiency in food, the winter arrivals of paddy were meagre and prices began to soar. This was mostly due to the export of the available surplus. To keep prices down and the rice at home, the Government banned the export of rice. But just when harvesting was in full swing, for no apparent reason the ban was lifted. The people took umbrage. It was again the women who sounded the tocsin.

The Maharaja, Sir Churachand Singh was away in Nawdwip on a pilgrimage. The Durbar was in session. A few thousand women came marching to the Durbar Hall demanding reimposition of the ban. The President of the Durbar, a man named Sharpe, pleaded inability to comply on the ground that the Maharaja whose prerogative it was to sanction the ban was away. He, however, reed to get in touch with the Maharaja telegraphically and obtain his sanction. He left for the telegraph office, the women following him, Sharpe sent his message and felt his duty was done but the women requested him to stay on till the Maharaja's reply was received. Their plea was that they were famished since the previous day for want of rice and if they could stay on arround the town on an empty stomach the President of the State Durbar could remain in the telegraph office for a few hours longer. It was a gherao, perhaps the first ever in India to make history.

On learning about the confinement of Sharpe, a British Major from the Fourth Assam Rifles and the Civil Surgeon, another Britisher, came to the telegraph office to help him. For the newcomers entry was easy, but exit, as in the case of Sharpe was denied. Tired, some of them stepped on to the office varandah to find out what was happening. Immediately, 'law and order' broke down. By afternoon, a platoon of Assam Rifles arrived led by a British officer. Some of the women were thrown out of the varandah; others were charged. Twenty women received bayonet wounds.

The crowd of women held their ground till one O'clock in the morning in the ice-cold Imphal.

They left only when it was known that the British civil and military officers had disappeared. But the women got their way for the very next day came word from the Maharaja sanctioning reimposition of the ban.

SELECT BIBLIOGRAPHY

Allen, P. 45 *The Kacharis*, 1903.

Allen, *The Tribes of Assam*, 1905.

Assam District Gazetteers Vol. VII P. 86-87, 1905.

Austin, A. John. Rev., *Beginning of Christian Work in the Hill Areas of North-East Region*, Calcutta, 1967.

Bose, Nirmal Kumar, *One State of Many States*, Calcutta, 1967.

Barpujari, H.K., *Political History of Assam*, Vol. I Govt. of Assam, Gauhati, 1967.

Basumati, Gahin, *Borolipi*, Asom Bani, Nov. 22, 1963.

Bhaskar, Barman 7th Cent. A.D.

Baker, *Assam Census Report*, 1891.

Barman, *The Kacharis*, 1968.

Bahadur, K.P., *Caste, Tribes and Cultures of India*, 1977.

Banerjee, Anjan K., *Assam A Look Back*, 1967.

Bhuyan, S.K., *Kachari Buranji*.

Bilear Journal in Assamese, 1923.

Bose, Saradindu, *Carrying Capacity of Land Under Shifting Cultivation*, Calcutta, 1967.

Brahma, M.M., *Tribal Culture and Folklore* Research Dept., University of Gauhati, *Folk Songs of Bodos*.

Census of India 1961, Vol. III, Assam, Part V, Vol. III, P. 260-269, 282-302.

Census Report of Assam, 1881.

Census of India, Tribes of Assam, 1951.

Census of India, Part II-C, 1961.

Col. Dalton, *Journal of Asiatic Society of Bengal*, V-14, Part I, 1845.

Col. L.A. Waddel, *Tribes of the Brahmaputra Valley*, P. 29, 1900.

Chatterjee, S.K., *Indo-Mongoloid Race*, 1951.

Chaliha, B P., *Assam and People*, 1967.

Chaudhury, P.D., *Arts and Crafts*, 1967.

Das, S.T., *People of the Eastern Himalayas*, 1975.
Dasgupta, B.K. and Pradyot Mitra, *On Tribal Life*, 1967.
District Census Handbook, United Mikir and North Cachar Hill, Census of Assam, 1961.
Edward Stock, *The Mikirs*, 1908.
Endle, The Kacharis, 1911.
Gait, E.A., *History of Assam*, 1963.
Gemini Paul, *People of Assam*, 1956.
Ghosh, *Dimasa Kachari*, 1964-65.
Gupta and Dutta, *Ethnographic Studies of Mikir*, 1966.
Grierson, G. Sir., *Linguistic Survey of India*, Vol. III, Part II, 1903.
Graham, U. Baver, *Cycle Migration of the Zemi Nagas*, N.C. Hills, 1946.
Haddon, *Tribal India*, 1893.
Hutton, J.M., *The Angami Nagas*, 1921.
Hudson, T.C., *The Naga Tribes of Manipur*, 1911.
Industrial Classification of Workers of Scheduled Tribes, 1961.
Jyoti K. Sarma, *On Eastern States*, Illustrated Weekly of India, 1975.
Lyall, C.J., *Assam Census Report*, 1881.
Lamkam Teron, *Mikir Jana Jati*, 1966.
Mahabharata, 10th Cent. B.C.
Mankekar, R. Dr., *Understanding the Tribals on the North-Eastern Border*, Tribal Situation in India, Simla 1972.
Martin Classification of Measurement.
Mikir Hill District (Jhuming) 1966.
Man in India, Quart. Vol. XXVI. No. 1.
Man in India, Quart. Vol. 48, No. 102.
Nair, C.N S., *Mizoram*, 1973.
Phillip, Puthuvail Thomas, *The Growth of the Baptist Churches in Nagaland*, Christian Literature Centre, Gauhati, 1976.
Pugh. B.M., *Politics in the Hill areas of North-East India*, Calcutta, 1967.
Roy Burman, B.K., *Demographic and Socio-economic profiles of the hill areas of North-East India*, Census of India, 1961.
Roy, Homdi, *Assam*, 1973.
Robinson, *Assam Census Report*, 1881.
Rustumji, N.K., *Meghalaya and Arunachal*, 1973.

Ramunny, M., *Manipur, Nagaland and Tripura*, 1973.

Sriniwas, M.N., and Sanwal, R.D., *Tribal Situation in India*, Simla 1972.

Swell, G.S., *Problems of the hill areas*, 1967.

Sword, V.H., *Baptists in Assam*, 1935.

Thaosen, Sonaram, *Why the hills and plains do not unite*, Calcutta, 1967.

Waddel, L.A., *Assam Tribes*, 1900.

ERRATA

Page 36	Read	CHAPTER IV	for	CHAPTER III
Page 42	Read	CHAPTER V	for	CHAPTER IV

1. A Naga chief

2. Young Zemi-Naga wife

3. A Warrier with head dress of Mithun horns (Mizoram)

4. Mikir girl spinning bark-fibre

5. Zemi Naga in ceremonial dress

6. Zemi Naga tribal chiefs

7. Hmar tribe (Manipur)

8. Naga tribal chiefs

9. Mikir girls

10. Garo dance

Hero's house (Nagaland)

 Mao Naga house

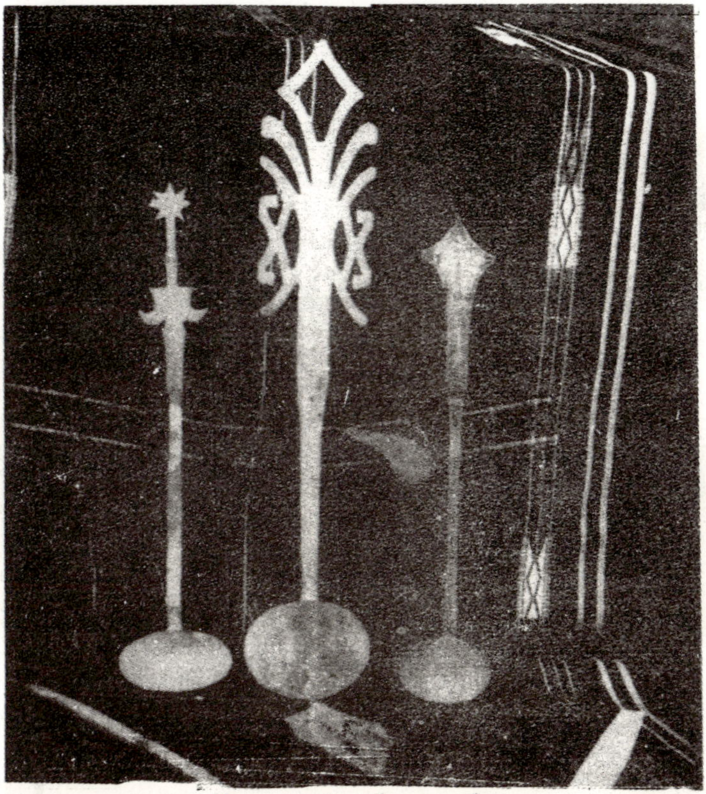

13.. Naga arton daily utensils

14. Author with Educated Kuki and Naga College Girls

15. Long drum—Zemi Naga

16 Drum long enough for a man to sit inside (Zemi Naga)

17. Zailaijong house (Manipur)

18. A Mikir village

19. Mao tribe

20. Khasi girls

21. Village industry (Nagaland

22. Mikir peasant woman

23. Maram health care

24. Maram health centre

25. Paddy husking dance (Naga)

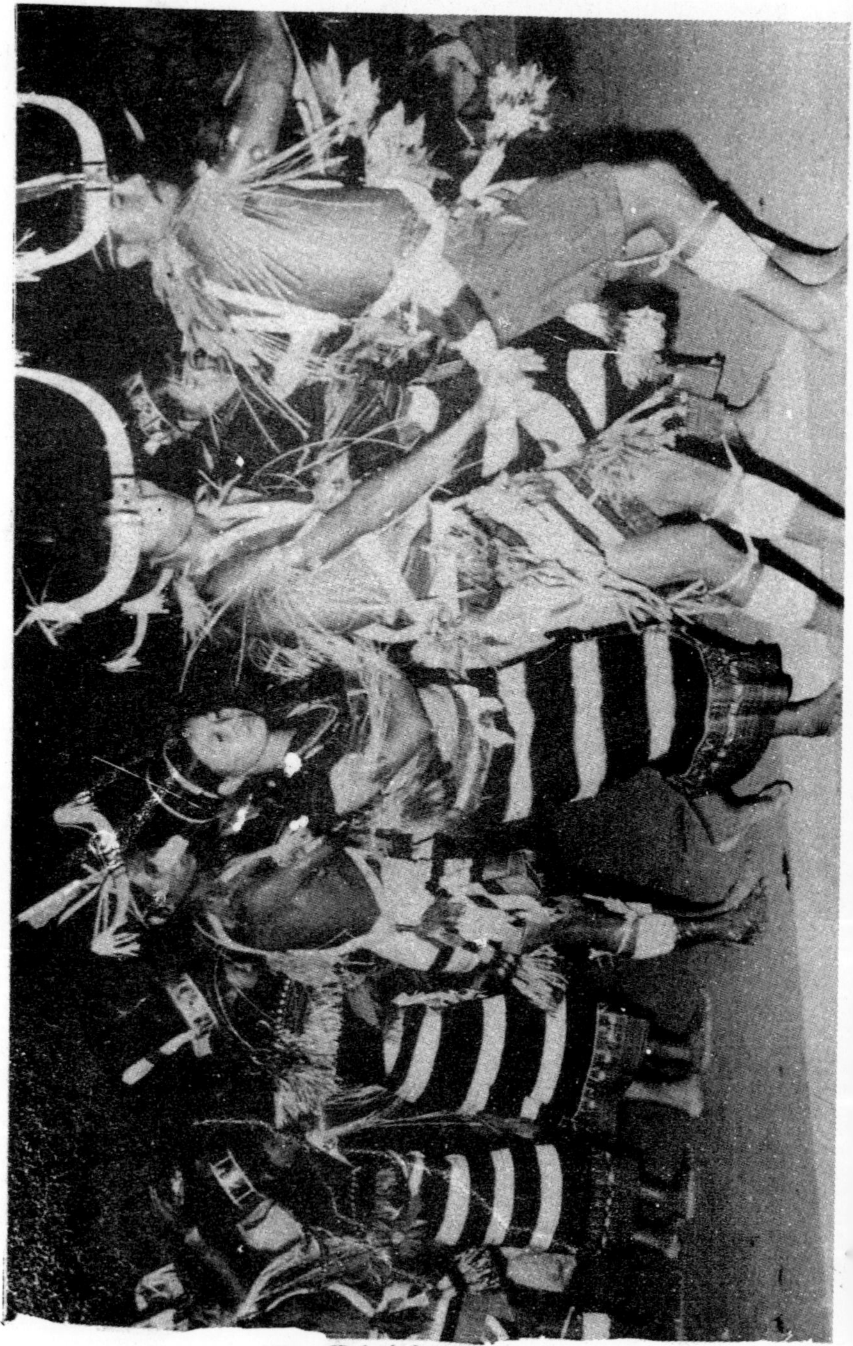

26. Kabui dance

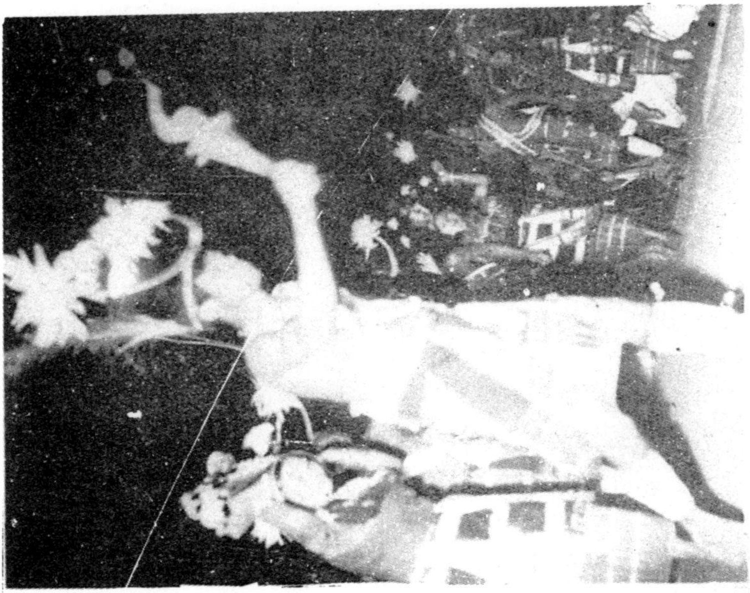

27. Konyak Naga dance

28. Naga dance

29. Kubui dance

30. Tribal dance (Manipur)

31. Zailaijong dance

32. Dimasa-Kachari dance

33. Semsa war dance

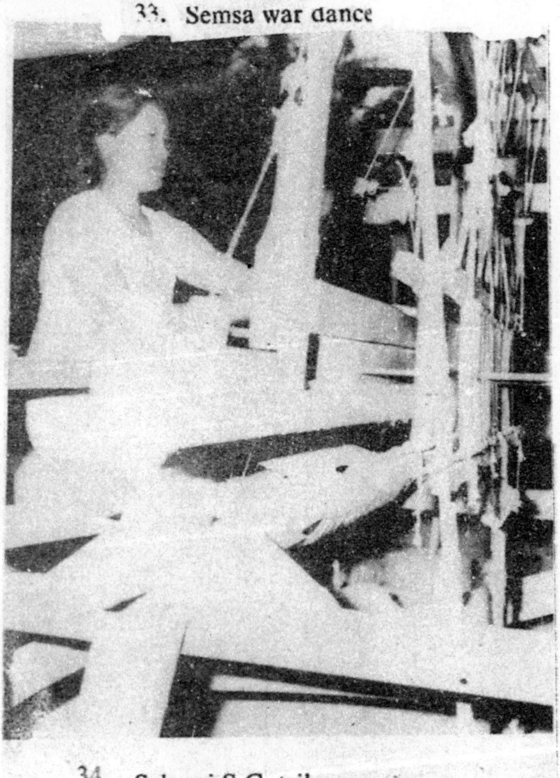

34. Sekmai S.C. tribe weaving

35. Kabui dance (Manipur)

36. Cheraw dance (Mizoram)

37. An Unmarried girl with short hairs, sign of virginity (Zemi Naga)

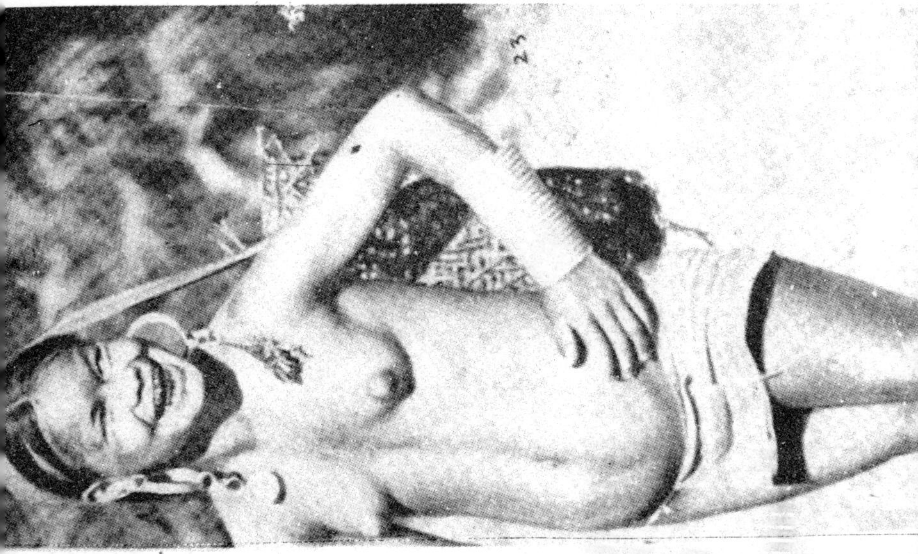

38. Mikir girl with blackened teeth

39. Mikir young man dressing hair

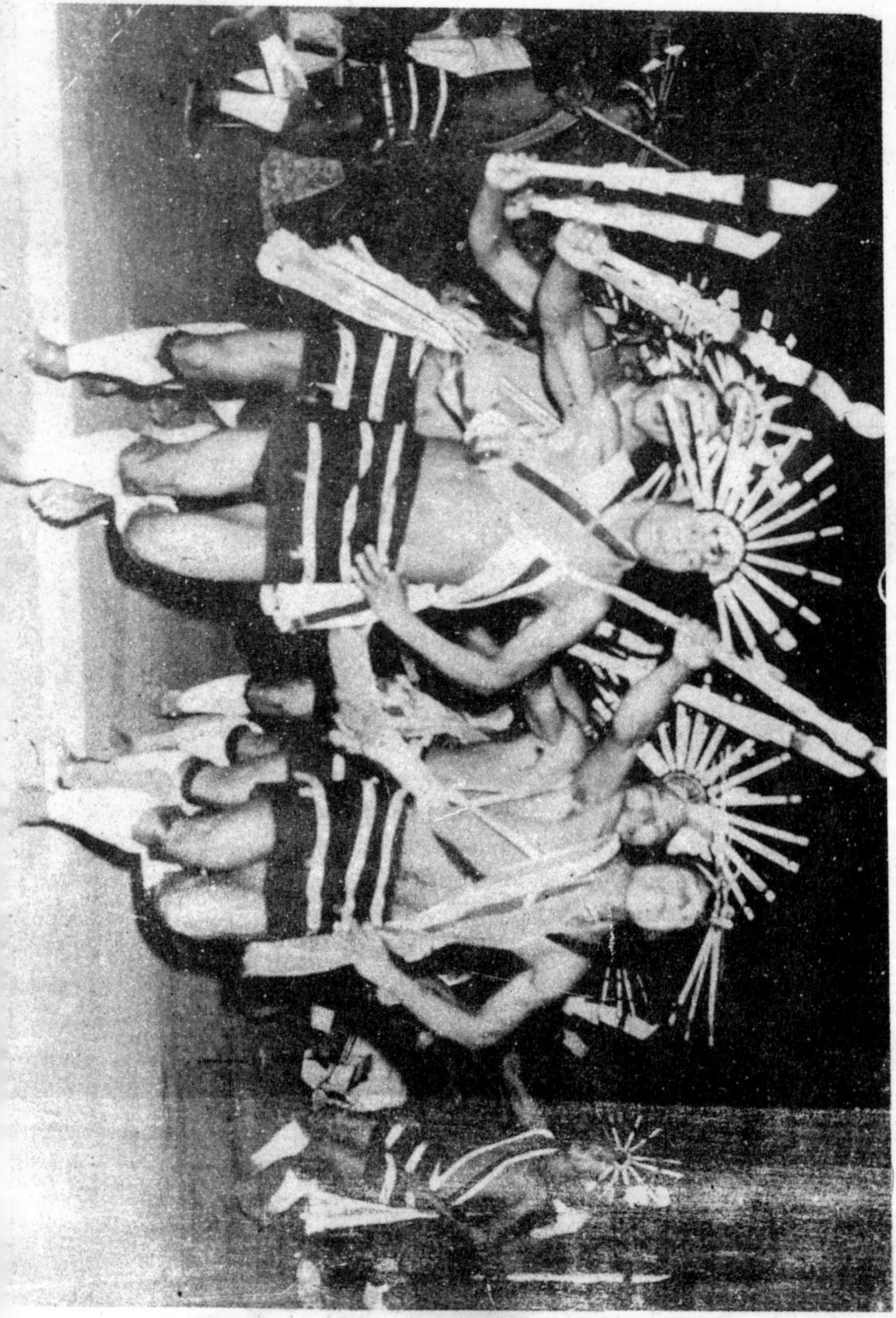

40. Kabui martial dance